# In the Middle of Now<sup></sup>

By

Peter Fl

Photographs by Peter Fleming
and Dawn Quinn-Havey

# Bounceabout Publications

## New Zealand

www.peteredwardfleming.com

## Printing history

2016 Bookwright – full colour hardback

2016 Kindle Direct Publishing – ebook

2017 CreateSpace - paperback

Copyright © Peter Edward Fleming

ISBN 978-1542583909

With sincere thanks to Dawn without whom this adventure would never have happened.

Thanks also to my wife Claire for her meticulous proof reading and editing of the manuscript.

# About this Book

This book is the story of a journey undertaken in 1980 and 1981. My original intention was to write and print just two volumes, one for my family and one for the family of my travelling companion. I had thought that an episode from so many years ago would have little interest in the modern world, but so many years have passed by and so many wonders have become everyday due to the advances in technology, that the world of 1980 is now of almost historical interest, particularly perhaps to the younger generation. In fact it is those very advances that now enable people like myself to write and publish a book and also be able to digitalise and revive old photographs that can be used to illustrate the manuscript.

This paperback is the third edition. The first was the original and was a glossy, full colour hardback. The second was a full colour ebook. Both are available through Amazon. Due to printing constraints this third edition is in black and white and consequently I have had to edit out many of the pictures in order to achieve a realistic sale price.

Readers will soon appreciate that I am a dedicated fan of the Land Rover and this book is my humble tribute to what I consider to be a truly great icon of British engineering. The less technically minded or interested may wish to start reading from Chapter 4.

*Peter Fleming*

# Contents

# Overall route map - In the Middle of Nowhere

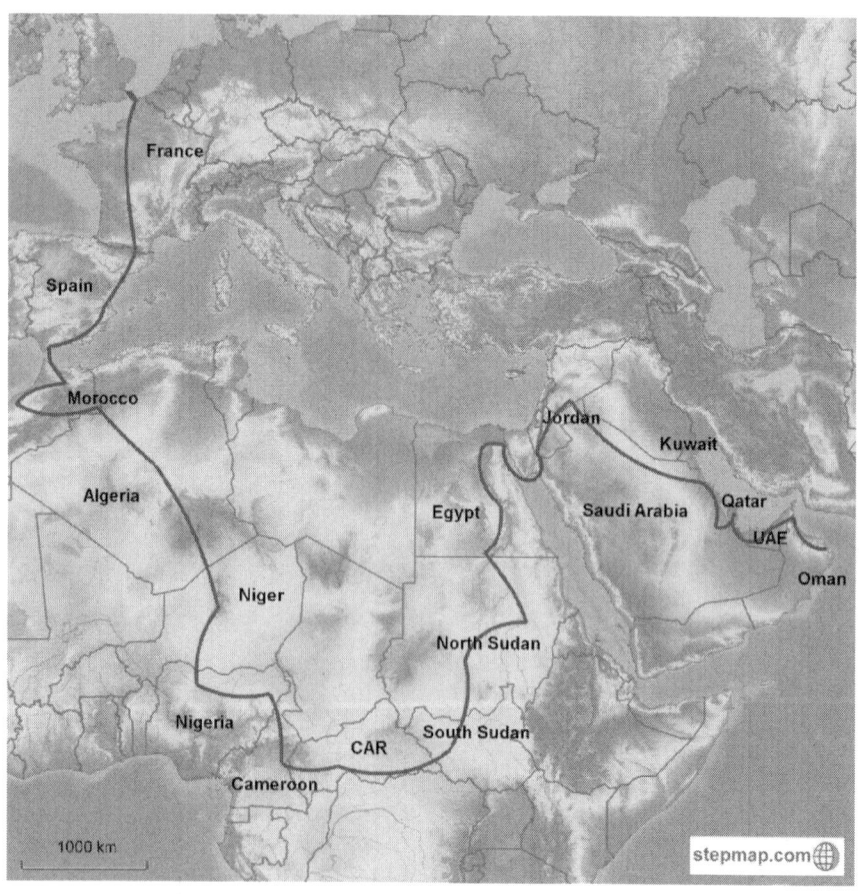

Departing from Oman in the east and ending in England in the west, a distance of 24,247 km or 15,154 miles over 5 months

# Chapter 1 - In the Beginning

I like to think that it all began in 1978 with a tiny piece of toughened glass.

I had arrived in the Sultanate of Oman in late 1978 and had been working there for 2 years as a field engineer with the British Aircraft Corporation (subsequently to become British Aerospace – BAe). BAC had sold the Rapier low level air defence missile system to Oman and I was part of a comprehensive support field team based there for several years. We had two locations, one near the capital Muscat and the other some 600 miles to the south on the huge but isolated air base at Thumrait, on the edge of the Arab Empty Quarter. I was based at Muscat.

In those days Muscat retained an irresistible atmosphere of Arabia in the Middle Ages. Not so many years before it had been shielded from the twentieth century by the reigning Sultan Said bin Taimur. The overthrow of Said bin Taimur in a British backed bloodless coup in 1970 placed his son Qaboos bin Said al Said on the throne. Then started a major programme to not only oust the communist guerillas operating in the Jebel (mountains) but also to improve the living standards of the country. By the mid 1970's the country had entered a period of peace which has since survived for many years under the sympathetic and even-handed rule of Sultan Qaboos.

By 1978 the north of the country around Muscat and the adjacent port of Muttrah had started to benefit from building programmes for schools and a hospital together with a couple of western style hotels. Shops and restaurants remained predominantly Arabic and Asian although we did have two small food supermarkets selling limited western fare. The traditional souk, or market, continued to be the focus of commercial business. Muscat and Muttrah are situated on a narrow coastal plain which starts at Muscat, where the barren Jebel drops dramatically into the sea, and then runs for many miles west along the northern coastline, gradually widening as the mountains retreat inland. Working on a defence contract meant that we were closely affiliated with the Sultan's Air Force, which was mainly comprised of British service contract personnel. We had automatic membership of the Air Force beach club, and swimming, sailing, scuba diving, water skiing and lazing on the beach with a beer or two or three was part of our normal, everyday life.

Against this very amenable geographical and climatical background we went about our daily business. Work started at 07.00 after a 20 minute drive to the workshops and finished for the day at 13.30. This six day routine stopped on

Friday, the Moslem day of rest. We worked in a purpose built, air conditioned facility in a barren area at the base of the Jebel and close to the main Air Force base and the new International Airport. The workshops were divided into specialist support areas for electronics, radar, hydraulics and optics together with a large mechanical workshop fitted with an overhead crane and equipped with a comprehensive range of tooling to support the Rapier generators. The availability of this workshop was to be a major factor in the preparation of my Land Rover over the next 2 years, and I was allowed full use of it by our resident mechanic, George, who was fortunately a kindred spirit when it came to 'extra-curricular' activities.

****

But back to that piece of glass. My close friend John (always known by his initials JVC) had produced it following long discussions about building motor vehicles from parts to be found on the many scrap heaps dotted around in the local desert. We regularly went on forays to these dumps, returning with spoils that we used to improve the workshop facilities. The piece of glass in question was the small block usually glued to a Land Rover side window and used to slide it open and shut. "Here you are", he announced. "That's the start, now build a Land Rover..........".

At the time I owned a Mazda 929 saloon, bought principally for my wife and son when they came over for 6 months. This six months sadly confirmed what we had expected for some time, however, and culminated in her return to the UK and the start of divorce proceedings. I had also 'acquired' an Indian manufactured Mahindra jeep, which JVC and I had found virtually complete on a scrap heap. I had rescued this, stripped it right down, repaired the engine, rebuilt it and registered it for use on the road. An amazing vehicle which had incredible performance under four wheel drive conditions.

Meanwhile, down in the south, two like-minded BAC engineers were engaged in similar foraging in the scrap heaps of Thumrait. Alan already owned a Land Rover 'Carawagon' which he had driven out from the UK, but Graham had assembled a long wheelbase Land Rover from a selection of abandoned Rovers scattered about the air base. With the end of both their contracts in sight, Alan and Graham decided to sell their vehicles, and as the market in Thumrait was very limited they drove them both the 600 miles across the desert to Muscat – an all sand track with no tarmac.

Once in Muscat Alan and Graham handed over their respective vehicles to JVC and myself in order for us to try and sell them, whilst they returned south for their remaining few weeks. John and I duly advertised them and drove them around to give them sales visibility.

Alan's Rover was very impressive. A Land Rover should always stir the soul of a red-blooded Englishman, and the professional Carawagon conversion produced a particularly intruiging and practical mode of transport for off-road conditions. The basic conversion was to take a long wheelbase pickup, build up the sides with aluminium panels with long narrow windows and fit a standard Safari rear door. The roof was an ingenious design of flexible flat aluminium sheets which lay flat for normal travel but which pushed up into a semi-circular shape with folding ends for camping. Inside, with the roof thus raised, there was plenty of room to stand upright. Down one side ran a padded seat that converted to a double bed and on the other side were cupboards, a refrigerator and a sink. A sort of stretcher arrangement could be slung at shoulder height to form 2 more sleeping berths in the roof space. The whole arrangement was neat and functional. An enormous roof rack spanned the width of the vehicle and from above the windscreen out forwards to vertical supports from the front bumper, creating a huge storage area for jerry cans and luggage. Finished in gloss white, this was a big, rugged vehicle with a beautiful sounding 6 cylinder engine. Unfortunately this engine was prone to overheating and Alan eventually exchanged it for a standard four cylinder unit – from a Thumrait dump, of course. I subsequently travelled in the deserts of Sudan alongside an almost identical Carawagon and experienced how the huge roof rack could easily be overloaded with little regard for the vehicle suspension – more later.

So we awaited responses to our advertisements but, of course, even in a country where off road driving was readily available it certainly wasn't *necessary* and therefore we were still appealing to a very small market. Then, one day, the 'phone rang and a lady with a delightful Australian accent expressed an interest in Alan's Rover and we subsequently met the most charming Antipodean couple who, I think, fell in love with the Carawagon at first sight. And so 'Lawrence' became the cherished possession of Pam and Geoff, who were planning an overland journey to the UK. This journey, in fact, was never to take place, but for many months Lawrence was Pam and Geoff's faithful companion, as fond of them as they were of him. Despite a sometimes temperamental relationship with Alan, Lawrence was as good as gold with his new owners. Alas, the time came for Pam and Geoff to fly to pastures new and Lawrence was sold to new owners – who changed his name. The immediate result was a series of breakdowns. A very concerned Pam called the new owners and urged a return to his former identity and, re-instated as Lawrence – believe it or not – the mischief ceased and harmony returned.

But what of Graham's Land Rover? Not, on close inspection, a pretty sight. To a rather battered pick-up body Graham had bolted a section of Safari side windows, a Safari double skin roof and a buckled back door. The whole, with the exception of a white roof, was brush painted in a matt grey/blue colour. The ensemble was completed with a couple of dark blue 'sand ladders' (Hunter aircraft cockpit access ladders) strapped to the sides and four non-standard wheels of small diameter but enormous width. Unfortunately, because of the ladders, the overall impression was of a window cleaner's utility vehicle, the only thing missing being a galvanised bucket. The inside would have made even a Spartan flinch. Two battered bench seats in the rear and equally battered squabs in the front. The internal décor was overall gloss black which, whilst blending the mismatched panels together also emphasised every dent and scrape. The noise whilst travelling was incredible. Anything that could bang or rattle banged or rattled, and through it all the transmission howled like a banshee. A journey of any kind was a boneshaking, shattering experience. How Graham coped with the journey from Thumrait I have no idea. Thank goodness I still had the jeep and the Mazda.

Well, nobody expressed any interest in buying the thing, but as the days passed into weeks I found myself starting to be strangely attached to this raw, unsophisticated brute. I was also aware of the tremendous amount of work that Graham had put into his creation, toiling and sweating beneath the unrelenting desert sun. The engine was as sweet as the proverbial nut and the gearbox, transmission and brakes were all in excellent condition after Graham's tender ministrations. Despite the cataclysmic rattles, nothing ever fell off and nothing ever broke, and as the weeks clattered by it slowly dawned on me that I didn't want anybody to buy it because I didn't want to part with it.

You can scoff at Fate but She now stepped in as I happened to be due for a periodic car allowance from the company, and so one thing led to another and following some haggling with Graham he ended up with £650.00 in his pocket of which I paid £150.00 and BAC generously donated the outstanding £500.00 – in return for a receipt for £1,050.00.............

I owned a Land Rover.

The Rover with my Mahindra jeep and Alan's Carawagon

# Chapter 2 – The Exterior

At this time I had no particular plans for the future. The Land Rover was bought on a whim because I wanted it. However, for some time I had been aware of a slight but niggling urge to drive back to the UK at the end of my contract. Not that this was anything special as the most direct route was even then all tarmac and well travelled, with petrol stations and hotels along the way. It certainly did not need a four wheel drive vehicle. In fact, the simplicity of the route is demonstrated in the following tale.

Jack was also a BAC engineer with us in Oman. He was accompanied by his wife Jacqui, who taught at the Muscat English Speaking School – a school for the children of ex-patriot gentlefolk. Jack and Jacqui decided after just one year that Oman was not for them and made plans to return to the UK. On arrival in Oman they had bought a brand new Isusu Gemini and now offered it up for sale. This Gemini was a small, two door hatchback in somewhat stunning Kermit the Frog green. Jack had put a rather high price on it but whether it was the price or the colour, nobody wanted to buy it. Anyway, with two weeks to go Jack and Jacqui decided to drive back to England. A frantic round of embassies secured the necessary visas and presumably Jack checked the oil level and tyre pressures – or perhaps he didn't. Following their last two nights spent in an hotel, Jack and Jacqui had a large gathering of friends see them off and after a few drinks they simply put their bags into the car and departed with no more fuss than if they were off to the local shops – and five thousand miles later they arrived safely and uneventfully in England.

This direct route through Turkey had little appeal to a man with a Land Rover, and Google (2014) states that the journey can be completed in just seventy five hours. Nevertheless I still felt that I wanted to drive somewhere in a vehicle in which I could eat, sleep and generally live whilst unconstrained by the need for bitumen roads. This persistent urge obviously had something to do with my decision to buy the Land Rover and I found myself planning its conversion to a camper long before the transaction was complete. So, now that I had the vehicle, where to start?

As it happened, I was not short of advice. Our accommodation was a purpose built site consisting of single storey, terraced rows of one, two and three bedroom villas. Each villa had its own walled garden but very little would grow in the intense heat. Outside the gardens and between the rows of villas were wide areas of graded and flattened dust and sand where we parked our cars. In the early days of Rover ownership I could be found pottering around it in the afternoons, poking under the bonnet or just sitting smoking and thinking in the back. Later in the afternoon some of the other chaps would come ambling over, hands in pockets and full of advice. Then someone would fetch a few beers and someone else would fetch a few more so that by the time it was dark and we stumbled off home the only material change to the Rover would be a pile of empty cans and some cigarette ends. This pattern of events would take place to a greater or lesser extent every time I worked on the Rover in the compound over the next twenty months, but these formative early days soon resulted in plans detailed in my head and I was ready to start.

The first move was to create more headroom in the back, so at least one could sit comfortably without one's head touching the roof. I accepted that any kind of raising roof was beyond my capabilities and I therefore decided to cut the existing Safari roof right across just behind the front seats and lift the rear section by just six inches in order to gain that essential extra headroom. Obviously I would not be able to stand, but the psychological effect would be considerable and the urge to sit hunched up would be removed.

I have already mentioned the scrap dumps in the desert around Muscat, and for JVC and me these dumps were fascinating places to roam and salvage all sorts of things. At that time the Air Force and civilian contracting companies dumped all manner of items from electrical and mechanical bits and pieces to complete, albeit damaged, trucks, and we had a wonderful supply of switches, lights, brackets, steel, aluminium, pipes, wood and vehicle parts. Probably just rubbish to most people but JVC, George and I would periodically sally forth and do the rounds of the dumps and collect anything that 'might come in useful'. In our defence I can state that the workshops benefited considerably from testing and handling aids that we manufactured from dump materials and in fact we collected so much that we had to create our own private store, complete with racking, on top of the office block in the corner of the workshop.

One of these dump runs had resulted in the collection of several brand new 18 gauge galvanized steel sheets about 2' 6" by 10' 0". These would be ideal for the fabrication of my new rear body panels and to create the 6 inch roof lift.

George had also acquired a Land Rover plus a second, damaged one for spares. The damage was mostly to one of the front wings but also the chassis was bent. The rear pickup body pan was good, however, so I decided to replace my old and battered one with it, and also exchange the box section on which the front seats are mounted and which covers the gearbox and transfer box. My basic Rover was an early Series IIA, circa 1963, with the headlights incorporated into the radiator grill panel. I decided to fit two later Series III wings which had the headlights mounted in them. Externally this is almost the only visible difference between the IIA and the III and therefore my Rover would look years younger and have 4 headlights as an additional feature.

It was apparent that a major strip down was going to happen. George was quite amenable to me using the workshop after work hours, but I had to be careful not to attract the unwelcome attention of either our own management or the Air Force. All went smoothly initially. The Rapier support equipment included several 1 ton trailers and these made ideal mobile workstands for me. First the Safari roof was unbolted (everything unbolts on a Land Rover) and craned onto a trailer to be hidden behind the workshop. Similarly the rear pickup pan was removed and wheeled out of sight on a second trailer. The unwanted rear windows were thrown into a third trailer to be dumped at a later date as was the aforesaid box section over the gearboxes. I unbolted and removed the body pan from George's scrap Rover ready to put it on my chassis and then thought that it would be a good idea to swap the gearbox as well as it presumably had less mileage on it than my original. The replacement body pan was therefore placed on a fourth trailer. I discovered that the rear of my chassis was in poor condition and had been badly repaired with some angle iron. I therefore hacksawed the back fifteen inches off the chassis and welded on a similar section from the damaged Rover – another improvement as this, too, introduced the later design of the Mk III. With the chassis so exposed it was a good time to clean it up and give it a coat of underseal.

So far so good until one morning all hell broke loose when the Air Force commanding officer came upon all my parts loaded onto his trailers and the skeleton of the Rover taking up half the space in his workshop. Perhaps he was in a bad mood anyway, but certainly made his anger known to my superior and the result was a flurry of activity to move all my items outside the compound, leaving only the Safari roof inside leaning against a building trying to look part of it.

Fortunately the chassis work was finished so the replacement body pan was hastily placed on it and all four trailers relieved of their temporary burdens. Even I had to admit that the compound looked considerably better.

The front wings presented a bit of a problem. The right hand wing from George's scrap Rover was useable but the nearside was beyond repair. I cast around my various military contacts and, lo and behold, a brand new wing appeared. Ask no questions!

*At this point I should mention the Airworks organisation in Oman. Airworks was a civilian company that specialised in supplying trained and experienced personnel to assist overseas developing countries with the technical support of commercial aircraft and military systems. Most of their staff were ex UK service personnel. In Oman, Airworks maintained the Sultan's air fleet which at that time included Hawker Hunters, Jaguars, Bell 212 helicopters and Jet ranger helicopters plus a couple of BAC 111's. Such a support task requires considerable workshop facilities, maintenance hangers and equipment. Our Rapier stores were run by Airworks and they also used the Beach Club so we had a close relationship both in and outside work.*

Throughout all these alterations the Rover remained road registered and I was now able to drive it about as an open pickup with no cab. The body panels were a mix of colours but it was much quieter and already seemed to be a much smoother ride.

I now needed some outside assistance to manufacture my new body panels from the sheets of galvanised steel tucked away out of sight in the workshop. Through a friend in the civil engineering section of BAC, I was introduced to a Greek Cypriot manager in the construction company Joannou and Paraskevaides (J & P) who gave me access to their sheet metal shop. I had made some detailed drawings of my requirements and produced my sheets of galvanised steel. I then stood back and watched whilst a skilled operator cut and bent the required 8 panels to shape. Each panel was basically a simple rectangle with 1 inch flanged edges which allowed them to be invisibly bolted together, sealed with mastic.

The roof was the original Safari roof, cut across at a forty five degree angle just behind the front cab such that the front section bolted onto the door pillars and windscreen as usual, and the rear section bolted on top of two new 6 inch deep panels which spanned from the door pillars to the rear of the vehicle. The resulting gap between the front and back roof sections was filled with a piece of thick plywood sloped back at forty five degrees and sealed and finished with fibreglass matting and resin. Both sections of the roof retained the double skin feature which plays such a huge part in keeping the interior cool in high temperatures. The sides of the rear were completed with the remaining steel panels which bolted into position and created a window opening on each side. The conversion was completed by raising the height of the back door to match the roof.

Stripped down and ready to start the rebuild

Starting the rebuild with the roof raised to its new height

So, there it was, my customised Land Rover. Maybe not the build from scratch that JVC had originally had in mind, but nevertheless a unique vehicle assembled from a wide range of component parts gathered from both ends of Oman.

The remaining job was to spray the whole thing in grey primer and then several coats of brilliant, gloss white cellulose. A transformation, and I relieved the blank whiteness with a three inch black stripe around at waist height with a one inch gold band in the middle. Pretty smart..........

The completed exterior – apart from the wheels!

........and the rear. Note the access panel to the tool box.

So much for the exterior, but the interior remained an appalling mess and it was to take a further year to convert it to a rather luxurious - but at the same time very functional - camper.

# Chapter 3 – The Interior

With memories of Lawrence it seemed a good idea to christen the Rover and give it a personality. Many names were put forward and discussed but I had never named a vehicle before and I think that such pet names should spring up spontaneously in order to be 'right'. As it turned out, whilst this vehicle and I were to have a very special relationship, it was to be strictly one of Man and Machine, and in keeping with its proud heritage the Rover was destined to always be known as ........The Rover. In the early days of the travel log there was an attempt to call it The Tardis but this soon fell into disuse. I could also argue that, like Lawrence, most of the problems occurred in this formative period and that once we settled on The Rover things went along much more smoothly.

And so to the interior. As I have said, the complete plans and layout were all in my head. I had designed the body to suit what I wanted to put inside. I had studied Alan's Carawagon and whilst some things were good I felt that much could be improved upon. I had spent a lot of my time on UK leaves in roaming around caravan centres, looking for ideas. However, caravans and commercially built campers were considerably larger than the space at my disposal and my original ideas remained unchanged. These nevertheless had to accommodate some indispensable commercial equipment and I had brought back a twelve volt/gas refrigerator, a plastic sink with tap and water pump, an extractor fan, a Gaz fuelled heater and a couple of strip lights. A suitable camping Gaz cooker was purchased locally in Oman.

I still had to resolve the question of the two rear side windows but one day, whilst nosing around a dump, I came across strips of aluminium extrusion of a complex cross section, used presumably for the installation of electrical equipment in buildings. Hacksawing down the length produced perfectly shaped sections from which I made the window frames and which came complete with a double channel in which to fit both a fixed and a sliding perspex window. Another problem neatly solved.

I had decided to fit out the rear of the vehicle first and leave the cab until last. The first thing to tackle was the roof, to insulate it against sound and line it with material. I had deliberately left the roof to be removable and so could now call in some assistance to lift it right off and support it upside down on my patio.

Up until this time, the flat, which I shared with another BAC employee, Jim Rix, had tended to have a few tins of paint and fibreglass and stuff kicking about in the kitchen and most of the work had been carried out in the Rapier workshop. Now that fabrics were to be used the lounge came in for more than its fair share of cottons, pieces of cloth, foam rubber, scissors etc, etc. There never seemed to be time to tidy it up. Jim was very patient, though, and fortunately spent most of his time out. I accept in retrospect that I was not perhaps the ideal flat-mate during this period.

I wanted the interior of the vehicle to be smart and cosy. There was going to be plenty of varnished wood and I needed a suitable fabric to go with it and something that would be relatively easy to fit. From one of the many Asian fabric shops I selected a gold material with a one eighth inch knap. Borrowing a sewing machine I set to and cut and stitched panels to fit the roof, supported by plastic strips sprung across the width. I stuck in thick felt for insulation and breathed a sigh of relief when we eventually swung the whole thing the right way up and put it back on the Rover and the lining stayed snug and tight. This time the roof went on once and for all and was sealed with mastic.

The interior design of my steel side panels was such that I could screw flat plywood panels onto them with self-tapping screws and cup washers, creating a 1 inch gap between inside and outside which could be filled with felt insulation. The wood panels were cut out of the sides of old packing cases and covered with the gold material which was simply folded over the edges and stapled into place.

With the upper sections panelled I could start on the 'furniture'. I started with the refrigerator housing immediately behind the driver's seat. I actually had to *buy* some plywood for this. The unit ran from floor to roof. The refrigerator sat on the square wheel arch leaving space above for a cupboard fifteen inches high by fifteen inches wide and eighteen inches deep. With this first unit installed I moved back down the side of the vehicle with a worktop leading to the cooker built in next to the door. The cooker was concealed by a hinged flap when not in use. It had two top rings and a small grill. Beneath the worktop was a long flap which hinged down to form a narrow table. Behind the flap was a storage recess and also a drawer for cutlery and the inevitable accumulated oddments. Below this a cupboard with sliding doors created more storage space and a place to clamp two five pound camping Gaz cylinders.

*The finished living accommodation*

This right-hand side installation was completed with another cupboard in the space under the cooker. Both the cooker and the narrow table were designed to be used whilst seated on a long bench seat to be fitted on the other side of the Rover.

Opposite the cooker I built the sink unit which was also concealed beneath a hinged flap. Below the sink was a small storage cupboard with double hinged doors. The tap on the sink was piped via an electric pump to a five gallon water tank which I mounted in the wheel arch space just in front of the rear left hand wheel. The drain from the sink was piped down through the standard Rover tool box, but with the sink unit fitted I had lost the normal top access to this toolbox. I solved this by cutting a hole in the outside of the Rover and fitting a lockable hinged door. This was a really neat modification and meant that the toolbox was always accessible.

All the working surfaces and some of the doors were faced with simulated wood grain Formica and the rest of the woodwork was stained fairly dark and varnished. It looked rather nice and a German traveller was subsequently to remark, "It looks zo English".

The next step was to construct the bench seat which would convert into a double bed. The resulting design was a seat which slid out from the side and across to the sliding doors of the gas bottle cupboard with the gap left being filled by dropping in the seat back. To give the bed a useable length I had to cut out a deep section of the aluminium bulkhead to allow access into the cab area. Then by lifting out the passenger seat squab, folding down the seat back and placing the squab back on top one half of the bed was extended to six feet six inches. The other half was extended by building a storage box with a padded top between the two front seats. An adequate and comfortable sleeping arrangement – although only really ideal with somebody that you had a close relationship with.

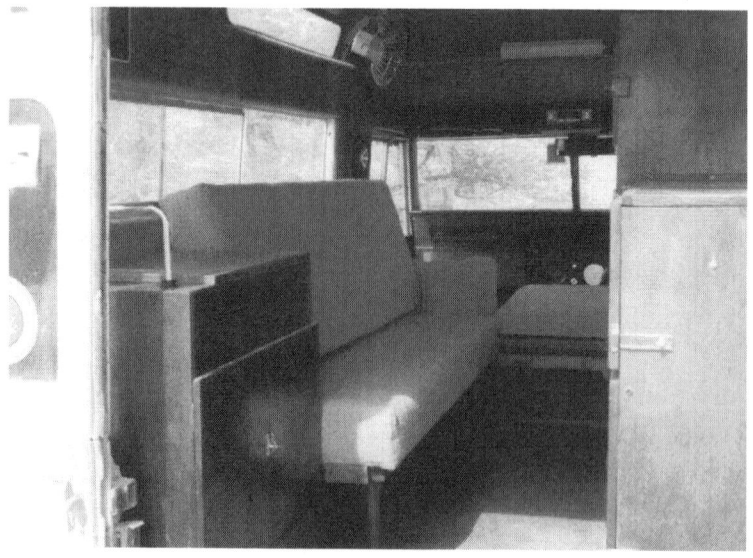

The sink to the left and the bed in sofa mode

I now had to have a dabble at upholstery. I chose a nice strong, rich bronze, corded material, borrowed a sewing machine and set to work. More mess in the lounge. The bench seat and the back of it were padded with pieces cut from a foam rubber mattress but the seat squabs and their backs I made from thick blocks of packing foam that had protected the Rapier equipment whilst in transit. This foam was very resilient and considering that that was all there was between one's bottom and a solid piece of plywood the result proved to be extremely comfortable throughout some very rough travelling.

I had decided to mount a radio/cassette player *above* the windscreen together with a panel containing all the vehicle electrical switches and warning lights, leaving the dashboard fitted only with the two standard Land Rover instrument clusters and the ignition switch and a cigarette lighter. This arrangement looked pretty good and also resulted in the benefit of the replacement of all the existing wiring loom in the cab with new cable. I well remember the day I completed the installation of this new loom. It was dark by the time I finished but I had successfully checked out all the circuits until I switched on the headlights and the ammeter shot to maximum discharge and all indications were ominous. An hour of fault finding traced the problem to a self-tapping screw I had used to secure a cable clip and which had *just* pierced the headlight supply wire.

I finally turned my attention to the dashboard and the rest of the cab. The dashboard in the Mk IIA was all metal and very functional and mine was particularly ugly with chipped black paint and dents. It was surmounted on each side with a bulky motor for each windscreen wiper.

In an attempt to resolve the issue of the windscreen wipers and also to find a replacement for the very ugly steering column indicator switch, I returned to the scrap Rover from which I had had so many bits and pieces and discovered that it still had the modern wiper mechanism consisting of a single neat motor and a cable drive to the two arms. This was removed without difficulty and, whilst glancing around I came across a neat steering column box of unknown origin. Fitted with two ex-Range Rover column switches for indicators and dip switch and tightly covered in black vinyl this fixed neatly to my steering column and admirably hid all the eyesores. With the 'new' windscreen wiper equipment fitted I made a new dashboard to cover the motor and which also gave me a small cubby hole to the left of the steering column and a wide, if shallow, lockable glove box in front of the passenger seat

The final hurdle was the upper half of the dashboard which had to slope backwards into the cab, following the lines of the existing metalwork. Behind this section of the dashboard the front bulkhead of the vehicle contained the two ventilation flaps below the windscreen which have been a recognisable feature of every model of the Land Rover. The problem was to find some suitable plastic grills to fit into a new inner plywood fascia board to allow the air to flow into the cab. I needed three neat grills two and a half inches high by twelve inches wide. I had a UK contact scour the BAC factory plus caravan and camping shops for something suitable but to no avail. This was, one must remember, years before the Internet came into being. I finally found, quite by accident and whilst roaming around a scrap tip, the perfect solution. In the doors of some VW minibuses were fresh-air vents, yes, two and a half inches high by twelve inches wide. Let into the varnished plywood they looked as if they had always been there, directing the air stream down to one's legs and hiding the mess behind. The new dashboard was completed with a top cover

– another length of vinyl covered plywood with two long grills from the dashboard of a Mk III Rover for directing air to de-mist the windscreen.

The transformed cab

With the insides of the doors insulated and covered in plywood and black vinyl, plus carpet front and back, the Rover was finally finished and was a far cry from the rattling monster that I had originally bought.

# Chapter 4 – Plans Start to Get Serious

Until this point I have omitted to mention a factor which had had a tremendous influence on my life and travel plans. This factor was meeting Dawn, who was a teacher at the Muscat English Speaking School and who I had first seen when I was operating the stage lights at a school concert and she was shepherding a load of children around. It was three months before I saw her again at a party and she actually looked at me and smiled and said hello. Blimey! In fact, I was subsequently to discover that she had mistaken me for somebody else. Not realising this I seized the opportunity and later in the evening launched into the old 'do you come here often?' routine, or something like that. Well, the result was a date the following week and after a couple of evenings out together things started to go along very nicely.

At this time the Rover was still very much in its infancy and whilst I, in my Land Rover euphoria of dreams and visions, thought it very impressive, I subsequently learnt from Dawn that she thought that I was a bit over-optimistic, to say the least, and that this rattling pumpkin would never become the golden coach that I airily described.

Well, love conquered all, and though Dawn kept well out of the way of the conversion business there was no doubt that the Rover had started to cast its spell in her direction. We used to go for trips into The Interior along with other members of the local sub-aqua club and in a variety of four wheel drive vehicles, and the benefits of a bed plus a cooker and insect proofing soon became apparent. All this well before the interior was finished, so things could only get better.

Dawn was a seasoned traveller, having covered the Asian route some years before, and soon became as keen as I was in making a long journey in the Rover.

She had moved from the Muscat school to The Sultan's School and her contract was due to finish at the end of June 1980. My BAC contract would be completed at the end of August. We both declined offers of extensions and early September was set for our departure, although we still didn't know where we were going! Basically I think that we decided to head for Kenya, having been there on holiday earlier in the year and fancying roaming the game parks at leisure in our own vehicle.

Unfortunately this was right at the time that the 'Death of a Princess' documentary was broadcast on UK television. This seriously upset the Saudi government and visas were not being granted to British subjects. Transit through Saudi Arabia was unavoidable for us and it was conceivable that we could set off and get no further than the border. We would then be left with no alternative but to return to Dubai and try to get on a ship to Port Sudan or Mombassa – a no doubt very expensive option and not in keeping with the aim of the trip.

Still, whilst these difficulties were being debated it was only May and there remained plenty of work to do on the Rover. I wired up the 'fridge and piped gas to it and the cooker. Dawn painted all the insides of the cupboards and started laying in the supplies that we would be needing. We reckoned to be on the road for some 4 to 5 months in all. She bought unbreakable plates, bowls and containers. We collected together all sorts of cutlery and cooking utensils. These all had to have stowage points and straps where necessary.

I still had several large jobs to carry out, not least the installation of a re-conditioned engine – well, after I had reconditioned it, that is. George had given me a spare Series III engine so I was able to get it rebored whilst still running on the old engine. I meticulously re-built the engine and replaced all the bits that I could. When it was completed I took out the original engine and then ripped all the old wiring out. I rewired all the engine compartment and thus the only original cable left was that running inside the chassis to the rear lights. The result was surprisingly neat and tidy. After two or three days I put in the new engine and breathed a sigh of relief – until the clutch thrust bearing started tapping. I just couldn't bring myself to start all over again and tried to ignore it. I couldn't but decided to do nothing about it and it was still happily tapping some 25,000 kilometres later when we arrived in England.

Three major jobs left to do. One was to make a roof rack. I searched all my favourite dumps for suitable material but could find nothing. I then remembered many lengths of strong aluminium extruded section known as Z Rail which had been supplied to Oman as part of the workshop installation kit for the hydraulic and optical areas. I couldn't weld it but it was very strong and I reckoned that it could be riveted into a suitable framework. I didn't want to increase the height of the vehicle any more than necessary so fabricated a flat platform the width of the vehicle and only about 2 feet long. There was a fair bit of discussion about where to place this but a technical article that I read said that any additional weight should be over the back axle, not the front so I duly fixed it at the rear of the roof, a decision I was to regret.

A couple of weeks later we went to a midday pool party and arriving at the venue I noticed a row of covered parking spaces. Shade was always welcome so I drove into one of them only to feel a slight jolt followed by the sound of clanging and ringing as the roof rack was neatly skimmed off and deposited in a heap behind me. Not only that but I was now firmly wedged under the shelter and after nonchalantly collecting my 'flat pack' roof rack I had to enlist a few heavy fellows to hang on the back of the vehicle to compress the springs so that I could back out again. I rebuilt the rack and refitted it.

Two major jobs to do. I was worried about the fuel carrying capacity and wanted to avoid having to carry too many jerry cans, inevitably on the roof. My original Series II had twin ten gallon tanks, one under each front seat with a cross-over selector valve. With the Series III rear pan fitted I could also fit the standard Series III fourteen gallon tank at the back of the vehicle. Another dump forage found a decent looking tank fitted to a bare Rover chassis so this was easy to remove and fit. Regrettably I didn't check it for leaks before I fitted it and soon found a major leakage problem when I poured some petrol in. My subsequent attempts at brazing up the leak failed miserably and I finally had to give up and throw the tank away and I was unable to find another one. However, I had had another idea. With no rear fuel tank there was a large empty space under the rear of the vehicle. I calculated that I could cut a hole in the body panel just behind the right-hand rear wheel and construct a compartment into which two jerry cans would slide side by side. Secured with a metal strap and a padlock this proved to be a very effective way of adding ten gallons to my fuel capacity.

Just one job left to do and that was to fit a storage box into the space on top of the chassis in front of the right-hand rear wheel. This took longer than I had envisaged but I ended up with a shortened ammunition box for mechanical spares neatly inserted and strapped firmly into place. To gain access meant jacking the vehicle up and removing the back wheel but that was a bonus anti-theft device.

We were now nearly in the middle of July and my scattering of building materials in the flat had been superseded by what appeared to be a mountain of provisions collected by Dawn. We were taking a minimum of heavy canned stuff and Dawn's emphasis was on dried soups and vegetables and all sorts of basic things that could be added to very little and yet produce a nourishing meal. Her theory proved to be spot on and despite many times on the journey when food was in very short supply we never failed to have a tasty meal every day.

So, it was the middle of July and we were off to England for four weeks leave. I was amazed that BAC let me go at such a time, with only two weeks of my contact to run on my return but our local manager was very sympathetic to my plans in more ways than one and I will always be grateful to him for the indirect assistance that he gave me – or perhaps I should say for not being as obstructive as he could very well have been.

For Dawn and myself, it was a last opportunity to collect items that were just not available in Oman – not least our International Driving Licences and a Carnet de Passage for the vehicle. We also had to collect our sleeping bags and Dawn's mum donated a couple of hot water bottles (!). I was also desperate for some curtain rails. The ones fitted in Alan's Carawagon were the ideal design and having been unable to find anything else suitable I ended up driving to the Carawagon workshop in Sunbury-on-Thames and buying some lengths there.

Mid-August and back to Oman for the last time. Dawn and I had arranged to meet at Heathrow and both arrived an hour before take-off. We then both stood waiting for forty five minutes before discovering that we stood only twenty yards apart but separated by a substantial pillar. Needless to say, a frantic scramble to get through check-in just in time!

# Chapter 5 – Final Preparations

There still seemed to be an alarming amount of work to be done. I resigned myself to the fact that the Rover would not be finished when we left and that any small jobs remaining would have to be completed en route.

Dawn was now working for an hour a day giving private English tuition to a Lebanese child and collecting a reasonable pay packet for her efforts.

We had attempted to acquire some visas before our departure and Dawn had visited the Jordanian, Egyptian and Sudanese embassies. She had no joy whatsoever at the Jordanian. The Egyptians took the money, stamped in the visas then promptly cancelled them and handed back the money when they realised that we didn't need them for another 3 months or so. The Sudanese consul was exceedingly polite and helpful but eventually admitted on her third visit that he really didn't have a clue on how to go about issuing a visa. We did learn, however, something of the restrictions on taking a vehicle into Sudan. The vehicle had to be inspected at the nearest Sudanese embassy before crossing the border, you couldn't pull a trailer, lots of vehicle spares had to be carried and checked by the Sudanese authorities and you had to travel across the Nubian desert in convoy. Last, but perhaps not least, thou shalt not drive on the railway line.......!

We had an AA booklet on driving through Africa and this was not very encouraging either, and gave the impression that the AA did not really approve of its members attempting it. It pointed out that to take a right hand drive vehicle into Egypt one had to have formal permission from the Egyptian Motoring Organisation in Cairo, but that you could not drive to Cairo to obtain it. I enquired about this at the Egyptian embassy in Oman and, like Dawn's friend at the Sudanese embassy, they were polite and concerned but totally nonplussed. I therefore wrote to the Cairo address given in the AA book and asked for their assistance, but never received a reply.

Our most pressing requirement was my transit visa for Saudi Arabia. Several visits to the embassy had been met with a shrug and "come back nearer the time". We knew that Dawn, being unmarried, would never get a visa so planned for her to fly to Kuwait from Qatar, stay with a friend whilst I drove to Jordan and then fly there to meet me. But what if I failed to get a Saudi visa? We would have burned our boats because by leaving Oman by road we would have had to return within two weeks or we could not gain re-entry. This would have left us stuck in the UAE.

I was aware of at least four people who had abandoned the idea of driving through Saudi at that time because of the repercussions of 'Death of a Princess'. In the end we left Oman without a single onward visa in our passports and with our fingers crossed. Happily our subsequent experience was that it was relatively straightforward to obtain a visa for a country by simply waiting and applying for it in the preceding country.

Meanwhile, back at the workshop I fitted and piped up the gas heater and also fitted a pipe to the water tank so that it could be filled from the outside.

The last job, then, was to fit the curtain rails and for Dawn to run up some curtains that would draw across all the rear windows and also round and across the windscreen.

The final result was, if anything, beyond the dreams that I had had at the beginning. I had produced a rugged camper with all the necessary amenities together with a very comfortable, practical and cosy layout.

It was now the end of August and time for my contract to end, but Dawn could carry on with her private tuition for another couple of weeks and we really were not ready to leave. I explained the situation to our manager and yet again he was very understanding and allowed me to remain in the flat.

I had been collecting spares for the Rover and now had to sort and package them. I carefully listed all the items and sealed them in stout plastic bags. I had a phobia about gearbox failure and ripped the innards out of my old box and packed all the useful looking bits in the theory that if I took lots then I wouldn't need them, but if I didn't take lots......... In addition there were things like gaskets, brake linings, clutch plate, prop shaft universal joint, water pump kit, a single long rear half shaft, oil filters, inlet and exhaust valves with springs, inner tubes, ignition coil and spark plugs. The list could be endless and it was difficult to know where to draw the line, particularly as I had access to so many items, albeit all second hand. These spares went into the ammunition box under the rear wheel arch plus a useful toolbox riveted to the front bulkhead under the bonnet.

On the roof rack was a second ammunition box with mainly our warm clothes in it (and the hot water bottles), three metal twenty litre jerry cans and two twenty litre plastic water containers. Also on the roof was a second spare wheel, the first being on the standard bonnet mounting, plus a folding camping table. All the items on the roof had a stout length of chain threaded through them and padlocked securely to the vehicle. The camping table was complemented by a pair of folding camp chairs that strapped inside the back door and which were quickly accessible at the end of a day's travelling. These were to contribute immensely to the simple pleasures of the journey.

We were finally forced to realise that we had better set a date for leaving or it would be just too easy to keep pottering on. We settled on Saturday the twentieth of September. This meant that we had a last weekend with our friends down at the beach. Closer to the day Dawn started transferring armfuls of stuff from the flat to the Rover. It looked impossible for it all to fit in but, sure enough, it all stowed neatly away and by midday on the twentieth we declared ourselves as ready as we would ever be. We had spread the word around about our departure and that we would be leaving at two thirty and that there would be beers in the fridge for well-wishers.

The point of no return

People started arriving at one thirty, the first being our very close friends John and Gill and Gordon and Barbara who appeared with a bottle of champagne.

Within half an hour we had twenty nine people crowded into the lounge bearing good luck cards and their best wishes for the journey. At two thirty (gosh, was it difficult) we said "right, got to go" and we all trooped outside to the Rover, which sat outside metaphorically champing at the bit. A barrage of photographs and Dawn at her window kissing all the men and me at mine kissing all the girls. The engine started first time and the proceedings were rounded off as we played 'Land of Hope and Glory' at full volume and slowly pulled away. I clearly remember being a little surprised that I was sweating so much, but then I glanced across at Dawn and saw the tears rolling down her face, too. As Dawn was to write in our first log entry – '… Pete and me groped for the box of Kleenex'.

Some of the crowd seeing us off

"Don't forget to write......"

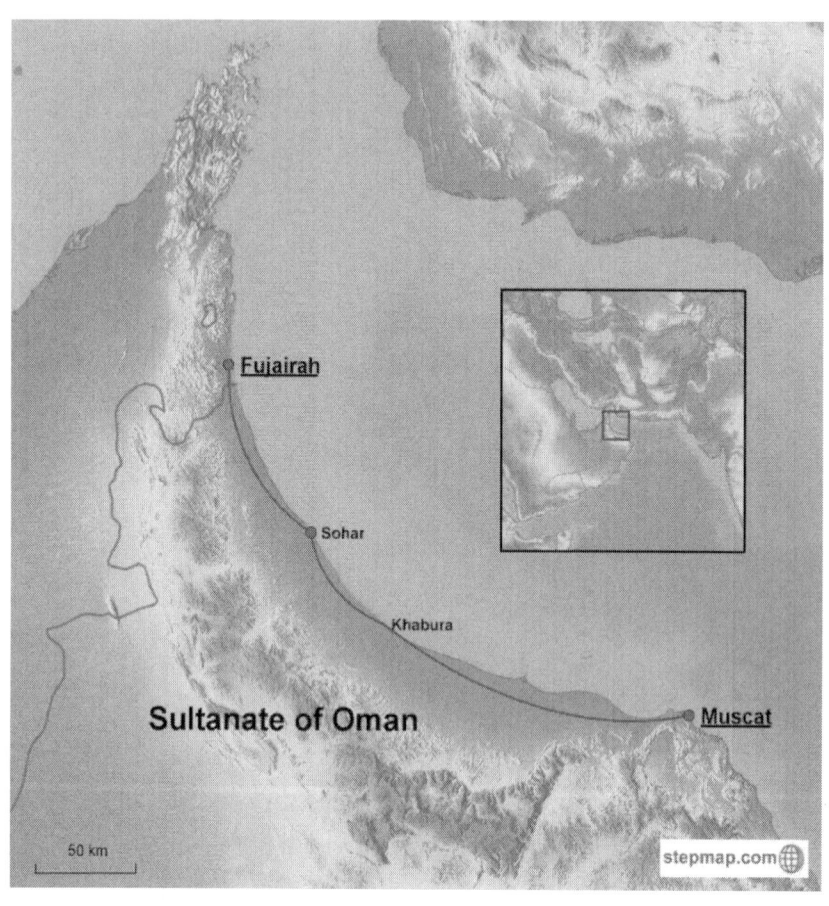

# Chapter 6 – Out of Oman

Saturday 20th to Sunday 21st September 1980

Journey days 1 and 2

As expeditions go, ours must have been one of the worst planned ever. As I have previously mentioned, we had no onward visas and could only get as far as Qatar on our British passports. I had purchased some Bartholomew's maps in Oman and these had adorned the walls of the flat for some weeks. I was subsequently to realise that whilst Bartholomew's maps are, indeed, ideal to hang on the wall they are of little practical use when it comes to navigating one's way across continents. We were to come across other travellers with amazingly detailed maps plus books stuffed with information on local customs, petrol stations, shops, currency, hotels and campsites. Our tourist information consisted of a Polyglot guide to Egypt and some handouts from the Sudanese embassy. Not that it really mattered in some ways as we still hadn't decided where we were going. However, we had a vehicle that could go virtually anywhere and all the amenities and provisions to live relatively comfortably for several months plus, of course, a firm resolve to drive back to England *somehow*. One item that was never considered or discussed was travel insurance.

Readers of this in the New Millennium should also bear in mind that mobile telephones, digital cameras, the internet and satellite navigation etc were but figments of science fiction imagination back in 1980.

On that first day we planned to travel only about 170 kilometres to the small town of Khabura on the coast of Oman. This was the road to the United Arab Emirates border and in the town lived a small group of young people who were running a small experimental farm. Two Brit guys were cross-breeding goats to try and provide a hardier local stock and an Australian girl, 'Sally the Weaver', was teaching the local women how to spin and weave the goat wool in order to obtain an income. We had been there a couple of times before and Sally had become a welcome visitor to us in the Muscat area. The main object of that first day was to make a clean break from our life in Muscat but not necessarily attempt to put too many miles on the clock. It was therefore ideal to arrange for our first night to be spent with Sally – coincidentally also putting off our first night in the Rover with no air conditioning. We therefore set off along the flat coastal road which gently curves with the coastline of the northern plain until it reaches the UAE border some 300 km from Muscat. We expected to reach Khabura after some three hours and Dawn dozed off. The road was extremely boring with the mountains getting further and further away to the left and the sea out of sight to the right. The plain was very flat and broken only by scattered, low scrub. There were many farms along the way and therefore some greenery, but all very repetitive. It wasn't too hot and the Rover was running smoothly. Mind you, during these first few days of travel I used up a lot of nervous energy listening for the slightest odd noise and I must have spent more time looking down at the temperature gauge and the ammeter and then up to the oil pressure warning light than I spent watching the road. I somehow felt that I could justify and cope with a breakdown once we had travelled a couple of thousand kilometres but could not face the embarrassment of a breakdown so close to home. Dawn, of course, was oblivious to all of this, ignorance of all things mechanical being bliss. As she slumbered peacefully on, my audio/visual faculties were turned right up, resulting in clenched hands on the wheel and I periodically had to make a conscious effort to relax.

*Is the battery charging? The ammeter needle is almost dead centre. Is it fully charged or has something failed? No good looking at the ignition light because it's on all the time (never did figure that one out!). But if the fan belt had gone then the engine temperature would be rising and – no – that's ok, but perhaps a little high, and it's not so hot outside now. Oil pressure ok? Yes, no warning light on (I had never fitted an oil pressure gauge as I find them more disconcerting than comforting. Watching your oil pressure vary is a sure way to early grey hairs so I was more than happy to rely on the friendly little green light being off). What about noises? Is that road noise or transmission rumble? I knew I should hixed that clutch thrust bearing. What about fuel consumption? Um, let's see, started off with ten gallons, less a bit, gauge is down to half but the gauge is a bit dodgy – let's say that I have used three gallons, kilometres covered, um, about eighty five which is just over fifty miles so averaging over sixteen miles to the gallon – wish it was nearer twenty.*

*Is the battery charging………………?*

Dawn returned from the Land of Nod and suggested a sandwich. Good-oh. She clambered into the back and deftly sliced the bread and made a snack whilst we continued travelling. I do remember thinking that the small town we were passing through looked familiar, but then turned my attention to my sandwich. There were villages and small towns dotted all along the route and they all looked much the same and certainly they did not all have a road sign to identify them. They also had no unique distinguishing features. It was only after a further forty five minutes and no Khabura that we did start to feel a little uneasy and realised that we didn't really know where we were – a feeling that I have to admit was to become all too familiar over the coming months. Well, we finally had to assume that we must have overshot and we turned around to retrace our steps. Sure enough, 55 kilometres back down the road we found Khabura, and, yes, this *was* where I took that first bite of my sandwich……..

What an ignominious start to our adventures! By this time it was dark and we thankfully lumbered down the sandy track to the farm where beer, food, air conditioning and a soft bed awaited us, plus a pleasant evening with Sally and Richard the Goat Breeder.

Stop the Rover, turn off the ignition, relax my audio visual senses and bring my nervous tension back to a normal level. This preoccupation with vehicle failure was to continue until I was through Saudi, by which time it had thankfully left me as my confidence in the Rover grew ever stronger.

The following morning Dawn went off with Sally to visit some of the women weavers and I stayed to help Richard with the goats. There was no particular hurry to be off and the whole idea was to get the most experience out of the opportunities that arose. Dawn ended up with some very good photographs of the local women and children and I mastered the technique of holding a nervous goat whilst it was injected.

The farm itself consisted of a small square of single story villas, leading onto a central area in which grew beautiful orange and red bougainvillaea. The goats were in pens outside the compound and next to the pens was a fairly large field cultivated with alfalfa. There was always a calm and serene atmosphere about the place, a pleasant farmyard smell and a feeling of being close to nature. Sally had her villa decorated with woven rugs hanging on the walls with huge brightly covered cushions on the floor. The walls were white with dark brown paint on the woodwork and the lounge was a lovely cool, restful place to be in, with the sunlight and the bright bougainvillaea peeping through the small windows.

It was all too easy to stay longer, and Sally was glad of the company as it was a rather remote posting. But, we had to make some effort to get to England so we left after lunch with a plastic shape of Australia mounted on a small magnet, a metal ashtray shaped like Australia and a Japanese hand fan. Plastic Australia ended stuck upside down in the roof of the Rover, metal Australia fell irretrievably into a space down the side of the cooker and the fan was stuck in the front curtain rail pending a decision on its future. It was still there when we landed in Dover but had proved useful en route. Note that, in yet another sign of the times, this was the first time that we had come across a 'fridge magnet.

And so on the road to Abu Dhabi, where we had friends working on another BAC Rapier contract. The journey from Khabura to the city of Abu Dhabi could easily have been accomplished in one day but I insisted that we spend one night in the Rover on the way. We had used the vehicle extensively in Oman for weekend forays into the desert but had not actually slept and eaten in it since it had been completely finished, and if there were to be any snags then Abu Dhabi would be the place to fix them. The plan, therefore, was to travel just over the border then camp for the night.

We left Sally at two in the afternoon and continued along the coast road in a northerly direction to the border. Audio/visuals on high alert again!

The most northerly town in Oman for us was Sohar, where a fine old Portuguese mud fort loomed over the squat houses. I had never been there before so we decided to detour for a quick look around. It was still only about 3.30 and everywhere was deserted under the hot afternoon sun. Sohar proved to be very similar to all the major towns in Oman with its central, round fort and rows of flat roofed, mud and straw – and latterly breeze block – houses all around with narrow sandy roads and alleyways between them. Built right on the coast, Sohar was long and narrow and the houses nearest the sea were but a few metres from the water at high tide. Oman was known for its ancient style of double house doors, each one no more than 18 inches wide and decorated with studs and carvings. Originally made of thick wood, modern doors are made from sheet metal and angle iron with decoration of wrought iron strips and painted in gaudy shades of red, green and blue. Each traditional style house had a pair of doors leading into the house or a high walled courtyard, and security was usually completed with a huge Chinese-made padlock. Being mid afternoon all the shops were closed, as were all the houses, and we were faced with sandy brown walls and solid doors and shutters of dry, grey wood that had withstood the onslaught of sun, salt spray and sand for centuries. Tall date palms loomed in places and at their base, sadly all too often, would be a pile of rusting Carnation milk and tomato paste tins with discarded blue, pink and yellow plastic bags to add a touch of colour. Much of the rock in Oman was dark brown, clinker-like stuff, and rusty, brown tins readily blended into the landscape.

Each town had its suq or souk, the market area which in the mornings and late afternoons was the bustling hub of life. Tiny shops sold basic supplies of tinned food and packaged foodstuffs with predominance given to tomato paste and large tins of Nido dried milk powder plus sacks of onions, rice and perhaps potatoes. Hardware stores sold brightly coloured plastic household goods and shiny aluminium pots and pans which glinted like precious metal in the sun, whilst other shops would be bursting with cheap foam rubber mattresses covered in the most incredibly lurid materials. Amidst these hot and dusty, and apparently dirt-poor, surroundings would be the goldsmiths and the silversmiths, with a small fortune in precious metals in each tiny workshop. Much of the crafted gold was of Italian origin, but the Omani silverware was usually made locally.

Sohar fort

A coastal town like Sohar was obviously a fishing community and would also have a fish market, identifiable from a distance by its distinctive odour. All manner of strange sea creatures found their way onto the thick, greasy wooden tables and sandy floor of the fish suq, from sizeable sharks to sardines. As with all fish markets the peak of activity was early in the morning. There was no harbour at Sohar and the fishing boats were simply hauled up the beach on baulks of timber thickly lubricated with fish grease. I was out with JVC once and we were prevailed upon to help pull a boat up out of the water and were rewarded for our efforts with the most appalling thick, black, smelly, rancid fish fat all over our hands.

The local Omani found in these towns would be dressed in his ankle length white 'dish-dash' with either a lace or embroidered skull cap, or a tablecloth sized square of usually red or black chequered material known as a 'shemag' which would be skilfully wrapped around his head in a traditional style. The shemag was a wonderful thing. It kept the sun off your head and could be partially unwound and tucked across the nose and mouth to keep the dust out. You could sleep in the desert on it, sit on the beach on it, use it as a towel or take it back to England to casually throw over your old, threadbare sofa. On his feet your Omani man-about-town would usually have plastic flip-flops or, occasionally, leather sandals – known by us as Nizwa Wellies after the name of the main town of manufacture.

Omanis away from the capital were friendly, kind and generous people who took delight in entertaining guests and visitors with tiny cups of delicious coffee made from beans roasted with cardamom pods. Despite their tough way of life they had a ready laugh and a proud heritage. These fine Arab traditions were sadly being lost in the capital area where the oil wealth was luring the young men from the villages and providing them with menial beaurocratic jobs and easy money which was resulting all too often in fast cars and arrogance.

Nevertheless, at that time it was a wonderful country and we were privileged to be there before the massive modernisation and building programmes that were to take place in later years, and which would inevitably change forever the delightful, unspoiled, exotic, romantic country that stole our hearts. To me it was always a heady mix of Beau Geste and Ali Baba with a bit of Lawrence of Arabia thrown in.

We drove along the deserted alleyways of Sohar and emerged onto the beach. Vehicles had obviously driven back and forth in the soft sand so we decided to take a short cut and do the same, and for the first time on the trip we ground slowly along in four wheel drive and low ratio until we came back to the main highway and finally headed off to the border, the excitement of our situation considerably tempered by the sadness of saying goodbye to our beloved Oman.

****

Distance through Oman – 434 km

Total distance travelled – 434 km

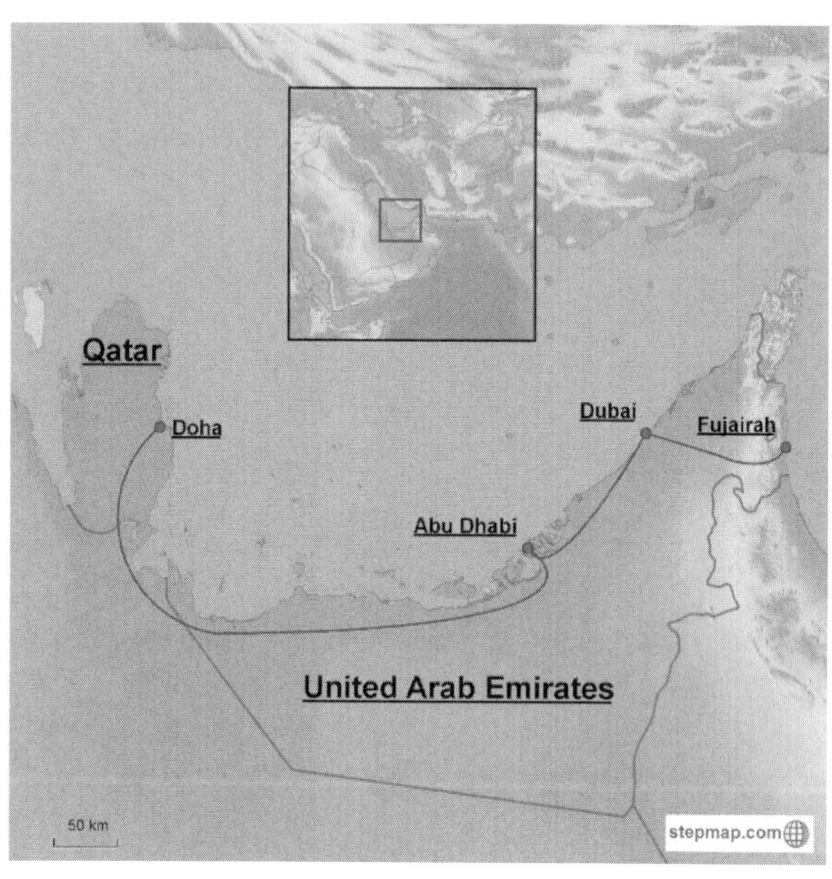

# Chapter 7 – The United Arab Emirates

Sunday 21st to Friday 26th September 1980

Journey days 2 to 7

From Sohar the border was still a considerable distance. As we progressed further north the mountains started to reappear, coming back to the coast again. Finally at about four o'clock we reached the end of Oman just south of Fujairah.

Border posts never seem to be the impressive places that you expect them to be, and this was no exception. I suppose that we are more used to the opulence of international airports, and it is often difficult to appreciate that you are actually at an official post when travelling by road. Pulling up by the side of the road and hoping that our papers were all in order, I nipped over to the hatchway of the tiny Omani customs building. I was not formally exporting the Rover and in order to leave Oman we had each obtained a road pass to allow us out and back in again within two weeks. We had to fill out embarkation forms and after the requisite stamps in our passports we were allowed on our way with a cheerful "Ma'a salaam, see you in two weeks time" from the customs official.

We were now in No Man's Land and drove for several kilometres before we reached the United Arab Emirates border post at Fujairah. Now we had to admit that we were not coming back as it was essential to have the vehicle Carnet de Passage (or Carnet de Douanes) stamped on entry. Our Carnet was a customs document for the Rover in the form of a large multi-page book. Each page was perforated into three strips and on entry to a country the customs official had to complete and sign the right hand portion and remove it and also complete half of the left hand portion. On exit the centre section would be filled in, stamped and removed whilst the left hand section was completed and left in the book. The Carnet demonstrates that a vehicle has passed through a country. Without the Carnet a country can demand a cash deposit be lodged on entry to cover any customs duties should the vehicle be sold en route. I had had to lodge £3,600.00 as security in the UK in order to obtain the Carnet and would claim this back on production of a fully stamped-up book at the end of the trip. This Carnet, or 'Triptych' as it was also known, made motoring into and out of countries remarkably easy and straightforward.

Mind you, I don't think that the UAE border had seen many Carnets before but we eventually obtained the necessary stamps and signatures and set off again.

So, here we were in the UAE. The Rover was coughing and missing a bit and I was going through my familiar trauma of mental fault finding and reaching no specific conclusions.

Fujairah was a surprisingly modern place after north Oman. There were multi-storey buildings and vast wide dual carriageways. There was even a Hilton hotel! We needed nothing and drove straight through and into the mountains and westwards towards Dubai. After a few kilometres we decided to stop and at five forty five pulled off the road into a deserted quarry and prepared for our first night 'on the road'.

The night that followed turned out to be nothing short of awful. The location appeared to be fine, tucked out of sight and sound of the main road. It would be dark soon so we decided to eat immediately. Whilst Dawn delved in the cupboards I clambered up onto the roof to fetch our table down. This had been manufactured at the last minute by our good friend Gordon, using the folding legs from an old battered camping table and a nice new plywood top. Dawn announced that our inaugural evening feast would be corned beef with reconstituted dried mashed potatoes and dried peas. Well, we forked our way through a plateful of claggy potato, dry corned beef and some rather hard, shrivelled green things. This first awful meal was a bit of a shock, probably more to Dawn than to me, and to her utmost credit she thereafter made it her business and very much a matter of pride to always produce an amazingly tasty and nourishing meal despite often struggling with a challenging lack of ingredients.

Well, having gamely fought our way through this gourmet course we sat back for a cup of coffee and a welcome cigarette. I don't think that either of us was particularly happy at that moment and we were both feeling a bit overwhelmed by what we had embarked upon. I was to find, however, that Dawn's resilience to adverse moods and situations was to prove a tremendous asset throughout the trip, and at no time would either of us admit to defeat or depression, consequently always keeping each other's spirits up when necessary – which really wasn't very often.

After washing up there seemed little else to do but turn in. It was dark by now and we were both tired, although it was only about eight o'clock. Everything was still very new to us, in particular pot washing and personal hygiene using a tiny sink in a confined space with a limited water supply. We had never made the bed up completely before either. Dawn had bought a pair of single sheets and sewn them together on 3 sides to form an inner bag for our double sleeping bag. During the day this sleeping bag was folded and stowed on the back bench seat with the seat back strapped down on top of it. Pillows were placed in plastic bags and tucked down behind the front seats.

Tidiness was to be all important because of the limited space and we soon adopted a strict routine for pot washing, drying and immediate stowage after each meal – not a routine that either of us was used to in our normal lives.

So we made up the bed and crawled in but it was so hot. I had fitted a small twelve volt fan in the Rover mainly for ventilation during the day but that night it stayed on and even with the back door open it was stiflingly hot – *really* hot. We just lay there and perspired and drank lots of water. Perhaps the quarry wasn't such a good idea after all, too sheltered and now radiating the heat soaked up by the rocks during the day. The problem of sleeping in such a small space in hot climates had always bothered me and I now had visions of many similar nights ahead of us but, in fact, we never experienced such hot and torrid conditions again – or such a stodgy meal!

Needless to say we did not lie in for long in the morning, neither of us having caught much sleep. The temperature hadn't really dropped and now it started to rise again as the sun appeared. So much for camp life, all we wanted to do was get to Abu Dhabi and air conditioning. After a simple breakfast we packed away and climbed in the cab and were ready to go – or almost ready to go. I now came across a ritual that was to be repeated every morning of the journey. My final preparations were always to check the engine oil, water etc, kick the tyres and hop in the cab with the ignition key at the ready – and there I would always find Dawn, calmly combing her hair and dabbing on a bit of make-up. This seemed to take for ages and I would sit quietly seething whilst champing at the bit to be on the move. Not very tolerant of me and I record it here as an act of contrition.

Anyway, this first morning I got on with my seething until finally Dawn sat back and was ready to go, but unfortunately the engine wasn't. It turned over on the battery with nary a sign of life. Out and under the bonnet to run through the standard procedure – check for spark at the points, check for spark at the spark plug. OK. Check for fuel at the carburettor – none. After disconnection of fuel lines and much manual pumping I finally raised some petrol and we were soon on our way at ten fifteen with sighs of relief and one very dirty pair of hands.

We arrived in Dubai at about midday and became lost there and initially failed to find the road to Abu Dhabi. Whilst stopped at some traffic lights the engine died and refused to start. Under the bonnet and much manual petrol pumping before we fired up again and went on our way but obviously something was amiss. The day had become very hot and I was keeping my usual anxious eye on the temperature gauge, which had risen alarmingly. Nevertheless we cruised smoothly along despite my fears of overheating and imminent engine seizure. The Dubai to Abu Dhabi road was even more boring than the one from Fujairah, flat, monotonous and littered with wrecked vehicles, new and old. We stopped halfway at a shabby café and transferred some petrol from a jerry can to the main tanks and then bought a couple of cold cokes, fortunately being able to use Omani currency. In fact the chap in the café was only too happy to serve us despite the potential currency problem, and he made us very welcome – a friendly reaction that was to be typical many times in many countries.

Back in the Rover I turned the key with some trepidation but the engine fired up instantly and we drove off happy and refreshed and comforted by the thought that we only had about 80 kilometres to go. At three thirty we rolled triumphantly into Abu Dhabi and drove along the rather pleasant Corniche to the Sheraton Hotel. Ah! The air conditioning! We strolled rather self-consciously across the opulent reception area, two rather dirty and dusty individuals in stained tee shirts and jeans, and telephoned Sean to announce our arrival. Sean came and led us back to his flat where his wife Pat plus a shower and a cold beer awaited us. Only a couple of days on the road and 780 kilometres and here we were reacting as if we had been away for weeks.

After an evening meal Sean and Pat took us to the BAC social club where there was a showing of Henry VIII on video – another relatively new technology in 1980. As an indication of the culture and sophistication of your average BAC engineer there was just the four of us and one other couple and after only forty five minutes we had all adjourned to the bar. Not a late night and back to a comfy, cool bed.

Up the next day and important things to do to prepare for the next stage of the journey. Sean was the in-country manager for the contract and he took us into the office to introduce us to his local 'Mr Fixit', Simon, a local resident of Sudanese origin and a very pleasant fellow.

As recorded earlier in Chapter 5, Dawn would not be eligible for a Saudi visa of any type, being an unmarried woman, but it was obviously vital that I obtain one. Dawn would bypass Saudi by flying to Jordan via Kuwait.

A telephone call to the British Consulate informed me that a letter from them was necessary to accompany my Saudi application. With this valuable information we set off with Simon, cashed some travellers cheques and then checked with the Jordanian Embassy about visas. We emerged only thirty minutes later with the visas stamped in our passports for a cost of just $5.00 each. At the British Embassy I collected my letter for a fee of $6.00. I have mentioned the problems caused by the 'Death of a Princess' TV programme and the effects were still rumbling on. The letter was an embarrassing, subservient, ingratiating document addressed directly from the UK Government to the Saudi Government. Not a letter to be proud of, but with much UK business – not to mention the dreams of one Peter Fleming – relying on the benevolence of Saudi Arabia, then we had to be grateful if such diplomacy did the trick. Lord Carrington had also recently poured some oil on the troubled waters and thankfully the situation had eased considerably.

By this time it was too late to go to the Saudi Embassy so we returned to the flat and I removed the carburettor and gave it a thorough clean before going to buy some petrol (less than $1.00 a gallon). There was no recurrence of the fuel problem of the previous day.

In the evening, Sean had arranged a get-together at the BAC Club so that we could meet up with some of my old friends from both Oman and Iran. Unfortunately nobody had advised the Iranians or the Iraqis of our intentions and they chose that day to declare war on each other, the result being that the BAC team was put on alert together with the Abu Dhabi Defence Forces, and they had to maintain a twenty four hour presence at the Rapier workshops. So much for our convivial evening.

The following day Simon took me to the Saudi Embassy. To my surprise this was a disgracefully dirty and shabby place, situated up a narrow alley in a block of rundown flats. Here I not only had the problems of inter-governmental relations to cope with but also an enormous rabble of Arabs clamouring for visas in order to visit Mecca for the forthcoming holy season. An hour and a half later we had fought our way to the application window and were then thankfully directed behind the turmoil to a more quiet and select area where my application was considered by a variety of officials. Consensus of opinion seemed to be divided between one gentleman who thought that I *would* get a visa and another who knowingly stated that I would *not*. Simon adopted the only attitude that works with these people and chattered away in Arabic - cajoling, pleading and arguing. Fortunately the optimistic official was also Sudanese and he advised us to get a copy of the Land Rover log book and submit everything to the Consul for his consideration. Just outside the building was an enterprising Asian with a photo copier in the back of his van powered by a small portable generator. Copy of log book plus the other application paperwork was therefore soon left for the hopefully sympathetic deliberations of the Consul.

BRITISH AEROSPACE NEWS, November, 1980

Picture above shows Pete Fleming and the restored Land-Rover in Abu Dhabi. They were photographed by the new BAe News correspondent there, Dave Smith. The vehicle seemed to have everything piled on it, says Dave — including the kitchen sink.

**OMAN**

# Trash tip truck in torrid tour

## BAe over -seas

OUR MAN in Oman, Pete Fleming, has set out on an overland trek that will take him thousands of miles across the Middle East, Africa and Europe in a Land-Rover rescued from a rubbish dump.

Pete spent two years restoring and preparing the vehicle for the journey while working with BAe in Oman.

His route is taking him across the desert via Saudi Arabia, Jordan and Sudan to Kenya.

After holidaying in Kenya Pete plans to drive north through Africa to Tangiers in Morocco and then across Spain and France to England.

The following morning Simon and I retraced our steps to the Saudi Embassy and, after some delay, were once again admitted to the inner sanctum of the Consular office where, somewhat to my surprise but certainly to my huge relief, I was granted a one month transit visa and at no cost. At a stroke the potentially biggest obstacle to our plans had been removed. We were able to celebrate our good fortune that evening when we were invited to a darts match at the BAC club, where I met many old friends and Dawn and I even reached the semi-finals of the doubles competition.

The next day was set for our departure from Abu Dhabi. At ten thirty my old flatmate from Iran, Dave Smith, and his wife Jenny came round to see us off and Dave took a photograph which he subsequently had published in the BAC newspaper, along with a short article entitled 'Trash Tip Truck in Torrid Tour'. Ouch!

Leaving the relative greenery of the capital behind, we soon found ourselves on the familiar flat tarmac stretching across brown desert, devoid of any landmarks. The horizon looked very close and with the mirage effect the land shimmered like water. We were heading west to cross the border into Qatar where we would then turn due north to Doha.

Here another comfortable flat and old friends awaited us and Dawn was adamant that we complete the journey that day. The distance was just under 600 kilometres and at our cruising speed of 80 kms/hour it would take several hours plus the time spent at the border posts. At one forty five we stopped for petrol, using up the remains of our Abu Dhabi dirhams topped up with US dollars.

The bulk of our money was carried in the form of US Dollar Travellers Cheques with a couple of hundred dollars in cash. In total we had $3,160.00 in the communal kitty, plus about another $500.00 each in individual pocket money. In those days Travellers Cheques were the accepted method of carrying negotiable currency and were not only secure but could sometimes even be used as cash. Together with our passports and other vital documentation, this money was locked in a modified ammunition box bolted under the rear seat. As it turned out it would probably have been better to take all our money in dollars cash as there were to be opportunities for very good exchange rates for cash and also times when changing Travellers Cheques would not be easy.

But, back to the filling station. Having taken the petrol on board the Rover refused to start. Under the bonnet I pumped and pumped but the petrol line remained as dry as a bone. Dawn took shelter from the heat in the filling station office and I set to and removed the petrol pump – like most things on a Land Rover, not a difficult job. Stripped to its component parts all seemed well. The base of the pump was a glass bowl clamped to a die cast body with a metal bracket and a thick cork gasket. When I reassembled the unit I put a thick coat of gasket goo on the cork and refitted the pump but still no petrol. Well, I took that pump off several times, stripping it and checking it carefully each time but to no avail. I finally looked closely at the bottom of the pump and discerned that it was slightly distorted and not offering a flat surface to the glass bowl, cork gasket or no cork gasket. I looked around and saw an abandoned inner-tube, from which I cut a new rubber gasket, and on completion of assembly and refitting the pump worked like a dream. Unfortunately this exercise took two hours out of our day and we set off somewhat behind schedule.

An hour and a half later we reached the UAE border post, slowed at the first barrier and the engine cut out again. Back to the petrol pump lever. Some local lads were hanging about and flip-flopped over to see what was going on. They peered under the bonnet, felt the ignition coil and jabbered away to indicate that it was too hot and that that was the source of the trouble. "Oh, no" sez I, the Land Rover expert, wishing that they would go away whilst I continued to agitate the petrol pump. But they insisted that I wrap the coil in a piece of wet cloth to cool it. Hmm. I then returned to my petrol pump and a dribble of liquid appeared at last. Quickly hopping into the cab I started the engine first time and we set off for the Qatar border post, the local Arab lads nodding at me knowingly as if to say "Ah, yes, we told you it was the coil" and me nodding at them and smiling as if to say "Ah, yes, I told you it was the petrol pump".

With some foreboding I turned off the engine at the border post and started on the embarkation card, passport, customs and Carnet procedure. Here we were somewhat taken aback when an over-enthusiastic young customs man insisted on looking in the back of the Rover and then demanded to see receipts and an export licence for 'the furniture'. I protested in amazement until a more senior official came over, glanced inside and then gave the original chap a disgusted glare and what sounded by a verbal Arabic kick in the pants, before waving us on with an apologetic smile.

Well, of course the Rover wouldn't start again. This time, however, a group of tough looking local lorry drivers sauntered over, indicated that I should get in the cab and who then gathered at the back and prepared to heave. I shrugged my shoulders. OK, but little point as there would be no petrol. I was knowingly explaining this to Dawn when the engine fired up and off we lurched. I waved my thanks out of the window, muttering under my breath and starting to think more seriously about the Hot Coil Theory.

300 metres on we had to stop again to have the passports stamped and this time Dawn was delegated to keep her foot on the accelerator and keep the engine revving. We finally left the UAE in a series of spasmodic leaps and bounds but once we achieved cruising speed everything was fine. It was about a quarter past six by now and it was not until eight o'clock that we reached the Qatar border, the sun having set an hour before. Definitely no stopping the engine this time and Dawn took up her station at the accelerator and I wandered over to a row of about five small wooden huts. Each hut had a one foot square hole about a yard off the ground through which one had to attempt to poke one's head and a fistful of documentation. Once again my white face and lack of the language was met with concerned help and assistance and I was carefully directed from one hut to another until the formalities had been completed.

We took the opportunity to spend our last UAE coins on a couple of cans of drink from a nearby snack bar, leaving the Rover ticking over on its own, but when we returned it had obviously become tired of waiting and had stopped again. I had to reluctantly concede that perhaps the coil *was* faulty. I rummaged in my front spares box, dug out my spare coil with a smug flourish, temporarily connected it and the engine fired first time. Hmm. But the petrol pump *had* also been faulty…………

Anyway, with the spare coil securely fitted there was no more misfiring and we at last cruised into Doha at about ten thirty (nine thirty local time) and found the Ramada hotel from where we could telephone our friend Carl

\*\*\*\*

Distance across United Arab Emirates – 736 km

Total distance – 1170 km

# Chapter 8 – Qatar

Friday 26th September to Thursday 2nd October 1980

Journey days 7 to 13

It turned out that Carl and Ellen lived just around the corner and Carl arrived five minutes later to lead us from the car park to their flat – except that the Rover was dead again. I climbed out to start my diagnostics in the dark but Carl brushed me aside and said that he would simply tow us. Oh, the ignominy of it. As it happened, one of my last jobs in Oman had been to fashion a tow rope out of a length of multi-braided helicopter winch wire and with a heavy heart I unwound it from the rear bumper and linked the two vehicles. Logically, I suppose that if you think about it, a helicopter winch would not be expected to heave a Land Rover around, so why design it for that amount of stress? Obviously they didn't and after moving silently forward for about twenty metres there was a twang and we just as silently came to a halt. Carl backed up and I furiously delved into the coiled up mess of my now *twin* tow ropes and joined them with a reef knot. Off we crept again until in the thick of the traffic and half way round a roundabout there was a double twang and Carl disappeared into the night. By this time I was in a foul temper whilst Dawn was hooting with uncontrollable laughter in the passenger seat. With traffic coming from all directions, totally unsympathetic to our plight, we awaited the return of Carl whilst I tied my now *four* pieces of cable together. Inevitably the tow rope was now much shorter and we ended up alarmingly close to the back of the car. However, within a couple of minutes and with no further drama we arrived at Carl's and while I fumbled to remove the now scrap length of cable, Dawn managed to recover from her hysterical giggling. Not an auspicious arrival but one soon put into perspective with a large gin and tonic, a hot shower, a hot meal and a comfy bed.

The following morning we were awoken at nine fifteen by a telephone call from Carl. Carl worked for Reliant, a large civil contracting company in the Middle East, and he was at that time Site Engineer (Mechanical Services) at the prestigious new Hamad Hospital which was nearing completion on the outskirts of Doha. Carl informed me that a couple of his men were on their way to collect me to take me to the bank and then to the Land Rover agency to enquire about a new petrol pump. The bank was no problem but the Rover agency was, quoting a staggering price of $85.00 for a petrol pump, so I returned to the house empty handed.

After breakfast, I tackled the pump for the umpteenth time and discovered that rubber inner tube material and petrol do not mix, and that my home-made gasket had swelled and distorted to twice its original size, becoming totally useless in the process. I had to admit, however, that despite it being an irritating episode the day before, we had been remarkably lucky to have reached the Ramada hotel and not ended up broken down in the dark on the side of the main highway miles from anywhere.

Whilst I was thus engaged, Dawn was inside doing some washing and ironing. Let me take this opportunity to say that it seems a shame that these mundane but essential tasks do not warrant more description. Perhaps if Dawn was writing this she would dismiss *my* efforts with 'Pete did some work on the Rover' and then launch into an interesting and graphic account of her washing and ironing. Reading our daily log I find plenty of details about the repairs and modifications I carried out on the vehicle, all too often simply followed by the bald statement 'Dawn did some washing'. The poor girl slaved for hours over a plastic bucket of foam during the coming months with the commendable result that we never looked overly dirty or scruffy at any time and I hereby pay tribute to her efforts.

After lunch Carl took me for a quick tour around the hospital. This was a mammoth building with apparently no expense spared in acquiring the latest in medical technology. In a few weeks the basic construction and fitting out would be complete and there would then follow a whole year of equipment installation and sterilisation. Carl took me behind the scenes and I was amazed at the scale of the machinery required to provide all the support services. Fascinating - and as a bonus I found some ideal neoprene rubber in the Reliant store so that I could make a decent gasket for the petrol pump. Carl encouraged me to take plenty but I just took a piece about ten inches in diameter. If only I had listened to him. I was to use every last scrap of that piece in the future.

That evening Carl and Ellen and their young daughter Nadia took us for a drive around Doha, so similar to Dubai and Abu Dhabi but not as prosperous looking. It was also a 'dry state' and alcohol was only available to approved expatriates with liquor licences, which restricted them to a monthly allowance. Unlike the rectangular street patterns of Dubai and Abu Dhabi, Doha was built on roads which radiated like the spokes of a wheel from the central sea front.

I had by now decided to seal the petrol pump glass filter bowl once and for all, and the following morning I took the unit off for hopefully the last time, cut a new gasket from the neoprene and reattached the bowl with lashings of Araldite.

Dawn spent the day giving some home tuition to a delighted Nadia, who had taken the day off school with a cold.

On the Monday we had a day off and went with Ellen to look around the Doha museum, but saw only part of it before it closed at midday. In the afternoon Dawn had a look around Nadia's school from a professional point of view and then we went water skiing with a friend of hers called Pete from Oman, followed by a party in the evening. It was as if we had never left Oman.

The following day we had to go to the Kuwait Embassy to obtain a visa for Dawn's stop over en route to Jordan. On top of a slight hangover from the night before, Dawn seemed to have contracted Nadia's cold and was suffering with a tight chest, stomach pains and general aches. Once again we had to divert to the British Embassy for a letter of introduction and to pay the inevitable fee. Back at the Kuwait Consulate Dawn was granted a visa on the spot. We were subsequently to learn that no more visas were issued after that day due to the Iran/Iraq war which had broken out a few days earlier on the twenty second of September. In the afternoon Carl took us to a travel agent and we purchased Dawn's air ticket for the following day, using a precious $300.00 of our funds.

For our last evening together for a while we went out for a meal with Pete and his girlfriend Chrissie. Chrissie was also a teacher and, not for the first time, the evening passed with an interminable and in-depth discussion of children's education. Beware the Ides of March and gatherings of two or more school teachers………..

Wednesday was the first of October, twelve days since we left Oman and Dawn was scheduled to fly to Kuwait at three in the afternoon.

We took advantage of the late flight in order to revisit the museum. It was based in a cluster of old houses once lived in by the Sheikhs of Qatar. Painted brilliant white and spotlessly clean, the ground floors were laid out with exhibits of rugs, chests, clothing and cooking utensils with a brief history of the previous occupants affixed to each dwelling. In the central courtyard was a full-size Bedouin tent, with to one side a large modern building housing the latest exhibits. Upstairs was totally devoted to modern Qatar and the transformation and progress following the discovery of oil. Qatar's maritime history was celebrated outside with several traditional dhows moored in an artificial lagoon together with an exhibition of the pearl and fishing industry and a magnificent aquarium.

Back at the flat Ellen had succumbed to Nadia's cold so we left her to rest and Nadia came with me to deliver Dawn to the airport. We were allowing four days for me to drive across Saudi Arabia and the plan was to meet up in Amman on Monday the sixth of October. It was a great shame to have to part at this stage of the journey but, of course, we had no choice in the matter.

Returning to the flat I filled all the Rover water tanks and did a bit of preliminary packing. Carl came in and we ended up watching a pirate video of 'Deep Throat' which had no sound track. I don't think that we missed much. (The reader must again bear in mind that in 1980 video recorders were still in their infancy and certainly a novelty in the Middle East. To put things into perspective, I had only seen my first electronic calculator a few years earlier, in 1975).

Meanwhile, Dawn had arrived in Kuwait and was met by her friend Marie who had been a colleague of hers at the Muscat English Speaking School. She spent five nights with Marie and managed to see quite a bit of Kuwait City in that time. Sadly, all the old buildings had been swept aside to make way for modern edifices and she was not impressed.

On Thursday the second of October it was my turn to leave Qatar. I rose quite early, breakfasted and finished packing the Rover. Dawn had carefully shopped for provisions for me and this included fresh eggs and vegetables plus four neat, cling-filmed packages of meat, thus ensuring my culinary independence across the wastes of Saudi. After my farewells to Ellen I drove to Carl's office and collected a spare petrol pump – which wouldn't fit but which might provide useful spare parts – and a three metre long wire sling which more than adequately replaced my inadequate helicopter cable. At half past ten I said goodbye to Carl and headed out on the long awaited trip to Jordan.

The road from Dohar led straight to the Saudi border, with a single left hand turn back to Abu Dhabi halfway along it. More brown, featureless desert. Just 100 kilometres to the border and once there, no problems with Qatar customs or passport formalities but yet again the Rover refused to start. This was getting beyond a joke. Back under the bonnet and it still seemed that there was a fuel problem. I removed the fuel pump and applied even more Araldite around the top of the filter bowl. Being rapid Araldite it was nicely set by the time I had re-fitted the unit. Fuel appeared and I was on my way by twelve thirty, negotiating my way around lumbering, overloaded Toyota buses packed with pilgrims and swaying under huge mounds of luggage roped onto the roofs as they slowly rocked and rolled their way to Mecca.

It was only a short distance to the Saudi border post and here, too, were many more vehicles crowded with pilgrims. It looked as if customs formalities were being rigorously enforced and some travellers had had to completely unload their cars, and their possessions were spread all over the tarmac. I therefore waited my turn with some trepidation, not only because of the two tins of ham that I was carrying (!) but more conscious of how much time and effort it would take me to unpack and repack the Rover. An Asian customs assistant in blue overalls came over and chatted with me, indicating that he was not impressed with the unsympathetic attitude of the Arab officials. We were joined by a Filipino assistant and an obnoxious looking, fat Saudi supervisor in a grubby white dish dash. I was curtly instructed to open the back door and my Asian friend climbed in and performed a perfunctory search of one of the cupboards and the 'fridge. The Filipino, however, started to take great delight in delving into the cupboards and I fought to conceal my annoyance. On the side of the cupboard under the cooker, and just inside the back door, were half a dozen round Tupperware containers lodged in brackets and containing salt, pepper, sugar, powdered milk etc. The Saudi selected a couple of these, tipped a small amount into his palm and sniffed. A pity he didn't select the pepper. Anyway, apparently satisfied, he collected his assistants and walked off to complete the Carnet. The Asian shrugged his shoulders apologetically - people like him maintain one's faith in human nature. I finally left the border post which was still teeming with delayed pilgrims and I retain a vivid picture of a big, red American car, doors and boot all wide open with an Arab family of four looking despondently at the contents of several large suitcases strewn all over the ground all around them. I've often wondered what they were being searched for, after all they were just devout Muslims intent on making their simple homage at Mecca. Not like me, an infidel Christian passing through their country with two tins of ham hidden at the back of a cupboard.

*****

Distance across Qatar – 409km

Total distance – 1579km

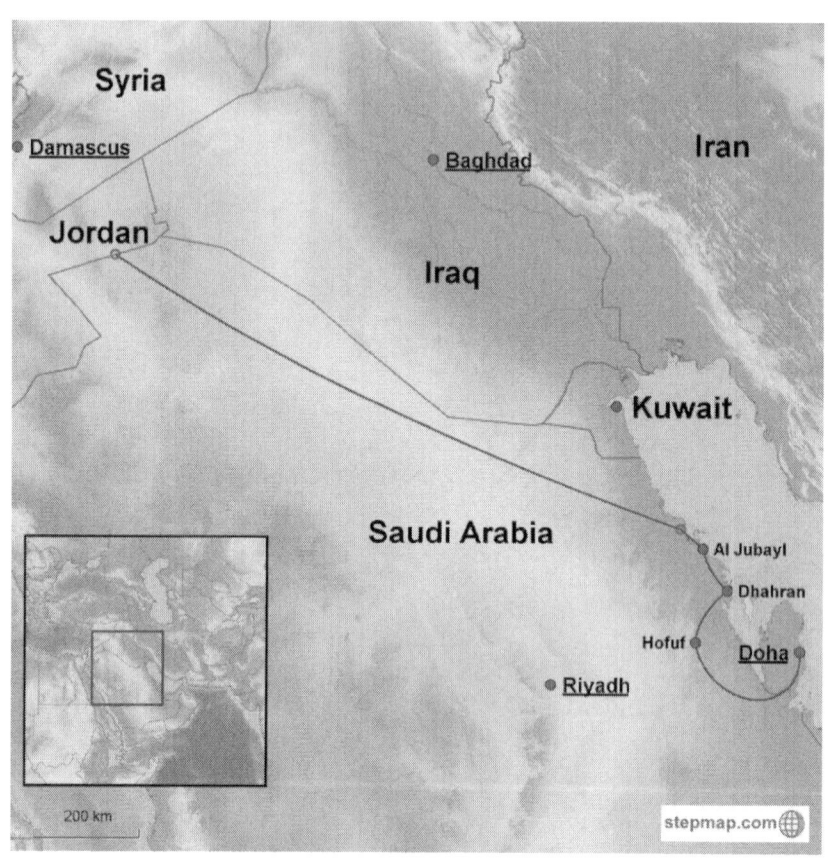

# Chapter 9 – Saudi Arabia

Thursday 2nd to Sunday 5th October 1980

Journey days 13 to 16

There were 2000 kilometres to Jordan, but after just 160 of them I entered the town of Hofuf and was slowing down to the speed limit when the Rover started to miss and lurch again. Aargh! This continued until I had to stop at a set of traffic lights and the engine died on me completely. There was little point in trying to start it so I hopped out and went back to face the hooting queue of traffic quickly building up behind me. I succeeded in getting over the message that 'big white Land Rover not going anywhere' and the stream slowly diverted around me with much heaving of steering wheels but with a remarkable lack of irritation. Perhaps this was a common event. After several changes of traffic lights it became obvious that nobody was going to offer to help and I certainly couldn't do anything on my own. I then espied a Land Cruiser with a couple of Orientals on board so flagged it down and indicated my predicament. With nary a word of English passing between us they quickly nipped in front, produced a length of stout chain and attached it to my front bumper. Oh dear, for the second time I found myself rolling silently along behind a towing vehicle, and this one a *Land Cruiser,* which really rubbed salt into the wound.

Just past the junction I was abandoned in a car park, so lit a cigarette and took stock of my predicament and my surroundings. I was pretty confident that I had finally solved the petrol pump problem and had therefore come to the conclusion that I not only had a suspect coil when we left Oman but that the spare had also failed me. As I have said previously, few of my spares were new, most just being second hand items that I had left over when I finished the building of the vehicle. However, looking around I suddenly realised that, incredibly, I was apparently in the middle of the motor maintenance area of Hofuf and all around me were shops selling spares, interspersed with little workshops fixing electrical and mechanical bits and pieces. On my third attempt I found a tiny store selling ignition equipment and for the modest sum of $7.00 I purchased a shiny new twelve volt coil, fitted it firmly in place and finally put an end to the engine problems that had dogged me since the Oman border and which had, indeed, proved to be as a result of both a faulty coil *and* a faulty petrol pump.

I headed for Dhahran in a much more confident state of mind, still guided by what was to prove my hopelessly inadequate Barthomew's Map of the Middle

East. As it happened there were not many roads in Saudi Arabia – and even less signposts – so I kept my fingers crossed and pressed on. Before reaching Dhahran and before darkness fell I pulled off out of sight of the road and stopped for only my second night in the Rover, despite it being the thirteenth day of the journey.

It was pleasantly warm and very quiet apart from the occasional lorry trundling past. As it became dark I became aware of all the huge flares from the oil industry dotted around the desert, strangely comforting in the otherwise complete blackness. I cooked a rather nice meal and sat swatting a huge cloud of moths transfixed by the Rover's interior light, and entertained by some huge ants and very large dung beetles that were industriously tidying up their patch of Arabia.

I slept soundly and was awoken at eight thirty the following morning by someone plodding past on a camel – well, what else? The postman presumably.

For the next two and a half days and 1,600 kilometres I bumbled my way across Saudi Arabia. The aim was to follow the big main road north east from Dhahran, following the coast until I came across a big sign to the left saying 'TAP Road' which would lead me straight to Jordan. Simple. The TAP road was the Trans Arabian Pipeline road. Well, 'twas not to be. The road from Dhahran via Al Khobar and Dammam was not a readily identifiable main highway and I have no idea where I went until I ended up in Al Jubayl which is right on the coast, in the right direction past Dammam but not on the main inland road where I wanted to be. There had been no helpful road signs anywhere and looking back I think I was lucky to have stayed basically on the correct route. The roads were just thick black layers of tarmac which appeared to have been laid straight onto the desert sand. They had no curbs and were pot-holed and lumpy from the heat and the incessant passage of huge Mercedes trucks belching black diesel smoke. Both sides of the roads were littered with wrecked vehicles and discarded tyres. Was this really the fabulously oil rich country whose wealth knew no bounds?

I finally located the TAP road but was then diverted towards Kuwait due to road works. By the end of the day I was back on the TAP road and confidently on my way to Jordan. The Rover hadn't missed a beat and all was well except that Nadia's cold was now tapping *me* on the shoulder.

*Camping by the TAP road*

What I didn't know at the time was that just over a year later Fate would see me living in Al Khobar and driving all over eastern Saudi in my new career in the oil industry. Places like Hofuf and Al Jubayl and the road up to Kuwait were to become all too familiar, although I was never to venture on the TAP road again. I was also to witness the replacement of much of the dreadful road system with magnificent new motorways.

On my second night by the roadside, *I* did some washing. This consisted of soaking dirty clothes in a bucket with a lid on and driving along so that the vehicle movement agitated the dirt out. Easy.

And so I passed through Saudi Arabia, not an exciting part of the journey. The country was so flat and boring that it was difficult to take any really representative photographs. I did miss one amusing opportunity when I passed a warning triangle on a brand new section of super highway. On the triangle was the black silhouette of a camel calmly sitting on the tarmac. This seemed incongruous until I rounded a bend and had to swerve around a camel sitting in the middle of the road. I spent a third night by the side of the TAP road and by this time could confirm that I had caught Nadia's cold.

At two o'clock on Sunday the fifth of October I arrived at the border. By this time the temperature had dropped considerably from forty two degrees when I left Qatar to just twenty eight degrees as I reached Jordan and I was driving with all the windows closed. The Rover was revelling in the cooler air and bombing along happily at an impressive 95 kms/hr.

Once out of the country with all formalities dealt with very quickly, I headed across No Man's Land to the Jordanian border post past dozens of intercontinental trucks coming the other way and queuing up to enter Saudi. Most looked as if they had been there for ages and I felt really sorry for them and the unsympathetic beaurocratic nightmare that they were heading into.

At the Jordanian side I was again concerned to see that all the car drivers (admittedly all Arabs) were having to remove everything from their vehicles and that the contents of their bags and suitcases were carelessly strewn all over the road as they underwent a very intrusive inspection. I pulled up into a vacant slot and resigned myself to a similar fate but then encountered the most amazing character. From a group of scruffy customs clerks in Western dress and agitated Arabs in white robes emerged a figure straight out of an episode of Starsky and Hutch. A lean Jordanian in his late twenties he was wearing immaculately pressed blue denim jeans with cowboy boots and an equally immaculate denim jacket. Underneath was a spotless yellow tee shirt and he had a large automatic pistol holstered at his waist. With neatly trimmed hair, the overall effect was perfectly completed with a pair of reflective aviator sunglasses. He spoke passably good English and I launched into my big smile and firm handshake routine, a little wary of what was to come. As it turned out he was very friendly, very helpful and very considerate, taking more of a curious interest in the Rover rather than an official one. He pointed me in the direction of the passport office, one of his assistants completed my Carnet and I was on my way.

Inspirational Saudi scenery

\*\*\*\*

Distance across Saudi Arabia – 1877km

Total distance – 3456km

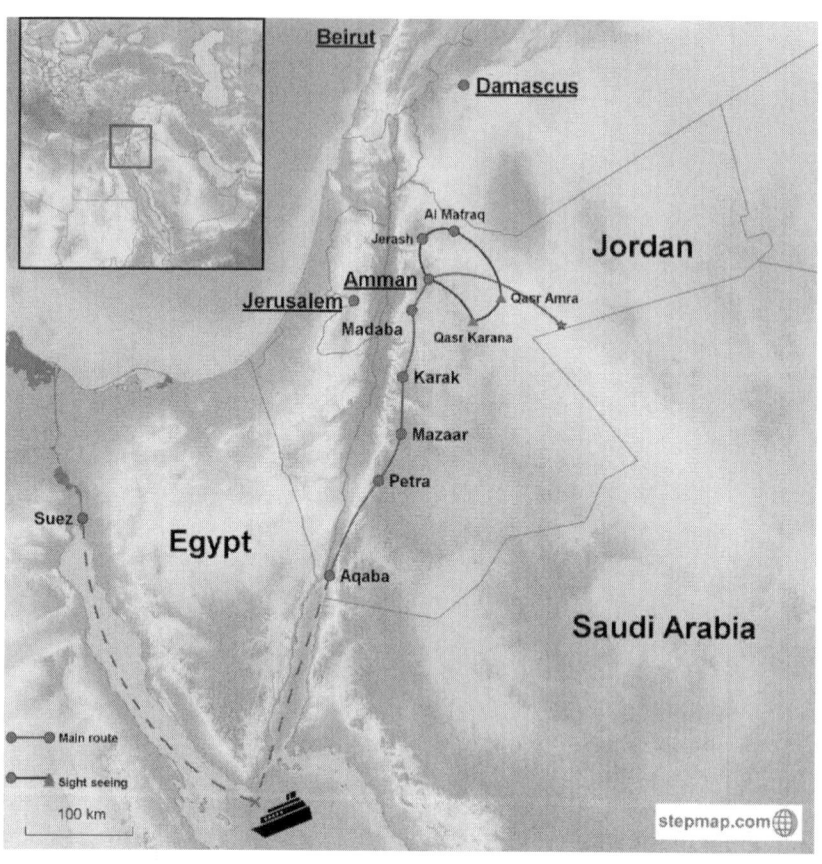

# Chapter 10 – Jordan

Sunday 5th to Tuesday 14th October 1980

Journey days 16 to 25

By half past three I was inside Jordan and heading for the mountains in the distance. It was only about 160 kilometres to Amman and the scenery started to undergo dramatic changes as the hills and then mountains supported the growth of vegetation. After the austerity of Saudi Arabia there was a noticeable atmosphere of westernisation, civilisation and hospitality. As I approached the outskirts of Amman, the military nature of the country was vividly illustrated by very many sizeable army camps and training areas, no doubt currently on high alert due the escalating conflict between Iran and Jordan's neighbour Iraq.

I headed into the suburbs where there was more and more housing and traffic. Dawn was due to arrive at nine the next morning and our timing was looking good. I wanted to camp as near to the airport as possible but in the end I had to give up that idea as I couldn't find any signposts and my enquiries of pedestrians met with blank looks. I headed away from the city centre to the pretty and hilly eastern outskirts, turned off down a side road and pulled off into a flat, thinly grassed area on the edge of a cultivated field. The sun was just setting with a pleasing red glow, and although it was a bit chilly it was very peaceful and pleasant.

One of the problems associated with living in a vehicle is finding a suitable place to stop each night when in populated places like towns, unless there is an official camp-site to be found. I had driven out of the built-up area and this place looked fine. I relaxed with a cup of tea and then with the sun gone it was time for dinner. Headlights outside and the sound of footsteps heralded a visitor who turned out to be the local bobby on patrol and who was not at all fazed by the presence of an Omani registered vehicle and an Englishman. He bade me a cheerful 'Ma'a salaam' and drove off.

I'd just made a cup of coffee when there was a knock at the door and I peered out to find an oldish, shabby, unshaven Jordanian chap with a filthy bandage wrapped around his left hand. For some reason my immediate conclusion was that here was the owner of the land on which I had camped, so I greeted him effusively in my limited Arabic and invited him to join me for a cup of coffee. It was cold outside so he heaved himself in and closed the door whilst I attended to his refreshment. We sat and chatted amiably, him in Arabic and me in English, not understanding a word of each other but illustrating fundamental points with intricate sign language. I must admit that I began to wonder if he was, in fact, the honest farmer I had taken him to be when he started to hint that he wanted some clothes. My doubts further increased when he pointed excitedly to a machine gun pictured on the front of a paperback book I was reading and indicated that the damage to his hand was a gun-shot wound. I decided to continue to play the whole thing cool, stiffened my upper lip and nodded with interest whilst racking my brains as to how to get rid of him without any trouble. I finally managed to convey that I was tired and ready for bed and handed him a couple of packets of cigarettes, with which he disappeared happily into the night – but not before giving me a parting kiss on the cheek, which probably placed the poor fellow next in line for Nadia's cold.

I was up at seven the next morning, anxious not to be late for my eagerly anticipated reunion with Dawn. I still had no idea where the airport was other than that I could see aircraft with lowered undercarriages descending into the hills on the far side of the city. I plunged into the traffic with one eye on my watch and the other scanning for signposts. I managed to pull up and ask a policeman and he gave me some vague directions but half an hour later I was still none the wiser. My uncertain progress came to the attention of a taxi driver who pulled up alongside me with lots of hooting and who looked across enquiringly.

"Airport?" cries I, with a spread right hand giving my best impression of a Jumbo jet coming in to land. Understanding flashed in his eye and he motioned for me to follow him so I did just that, blinkering myself to the Kamikaze drivers all around me and keeping my eye firmly fixed on my new friend. I can say that I have driven in some cities in the world notorious for traffic but I still maintain that Amman was the worst.

With more hooting and a wild gesticulation I was pointed in the final direction and the taxi shot off in another. I arrived at the airport soon after, having been driving for one and a half hours and covering 32 kilometres since leaving my camp site. However, I was bang on time at nine o'clock - which was excellent until I found out that the flight was delayed until eleven! I changed some travellers cheques and then saw a Penworld travel bus with UK plates pull into the car park and offload half a dozen occupants. I nipped over and introduced myself to the driver, who was sorting through his paperwork. It transpired that George had just completed a tour and was soon to drive down to Aqaba to catch a ferry to Egypt, which is just what we had in mind. Eager for information from an experienced traveller I bombarded George with questions and he gave me lots of useful advice on what to see in Jordan, backed up with a handful of travel brochures.

At eleven o'clock Dawn duly arrived and we sat for some time happily swapping tales of our individual experiences. She had some friends in Amman, another couple from her Oman days, and we were going to take the opportunity to look them up. In the past Dawn had spent a couple of days in Amman and she suggested that we go to the Hilton hotel to find the telephone number of said couple, Mick and Val, who at this time had no forewarning of our visit. We eventually obtained their number from the British Embassy and arranged to meet them in the Hilton foyer that evening.

We spent the afternoon sightseeing around the city, Dawn doing her "I've been here before" guidance bit. Amman was well known for being built on seven hills and these rose all around and appeared to be packed with slums. In the relatively narrow valleys between the hills the quaint old streets designed for the donkeys and carts of yesteryear were choked with smelly, noisy traffic. The pavements were filled with milling crowds of people, all intent on their business and the overall effect was of industrious bustle and excitement. I've never been much of one for hooting but in this impatient, jostling confusion of vehicles I was grateful for the twin air horns that I had fitted.

After a couple of false starts we eventually found the Roman amphitheatre and nosed our way into a lone parking space in front of the nearby Philadelphia hotel where Dawn had previously stayed – known to her affectionately as The Filthy Delphia. The amphitheatre looked to be a typical piece of Roman architecture but its spectacular position halfway up one of the seven hills meant that there were excellent views over the adjacent hills with their teeming dwellings. After roaming around the amphitheatre, Dawn guided us across to the Citadel. Built on the site of a temple to Hercules, the Citadel also commanded impressive views across the city.

Back down into the traffic, we eventually emerged unscathed from the confines of the old town and joined the more modern roads to re-trace our route to the Hilton, where we were to have dinner that evening. Well, in the Rover in the car park on the waste ground next door. After a fruitless search for fresh meat, dinner that evening was oxtail soup stew – the first of many meatless dishes that Dawn was to develop and perfect. After this exotic repast we dressed in our 'going out' clothes and emerged from the Rover looking as smart as possible for our evening rendezvous.

I hadn't met either Mick or Val before. Mick proved to be a somewhat dour Brummie but Val had a sparkling personality once we had all relaxed. We had not made any plans, and in order to demonstrate that we were not just a couple of poor, scrounging travellers (which we were), I suggested a drink from the Hilton bar. I had cause to choke a bit when the bill came to $14.00, which would probably have fed and watered us for a week, but the gesture had been made and fortunately we called it a night after just the one round. Mick and Val wouldn't hear of us sleeping in the Rover and invited us back to their place – typically spontaneous expat hospitality. There was a huge look of relief on Dawn's face.............and on mine, at least I would get a welcome shower. This was to be the seventeenth night of our journey, Dawn had spent just one night in the Rover and I had spent four.

The priority during the next day was to obtain our visas for Egypt. The embassy was very close to the Hilton and it was to take all the morning to complete the business. There was the usual rag tag queue of individuals applying for visas. A first queue formed outside the gate to the compound and a policeman controlled the movement from this queue to a second one inside the compound. Quite innocently we walked in through another gate and consequently missed the outside queue, eventually arriving at the application window amidst the inevitable pushing and shoving. We were immediately directed inside, which meant squeezing through a narrow door whilst preventing anybody else from slipping in, too. Once inside it was calm and uncrowded and an official attended to our applications. We impressed upon him the urgency and he agreed that they would be ready for collection after lunch. We pushed our way back through the heaving melee and went off to buy some food. The weather was lovely, warm and sunny and comfortable unlike the relentless heat of the Gulf that we had left behind us. After lunch in the Hilton car park I returned to the embassy, and after a repeat of the pushing and shoving I emerged triumphant with our stamped passports.

On the advice of George of Penworld we were going to spend some tourist time in the Amman area, making a loop to the north to the Roman remains at Jerash and then circling out into the desert to the east to visit a couple of old castles.

It was not far to Jerash and we spent a pleasant couple of hours there after a drive through rolling hills with an abundance of trees and greenery and very pretty views. All very Mediterranean. We found the ruins to be very impressive, the streets and remains of the buildings readily indicating how the town used to look. The centrepiece was the oval, rock-slabbed market place with standing columns spaced around the edges and continuing down either side of the main thoroughfare which ran right through the town. Each row of columns supported a continuous line of long rectangular stone slabs which originally had been an aqueduct system. There were two amphitheatres, one at each end of the town, each remarkably well preserved and restored. Along the main street, which must have been about a quarter of a mile long, there were the ruins of houses, shops, temples and baths.

Market place at Jerash

To one side of the ruins was a small restaurant and we took a breather to have a cool drink. The only other people in our area were what looked like a very rich Saudi youth and his two minions, one of whom was dressed in Western clothes with some incredibly big, old fashioned and heavy looking camera equipment hanging around his neck. The youth came over to us, beaming broadly and displaying an impressive array of gold teeth. He informed us that he had been studying in England and thought that the English were wonderful etc.etc. He offered us a beer, of which he had evidently had several already, but we politely declined and started to make our excuses prior to scuttling off. He insisted that he have his photograph taken with me – no interest in Dawn – and seemed to be tickled pink because we both had beards. After the photograph, taken after much concerned camera juggling, we managed to escape but came across the trio some time later amidst the ruins and I had to go through the posing routine again.

In addition to the antique equipment our hero also had a modern Kodak Instamatic which he spent much time turning over and over, round and round whilst peering through every aperture in an effort to discover how to use it.

I'm sure that he took more than one shot of his left eyeball. Meanwhile the cameraman was frantically twiddling knobs and looking in vain for a 'ready' light on his enormous flash unit which was cabled to a huge, varnished wooden box which presumably held a lead/acid accumulator. Our hero still took no notice of Dawn and insisted on draping his arm over my shoulders and breathing beery fumes over me. After some minutes it became apparent that the photographic system was not going to oblige and we managed to make our escape, much to my relief and Dawn's amusement.

*Audition time....."Thank you, Dawn, don't call u,s we'll call you"*

It was late afternoon and we set off into the hills again, heading for Al Mafraq. Stopping for the night proved difficult as there were farms all along the road and it was dark before we found an apparently uninhabited stretch and were able to pull off and camp. I don't like stopping after dark as you have no real idea of your surroundings, and what you discover in daylight when you awake can sometimes come as a bit of a shock. This time we came across an old quarry and we spent a peaceful night there, this being just Dawn's second night in the Rover, but this time complemented by a super meal of fresh lamb chops and vegetables, a far cry from the dreaded corned beef and rehydrated potatoes of the first night.

We awoke to find a herd of sheep next to us, guarded by a shy old man and a not-so-shy young boy. We gave the man some bread and the boy some sweets and after breakfast headed for Azrak and the desert forts. This meant retracing part of my previous route from the Jordanian border to Amman and the countryside flattened out into the familiar featureless desert. At Azrak we left the tarmac and headed south on a barely recognisable track. We had a rough idea of the route from a tourist pamphlet, which seemed to indicate obvious forks in the road. Coming to one such fork our map said turn right but the left fork was clearly marked every few metres with large concrete blocks. We decided to trust the map (why??) and meandered off to the right, rising and falling over the sun baked rocky desert which undulated all around us. Our faith in the map gradually faded and we eventually decided to cut back across country, working on the theory that there must be a better, more frequently travelled road to these noted tourist attractions. We came across a totally isolated Bedouin tent and stopped some distance away to walk over and enquire as to our whereabouts. The Arab occupant did not seem overjoyed to see us but pointed us in the direction that we needed to go.

Fixing the starter solenoid

Back at the Rover there was a deathly silence when I turned the ignition key to engage the starter motor. Bother. Out and under the bonnet where I discovered that the starter solenoid had fallen off the bulkhead. Nothing serious except that it was mounted in a cunning position which prohibited the use of a normal spanner. As I struggled to refit the unit a Bedouin woman appeared from the tent and engaged Dawn in sign language which seemed to translate as "Give me your watch". Fortunately I was soon finished, the engine burst into life and we rapidly took our leave, soon espying a building in the distance which gradually took on the shape of Qasr Amra according to the photograph in our pamphlet. Before reaching it we had to negotiate an awkward area of bushes and dried up water courses, and we zig-zagged and bumped the final two kilometres before coming across what was obviously the correct route – clearly marked by large concrete blocks.

Qasr Amra was, in fact, not a fort but a hunting lodge built between 705 and 715. For the refreshment of the hunters, there were baths based on the Roman hypocaust design of hot, tepid and cool rooms. In those days the land was roamed by lions, deer and gazelle and these were depicted in some amazing frescoes painted all over the interior, including three impressive domed roof sections. Some restoration had taken place but nevertheless the original colours still remained vivid.

Qasr Amra

Painted ceiling in Qasr Amra

From Qasr Amra we drove on to Qasr Kharana, this time faithfully following the concrete markers. Qasr Kharana appeared in the distance, a solid, square structure of stone with that impregnable air of such old fortresses, vertical walls pierced only by tiny narrow slits, a round tower at each corner and just one single huge doorway. This doorway lead into a large caravanserai with stabling for horses and camels arranged around a central courtyard. Flights of stone steps led to the first and second floors, everything in excellent condition and restored where necessary to show how it all would have been back in the first century. From the roof there was a three hundred and sixty degree, commanding view of the empty desert. As the afternoon sun started to sink into a dusty, red sunset it was easy to vividly imagine the relief of the traveller of yesteryear arriving at the end of a long day's lonely journey, to be greeted with the door opened wide and the welcoming glow of a fire in the courtyard with robed figures bent over cooking pots and tethered animals shuffling and rustling in the gloom.

Qasr Kharana was looked after by a tall, friendly Jordanian in a striped Arab robe who spoke not a word of English but who was evidently used to all sorts of people arriving in a cloud of dust. It was time for a late lunch and as we were the only visitors Dawn invited him to have a bite to eat with us. This pleased him and he called over a friend to share his good fortune. This was an older man dressed in an old army uniform, presumably a relic of his younger days. We all tucked into cheese sandwiches and drank cups of tea whilst Dawn and I amused them with our attempts at conversing in Arabic. They seemed to find my efforts particularly entertaining but at least there was no embracing and kissing for a change.

Qasr Kharana

It was only 60 kilometres back to Amman but the road deteriorated after Qasr Kharana and vehicle tracks spread out either side of us as evidence of the attempts of previous drivers to find a decent route. It was low, rolling desert but the rocky surface gave way to dirt and finally to fine dust and we kicked up an almighty cloud as we bounced along. This dust easily found its way into the Rover and everything became covered in a gritty layer. We reached tarmac after about 35 kilometres and soon, as darkness approached, we pulled off for the night. The whole area was cultivated land which had had some sort of cereal crop grown on it, but this had been harvested leaving just crackly, dry stubble. Dawn set to before it got dark and brushed out the dust and cleaned out the refrigerator before preparing a tasty beef stew. We were just about to tuck in when two men came over from a nearby farmhouse and indicated that we would be welcome and safer to move nearer to the house, there apparently being a possibility of ne'er-do-wells roaming about in the night. By this time we were pretty well settled so I politely declined and they retraced their steps. Nevertheless I remember their kindness and thoughtfulness and this was, in fact, to be typical of so many people that we were to encounter in all the countries that we travelled through. It is often natural to be suspicious of people's motives but our experience was to be that easily the vast majority of people were just kind, straightforward, honest and generous.

We were becoming a bit concerned about the cooking Gaz situation, with one cylinder empty and one nearing empty. We therefore set off into Amman the following day to try and replenish our stocks. Though many shops looked promising we could not find a Gaz stockist. We bought a load of food then called in to see Val again. Dawn, ever the opportunist, used her washing machine to catch up with the laundry before we bade farewell in the early afternoon and headed south for Madaba and the Dead Sea.

*****

We navigated successfully to Madaba but then couldn't decide which was the road to the Dead Sea. We had been assured that the route went via Madaba but there were no signs and we had no success in asking the locals. We eventually decided on a likely direction, however, and set off.

From Amman to the southern tip of Jordan the barren desert that encroaches from Saudi Arabia in the east gives way to mountains which fall away to the valley of the Dead Sea, far below the desert plateau. Two roads ran north to south through this area. The Desert Highway was the main, fast, commercial route in the east, passing through featureless countryside. The King's Highway, further west, was one of the oldest trade routes in the world, running from Babylon to Egypt and winding through the enormous wadis cutting into this western edge of the Jordanian desert plateau. For those in search of history, this was a route of ancient mosaics, Crusader castles, tales of Saladin, the dancing Salome and the site of the beheading of John the Baptist.

Heading the wrong way to the Dead Sea

Madaba lies on the King's Highway and heading due west from there had to take us to the Dead Sea. We drove on, gradually winding down into a deep wadi. The tarmac ended and we continued along a graded track which descended steeply to the bottom of the valley, crossed the dry river bed via a small bridge and then proceeded to follow the course of the valley down to (we presumed) the sea. The track got narrower and was very steep in parts and still no sign of glittering water beyond the endless slopes surrounding us. Some of the slopes were seriously steep and I began to become a bit worried about getting back up them again if we had to. Possibly fortuitously, the track ran out at this point and we abandoned our goal, executed an umpteen point turn and started to retrace our route.

We *did* manage to climb back up and crossed back over the bridge where we came across a group of three Bedouin tents which we had not noticed on the way down. The occupants waved cheerfully and flagged us down. There followed a very pleasant half hour sitting cross-legged with our hosts whilst they entertained us with tiny china cups of hot, sweet tea. They enjoyed a cigarette and insisted that we smoke theirs and only accepted ours after a delightful charade of polite refusals. I let Dawn do most of the talking, her

Arabic vocabulary of about twenty words being virtually fluent compared to my seven or eight. We gave a handful of sweets to their little girl and they then presented us with ten chicken eggs – an incredible gift. We offered to pay for them but at the same time didn't want to offend them and their customs. They would not accept any money and added to their gift with two conical white lumps that looked and felt like pumice stone. This, apparently, was dried goat's milk cheese. All we could do was show our appreciation with some more sweets and a packet of cigarettes and hope that we had satisfied their cultural requirements. We parted with waves and smiles. A genuine encounter with old-fashioned Arabic hospitality. We stopped for the night a little further on, still in the awe-inspiring wadi, and Dawn demonstrated her growing mastery of Land Rover cuisine with a superb curry.

The next morning we continued back to the King's Highway and headed south in order to try for the Dead Sea further on. It was Friday, and scattered all along the road were men and youths walking slowly with their heads bent, intent on studying the Koran. We reached Karak and this time easily found the tarmac road to the Dead Sea. Karak (or Kerak) was a large town with an imposing ruin of a Crusader castle dating back to 1136 and perched on a mountain spur jutting out towards the sea, which was still several kilometres away.

Winding down and down, we at last reached the shoreline and left the road to drive along the top of the beach, passing a small army post on the water's edge. We stopped for lunch amidst thousands of flies then changed into our cozzies for the obligatory swim.

The author catching up with Noddy's adventures

70

Lo and behold, as Dawn emerged from the Rover in her bikini, a Land Rover from the army post rolled up and a young, smartly uniformed officer emerged and casually strolled over. He was very polite, spoke some English and hoped that we were enjoying Jordan and if there was anything that he could do to help? Well, yes, he could clear off and leave us in peace but you don't say that, do you? We assured him that we were fine and waded into the water with cameras and books for the classic Dead Sea photos. It *was* an odd sensation. The water did not strike us as particularly clean and the high salt content made it feel greasy. Nonetheless a unique sensation and easy to lie reading a book whilst floating almost on top of the water.

We took some snaps of each other but our army officer remained looking on and we soon abandoned the water and Dawn was glad to regain her modesty and cover herself with a towel. The officer summoned his driver who came over bearing a gift of two huge, sweet grapefruit. The officer then decided to take an interest in the gear piled on our roof rack and climbed halfway up for a better view. Apparently satisfied he jumped down and casually wiped his inevitably dirty hands on a skirt of Dawn's that she had washed and hung out to dry. To our relief he then at last took his leave. He probably didn't intend to upset us, but his presence rather spoilt our Dead Sea experience. By this time we had dried out and it felt as if we were covered in sticky grit. Most unpleasant. Thank goodness for plenty of fresh water on the roof and a hose for a shower. We were soon rinsed off and ready to go, spraying copious amounts of insecticide to evict the swarms of flies that had by now taken up residence in the Rover.

Needless to say we took a wrong road coming out of Karak and got lost again and ended up on a meandering country road to the town of Mazaar which was finally back on the King's Highway. We drove into Wadi Hasa and stopped for the night at the bottom. Mm! Chips for dinner.

October the eleventh was my birthday, and there was a card on the mat! Today we were going to visit the rose red city of Petra en route to the port of Aqaba at the southern tip of Jordan, so up and away early (!) at eight o'clock. There were more enormous wadis to cross. Each one entailed a long, long run down the side and into the vee of the valley with the engine and gearbox whining in second gear, dabbing the brakes to negotiate endless hairpin bends. At the bottom a short flat run across a modern concrete bridge then the grinding crawl back up the other side in second or even first gear, with a careful eye on the temperature gauge. The climb out of the colossal Wadi Mujib – Jordan's Grand Canyon – took a steady half hour, giving some idea of the massive scale of these awe inspiring gorges.

71

We arrived at the Petra visitor's centre at eleven thirty. It seemed many months ago – in reality just 3 weeks – since we had studied our Bartholomews map on the wall of the flat and Petra had been earmarked as a major milestone on the journey. If we could reach Petra, we thought, then we could reach anywhere, and here we were, safe and sound and feeling like very experienced travellers.

Though not the height of the tourist season, several coaches started to arrive at midday having travelled directly from Amman on a day trip. From the car park one found oneself in a broad rocky area with dozens of saddled horses, and their attendant guides now swooped on the new arrivals, who seemed to be predominantly Americans, and practically bullied them into hiring their services. Dawn and I were in no financial position to pay for such luxuries even if we had wanted to, but anyway preferred to walk. The locals soon identified us as 'poor Brits' and accepted the futility of approaching us. The trail into Petra headed along the valley, at the end of which the rocks started to rise steeply on either side. We passed some dwellings carved into the rock and then came to a narrow cleft in the rock face which now rose some fifty feet above us. This was the Siq, the only entrance to the ancient city. Entering the cleft the immediate effect was of coolness and awe, staring upwards to the narrow slit of sunlight now 100 feet above us. On average the walls were just twelve feet apart and it was perhaps a quarter of a mile walk through the twisting gorge until suddenly we came around a bend and saw our first glimpse of the ornately carved Treasury glowing pink in the reflected afternoon sun – the classic image of Petra.

The cleft ended as suddenly as it had begun and we stepped out into the sunshine again. All around, the virgin rock rose steeply but everything was eclipsed by the magnificent Treasury with its beautifully carved façade of columns and balustrades with a broad set of steps leading up and into the entrance cut deep into the rock. High above us the top culminated in a temple style roof with a central sculpted vessel known as the lantern. The Bedouin had caused considerable damage to the lantern over the years, firing at it in the belief that if shattered it would reveal a hoard of gold.

We turned right and then left and out of this enclosed area into the more open spaces of the city. Here, all around the cliff walls were rooms and dwellings cut into the rock. At the far end were enormous temple buildings high above the ground level and opposite was an amphitheatre and stage, all carved out of the solid rock.

The carved rock buildings of Petra

In retrospect I don't think that we really did justice to Petra and should have explored it more enthusiastically, but we were feeling somewhat lazy and the sheer size and spectacle of the place was quite overwhelming. We sat for a while watching the younger guides showing off as they galloped along the rock strewn road, their robes flowing behind them and the hooves of their mounts clattering on the stone, before we headed back through the Siq. Here we found streams of tourists of all shapes and sizes sitting determinedly astride their unaccustomed mounts. Many voiced their cheerful surprise that we were walking but we couldn't help thinking that there would be more aching thighs in the hotels of Amman that night than in the Rover.

Back at the car park we were further amused by the furious haggling going on as the returning tourists were now pestered by their guides for tips and extra money. In fact it turned out to be a good place to buy dollars with Jordanian dinars as the Americans tended to tip in dollars and the locals were desperate to convert them to local currency.

*"...and then, my brothers, we grab the Americans' dollars and run!"*

We left Petra early in the afternoon as we wanted to reach Aqaba that day. We left the mountains with their east/west wadis and started dropping down to the coast along broad north/south valleys, the mountains either side of us becoming long ridges like outspread fingers pointing down to the Gulf of Aqaba and the Red Sea. I have no idea of the height that we had been at, but the last 100 kilometres or so were an almost continuous downhill gradient. The Rover bombed happily along and Dawn dozed off. I noticed an occasional squealing noise and a slight rise in engine temperature but put the noise down to the high wind that was blowing across the road, and the temperature rise was not too great. Dawn opened an eye and asked what the noise was. I reassured her with my theory of the wind but she frowned and said that her car had made that noise once when the water pump failed so perhaps we should stop and check. Well, anything for a quiet life so I pulled up, hopped out and – blow me - the water pump *had* gone. I'd left the engine running and when I opened the bonnet I was met by a stream of steaming, dirty brown water. We heated some water to top up the radiator but this ran out of the water pump as quickly as I poured it in. In my Goody Box I had a water pump kit but I would need a vice with which to carry out the repair. A Landcruiser pulled up and the Brit driver offered his assistance. With nothing I could do to the pump I said that we would attempt to reach Aqaba, but would appreciate it if he would accompany us and perhaps give us a tow if necessary. We therefore set off rather gingerly, but with the continuous downhill gradient we actually coasted all the way with just a couple of places where I needed to start the engine. Still trundling silently, we saw the sea appear before us, rolled down onto the coast road and finally came to a stop having freewheeled thirty kilometres.

In Aqaba we were aiming for a hotel which George of Penworld had told me about and we now found ourselves only about a kilometre from it on the same flat road. It was possible to drive that short distance without overheating and we pulled up outside the Palm Beach Hotel with two huge sighs of relief, bidding farewell and thanks to our faithful escort. Parked outside was George's vehicle, a special conversion with a bus body mounted on a Bedford 4x4 chassis.

The Palm Beach proved not to be as exotic as the name implied, in fact it was decidedly run down. At the back and just on the beach was a patio and bar. Here we found George in the company of a rather vivacious Australian girl called Mary who was also staying at the hotel and who was awaiting a visit from her boyfriend, currently working in Saudi Arabia. Dawn and Mary were to be excellent company for each other over the next couple of days.

It was still my birthday so we treated ourselves to a couple of beers and settled down to relax and chat with our new friends. Mary had been in the hotel for several days and it was a meeting place for local ex-patriates and the management also allowed camping in the limited grounds. A resident Brit called Bill dropped in for a drink. An older chap, he was apparently King Hussein's Number One at the port of Aqaba. A bit of an odd character who gave the impression that if the Iran/Iraq war spread to Jordan he would be only too happy to get back into action again. He was on his own in Aqaba and sadly seemed rather a lonely individual.

The Rover was, of course, hors de combat so we resigned ourselves to a night by the roadside in a fairly major town. Nobody took any notice.

*Fixing the water pump on the seafront at Aqaba*

First thing the next day I tackled the water pump and soon had it out on the pavement. As suspected it was impossible to take apart without a vice so George took me to a small vehicle workshop where the owner kindly allowed me free use of his bench and vice. By midday the pump was repaired and refitted and we were back in business. Dawn went shopping with Mary and then they both lay sunbathing on the beach – Dawn having done some washing first, I hasten to add. I had at last managed to find a shop that would fill our empty Gaz bottle and arranged for it to be done the next day. We invited Mary for dinner that night, intending to drive to a public beach just outside the town limits, have our meal, take Mary back to the Palm Beach and then return to the beach to spend the night there. Our plans were thwarted when the police stopped us before we even reached the beach – no passage after dark, which by this time it was. Driving back into Aqaba we scanned the beach area for a likely camping spot. Not far beyond the Palm Beach we came to a large open space and pulled off under some palm trees next to the ruins of an old house. It looked ok so the girls set to and prepared dinner, based on a ready cooked chicken. All very civilised and afterwards we settled down and listened to Episode One of the radio series 'The Hitchhikers Guide to the Galaxy', thoughtfully taped and provided to us by my old friend JVC before we left Oman.

We now had to find and book a ferry to Egypt. George was also heading for Egypt and directed us to a reputable shipping agent. It seemed that the ferry schedule was a bit unreliable and when we visited the agent he could only shrug his shoulders and suggest that we returned the next day.

On the previous day an Exodus overland tour had arrived at the Palm Beach, and the group of ten passengers were camped in the grounds, or rather, back-yard. We met the driver of this bus whilst in town and he told us of a small bar that he used, the Omar Sharif, and suggested a quick beer. Sounded like a good idea and so we ended up meeting yet another unusual character. The Arab that owned the bar had apparently been some kind of stand-in for Omar Sharif when he was filming Lawrence of Arabia in the local Wadi Rhum some twenty years earlier. The walls were covered in photographs of him during filming but unfortunately the passing years had not been too kind and the resemblance to Omar was fading and sadly our 'star' was starting to look not a little seedy and somewhat older. Anyway, as newcomers to his bar he welcomed us with some sort of cocktail and a Pepsi and then produced a lady's vanity case from which he carefully extracted the black cotton robe and hood which he had worn during filming. I was prevailed upon to don this garment and was then directed on how to strut around the bar, striving to look like Mr Sharif whilst peering out threateningly from under the hood. The effect was probably more like a cross between a poor man's Sheikh of Araby and the Scarlet Pimpernel but fortunately there were only a few people in the bar at the time. It was then Dawn's turn but our star allowed *her* to use a back room to change and even kindly assisted her, brushing obviously but inoffensively against her during the process. So Dawn strutted about a bit and we all laughed politely before handing back the hallowed gown and making our escape.

I wanted go diving in the Red Sea as part of our adventure so we went to the Aquamarine hotel where I booked a dive for the following morning before returning to the Rover for chili-con-carne and an early night. I keep mentioning the meals in order to give Dawn the credit to which she is due and also to illustrate the sophisticated range of dishes that she produced on just a couple of gas rings.

I had joined the British Sub-Aqua Club whilst in Oman and had spent three very enjoyable years diving there. The intention was to dive in places during the journey, and space had been allocated in the Rover for my wetsuit and basic gear. In fact this was to be the only time I was to use it. The diving facility at the Aquamarine was run by a young Frenchman and after filling in numerous forms and hiring an air cylinder and demand valve, I and two others were taken in the hotel mini-bus to a dive site a few kilometres outside the town. I had a pleasant dive with excellent visibility but there was very little fish life around the very beautiful coral.

..........and Dawn did some washing.

Meanwhile Dawn had been busy washing again (!), this time taking advantage of the Palm Beach facilities, and had then set off into town to retrieve our filled Gaz bottle and hand in our second one which had now also run out. She also checked with the shipping agent and was again told to try again the next day. However, in her travels she came across another agent and in response to her enquiry was informed that a suitable vessel was leaving that afternoon at three o'clock, and that we could probably get on it. Whilst we had no timetable to meet, there were rumours of an influx of refugees fleeing the Iran/Iraq conflict and a potential high demand for ferry places out of Aqaba. We therefore thought it prudent to take the first opportunity that arose. This set off a frantic series of events. Dawn first tried to retrieve the second Gaz bottle but it had already been dispatched to the depot. She then drove to the Aquamarine to await my imminent return and inform me of our early departure. I hastily sorted my gear out (it was not rinsed in fresh water until we reached the UK) and was bundled off to the Palm Beach to grab a shower in Mary's room whilst Dawn and Mary set off in pursuit of the Gaz bottle. They tracked it to the depot where they were advised that such a bottle could not be filled there – although surely they had filled the other identical one the day before? Collecting me from the Palm Beach Dawn then drove us to the shipping agent. At this stage there was some doubt as to whether or not the Rover was too high to fit on board the ferry. According to a comparison of the measurements of the ship and those of the Rover it wouldn't fit, but despite our concern the agent cheerfully told us to report to the embarkation office near the port. In situations like this, one tends to surrender to the lack of logic and organisation and get carried along in the confusion.

We said a hasty goodbye to our friends at the Palm Beach and hurried to the embarkation office – a shabby concrete waiting room inside a fenced compound where a mass of other prospective passengers was milling around. There were quite a few cars around, too, all equally eager to board the ship. We hadn't bought any tickets and were rather pessimistic of our chances but all of a sudden a Mercedes rolled up and out jumped our agent. Brushing aside our anxious questions with a 'don't worry' smile he strode into the office. The gate to the harbour was across the main road, guarded by a couple of armed policemen. A signal came, the gate opened and the pedestrians scrambled across and into the harbour buildings. The cars also started to move, their occupants waving tickets or some such which granted them admission. At last our agent reappeared, shouted for us to follow him, jumped into his Merc and headed into the port. Leaping into the Rover we lurched after him, careering through the gate with an apologetic look on my face which I hoped the policeman would accurately interpret as "Sorry, can't stop, got to follow this chap in front, haven't got a ticket, might not fit in the ship, but if we do fit we will buy one and if we don't fit it doesn't matter anyway, does it? Please don't shoot us".

Well, no shots were fired, and rounding a corner we pulled up in the queue of cars waiting to embark. We could now see the ship, a sizeable one reminiscent of an English cross channel ferry. The rear doors were open and cars were slowly being manoeuvred up the ramp and into the bowels. It was plainly obvious even from this distance that the jerry cans and boxes on our roof rack, plus the spare wheel on the roof, would not fit so I started to unload them all. This was not as easy as it might sound. Everything was securely lashed and strapped in a rather complex fashion. To make matters worse a gallon can of engine oil had been slowly leaking ever since we left Oman and half the ropes were now covered in filthy black oil and dirt. As I fumbled about on the roof the situation wasn't helped by a hurricane force wind that was whistling in off the sea, whipping the waves into whitecaps and trying to blow me over the edge. It all seemed so unglorified compared to the smooth characters sitting neatly dressed in their Mercedes and Peugeots, windows tightly closed against the wind and noise. Some of the port guys gave us a hand and everything was heaved into the back of the Rover and I dug out my rapidly diminishing tin of Swarfega. We dived back into the cab and were then approached by an official wanting our Carnet. This alarmed me because if he completed it and then we couldn't get on the ship it was going to complicate matters somewhat. Blithely ignoring my protests the customs man scribbled in the appropriate places, tore out the requisite section and handed the remainder back to me, but without stamping it. I could see no point in pursuing the matter and we sat back to wait for the next instructions. The queue of vehicles gradually moved forward but because of our size we were kept at the back. At last it was our turn and I ground up the ramp. Well, we got three quarters in but further forward motion was prevented by two inches of roof rack sticking up. Expecting some anger and impatience I was very pleasantly surprised when a couple of friendly and un-fazed crew members took stock of the situation, motioned us back down the ramp and even gave me a hand to remove the rack, held on by just four bolts. All this provided considerable entertainment and amusement to the several hundred Asians and Arabs who were now leaning over the stern rail watching us. The rack was carried into the ship and I slowly eased up the ramp again, now prepared to let the tyres down if necessary, but we just scraped in with no more than an inch of clearance. Phew! Stop all engines and we flopped out.

We grabbed papers and passports, locked up and found our way up to the lounge where our helpful agent found us and proceeded to relieve us of an incredible $450.00 for our passage to Suez. We had a choice of Second Class or Deck Class. Anxious not to strain our budget any further we opted for the deck, assuming that this would include the lounge. I explained to the agent that our Carnet had not been stamped but he did not seem very concerned. I finally persuaded him to stamp it with *his* rubber stamp – well, a stamp's a stamp, isn't it?

The express ferry Najd

\*\*\*\*

Distance across Jordan – 1252km

Total distance – 4708km

# Chapter 11 – The Red Sea

Tuesday 14th to Wednesday 15th October 1980

Journey days 25 and 26

After the mad scramble we now hung about for an hour before casting off. We popped back to the Rover and having been assured that we could have access to it at any time during the journey, returned to the lounge and relaxed. The vessel was Saudi owned and looked like an ex English Channel ferry. The lounge was finished in rich dark wood, brass fittings and a deep shag pile carpet with a central circular 'bar' dispensing tea, coffee and cans of 7 Up at high prices. Two sets of double doors at the forward end led into a dining room and then on to long corridors of cabins plus some European style toilets. Right for'ard were the first class lounge and cabins. All looked very tired and shabby.

Having explored the interior we headed up on deck. Here were the rabble, who were not allowed into the lounge area. Poor people of all ages, their facilities consisted of a couple of tanks of water and a row of metal Asian toilet cubicles welded across the rear deck, half of which were inaccessible. The deck above the lounge and cabins was clearer, with lifeboats and seats and apparently lots of space to lay around in the cool evening air if it became too stuffy down below.

By now we were under way, and retracing our steps to the lounge met a Scottish couple of about our own age. Mike and Daphne were travelling using public transport. They had originally left England on an old motorcycle combination, loaded to the gunnels and headed for Africa and Australia. With all the weight and the strain the bike constantly overheated and gave problems. Not far into Europe they decided to turn back. On their return they were persuaded to remove the sidecar, reduce their luggage and travel on the bike alone. This they did and set off again, reaching Greece this time before persistent ignition problems forced them to abandon the bike completely, shipping it back to England and continuing 'a pied'. Here they were heading for Egypt and then down through Africa. It was nice to have company and we sat and chatted until hunger overcame us and Mike and Daphne headed for the dining room and I popped below deck to fetch some food from the Rover. To my dismay I found all the doors to the car deck securely locked. So much for constant access. I managed to locate the bosun, a cheerful African, who kindly unlocked one of the doors and allowed me to get to the vehicle where I collected cold chicken and salad. We ate this in the dining room with Mike and Daphne and then went back on deck. Our friends had already 'reserved' a bench for the night and had their sleeping bags with them. We bade them goodnight, picked our way over sprawled bodies and found ourselves a bit of deck to lie on.

It was really rather pleasant, with a gentle cool breeze and the faint vibration and muffled rumble of the engines. We had brought a couple of sweatshirts up with us and with them bundled under our heads we soon dozed off. It was about ten thirty. By one o'clock in the morning we were both awake, shivering even in our sweatshirts and desperately trying to get warm in the cold blast of air that was now sweeping relentlessly over the deck. Time to retire to the shelter of the lounge but....Deck Class meant Deck Class and all the doors to the interior of the ship were firmly locked. We trailed all over but couldn't find a sheltered spot anywhere. There were huddled bodies all over the place, but most of them had their possessions with them which included blankets. The air temperature probably wasn't too low but it was the powerful buffeting wind that gave real meaning to the term 'wind chill' and we were shaking with cold. We looked ruefully at other travelers cosily tucked up in their sleeping bags and thought of all our gear down below, totally inaccessible. It was Dawn who finally noticed a small wooden door with a bolt on the outside. She slid back the latch and the door whipped open in the wind to reveal a tiny, dimly lit air conditioning plant room. Sanctuary! We stepped over the sill into a quarter of an inch of water and an available space about two feet by four feet. Only trouble was that the door had no handle on the inside and the wind was continually blowing it open. Shuffling around I found an old fan belt on the floor and by looping this around the end of the bolt and the edge of the door I was able to hold the door almost shut from the inside. The relief of being out of that wind was indescribable. In fact we were so overjoyed that it was a few minutes before the reality of the situation became clear, and we began to wonder how we would survive the next few hours, desperately tired now and with nowhere to sit or lie down and hanging on to the fan belt all the time to keep the door shut. Beyond a mass of pipes was a similar space and door on the other side of the room and two or three Asian chaps were crouched in there. After a while one of them gallantly offered us a stool that he had found, and leaned over to pass it through the pipes. Whilst this improved our position considerably, it only had three and a half legs and demanded continuous bracing to keep it upright. With our leg muscles tensed to prop up the stool and me clutching the fan belt we settled down to survive the hours until daybreak.

Oh, the joy of dawn and the heat of the sun's rays! We stumbled out of our black hole and soaked up the warmth radiating from just above the horizon. We both felt lousy. The lounge doors were eventually re-opened and we gratefully left the outside for the snugness of the interior. Mike and Daphne appeared and announced that they had had a decent night's sleep on the deck in their sleeping bags. We headed for the dining room, had a basic breakfast of boiled egg and bread and a cup of tea then went back to the now windless deck to read books and doze.

We arrived at Suez at eleven but it was to be four o'clock before we finally docked. Vehicle owners were requested to report to the dining room and we all assembled in a crowd around a couple of men at a table with a cash box and a stack of printed forms in front of them. It was the usual bedlam with every man for himself – whatever it was that we were fighting for. In the midst of all this confusion someone appeared at the door and demanded that the owner of the white Land Rover move it out as it was stopping everyone else from getting off. I tossed the keys to Dawn and she nipped below. A big, fat, angry Egyptian wanted to grab the keys and move it himself, but though Dawn may be small she could be quite forceful and she calmly but firmly refused his demands and climbed into the cab through a seething crowd of passengers struggling with huge bundles of luggage. With other engines revving all around and the fat Egyptian still shouting, she carefully backed down the ramp until she was stopped with a rear wheel lodged against a rock, throwing him into a fresh paroxysm of fury. At that point the friendly bosun stepped in, smiled encouragingly at Dawn and calmly removed the offending rock. With great satisfaction she continued backwards quite quickly, forcing the now wildly beckoning Egyptian to leap for his life and unleashing a stream of impatient cars from inside the ship like water out of a breached dam.

Meanwhile, back in the dining room, I had been informed that it was going to cost a further $70.00 to get the necessary piece of paper to allow us to leave the ship. This was a bolt from the blue and I argued in vain, not least because

I didn't have $70.00 on me, just $20.00 in Jordanian dinars. In the end I went down to Dawn to discuss the situation, finding her still being ranted at by the fat Egyptian who was demanding the piece of paper that I was trying to pay for. We finally paid the bill with a $50.00 Travellers Cheque and the Jordanian dinars. Added to the original cost of the ferry this meant that this boat trip had now cost us as much as the rest of the journey all together from Oman to Aqaba – including Dawn's air fare.

Whilst negotiating my piece of paper I had been approached by a tall Egyptian youth who spoke a few words of English and who offered his assistance with the usual "You my friend. I help you". I was immediately on my guard and indicated that he should leave me alone. I couldn't understand what he was on about, anyway. Emerging with my piece of paper we at last got rid of Dawn's fat Egyptian and in the relative calm that followed we discussed with Mike and Daphne what to do, having offered them a lift to Cairo. The first thing was to get out of the port. At this point Mr Fixit reappeared at my elbow. "You my friend. I help you". Well, at this point I honestly thought that he was something to do with the shipping agency and having coughed up $70.00 decided that he might as well earn some of it.

Let me say now that at every other port, harbour, ferry or border that we encountered it was always possible to find one's way through the beaurocracy without the help of a third party. Not so at Suez. Here the whole process was so complicated and involved that it would be impossible for a non-Arabic speaker to proceed unaided. There were numerous clerks and officials to be seen and they were hidden away in dirty, smelly, ill-lit, bare offices scattered all over the place. At the time, of course, we were unaware of this, and of the four and a half hours it would eventually take to negotiate our way out of the docks.

Mr Fixit pointed us in the direction of a large shed and said that that we should go there and see the customs people while he took Mike and Daphne to the passport office. No problems at customs except that by now we were very much on our guard and refused point blank to co-operate with the plain clothes customs official until he produced evidence of his authority. He fortunately accepted this with good nature and we passed through with no trouble. We were going to need money before leaving the docks so Mr Fixit arranged a taxi and he and I drove into Suez, about ten minutes away, to change some Travellers Cheques – at a good rate, as it happened. Back to the docks and the passport office where there was a considerable delay, not that it was busy, just us and four German lads. Mr Fixit and I drove to another office to get the Carnet stamped but this was closed until later. He now informed me that we would need Egyptian insurance so back into Suez in another taxi and down some shady back streets to a gaudy open office where everything was in Arabic and I obtained some sort of insurance certificate for $7.00, then back to the port. It was dark by this time and not the most inspiring time to be roaming around a gloomy, deserted Egyptian dockyard. Mr Fixit wanted to know if I had any sex magazines or sex tapes. No. We hung about waiting for the carnet office to open. When it eventually did, the doors of a large warehouse slowly creaked open to reveal a dusty collection of ramshackle desks and filing cabinets in one corner, dimly lit by a couple of twenty five watt bulbs high in the roof. A scruffy man came out and insisted on checking the engine and chassis number. To combat the dark he had a torch which struggled to glow feeble and yellow as I scraped off dirt and oil to try and reveal the elusive numbers. He was at last satisfied but then proceeded to partially demolish my Carnet book in the process of scribbling in it. He did remark on the fact that the Rover was right hand drive, but made no reference to the special pass from the Egyptian Motoring Organisation as had been indicated as essential in my AA advice book, and *I* certainly wasn't going to mention it. The stamping of the Carnet lightened me of a further $25.00 – a process that was free everywhere else that we went.

Mr Fixit was gradually collecting a fistful of papers and receipts and I was completely confused and bewildered. Back to the passport office and an office next door. We ended up parked outside the office toilet and sat gagging on the stench. I don't know why we were there, but another man appeared and checked the engine and chassis numbers again. I then had to pay another $3.00 for a postage stamp (just 2 Egyptian pounds but Mr Fixit tried to convince me that it was 20). We took the stamp to another office to be stuck on a form. I was then issued with a pair of battered metal plates with barely legible Arabic numbers and covered in rusty scratches. These were our Egyptian number plates, to be worn at all times and costing a further $4.00. A smelly old man was summoned to attach the plates to the Rover and he started to try and remove the Oman plates first. I soon put a stop to that and tied the Egyptian plates on top with some string. Mr Fixit then demanded that I give Mr Smelly a $1.50 tip. By this time my patience was running pretty thin, not helped by a lack of food and sleep, so I'm afraid that Mr Smelly was left empty handed.

We had our passports back, we had insurance, we had the Carnet stamped and we had Egyptian number plates but there were still more signatures and stamps to obtain. At last, at about nine o'clock, we drove to the gates and hung about whilst everything was checked and a final signature scrawled on a final document. Almost unbelievably we were free to go! Of course Mr Fixit came out of the gates and inevitably asked for money for his trouble. I look back and still remain unsure of his real role in all of this. He was an obnoxious, sly character who I didn't like and who had blatantly tried to con us out of money.

Nevertheless, he had spent four and a half hours with us and had led us through a totally mind boggling maze of a system that would have been impossible to navigate without his help. Unfortunately I was very tired and had had more than enough, so flatly refused to give him any money, insisting that he must be part of the organisation that took $70.00 off us on arrival so was being paid anyway. I was really angry – most unlike me – but he didn't argue, just stood there looking a bit pathetic and I actually started to feel a bit sorry for him. It would have been easier if he had shouted back at me. Anyway, right or wrong, I ignored his request, climbed in the Rover and we drove off, his outstretched hand still through the window as we started to move.

In hindsight I have to say that I have always felt very guilty about not giving him anything.

Coming into Suez

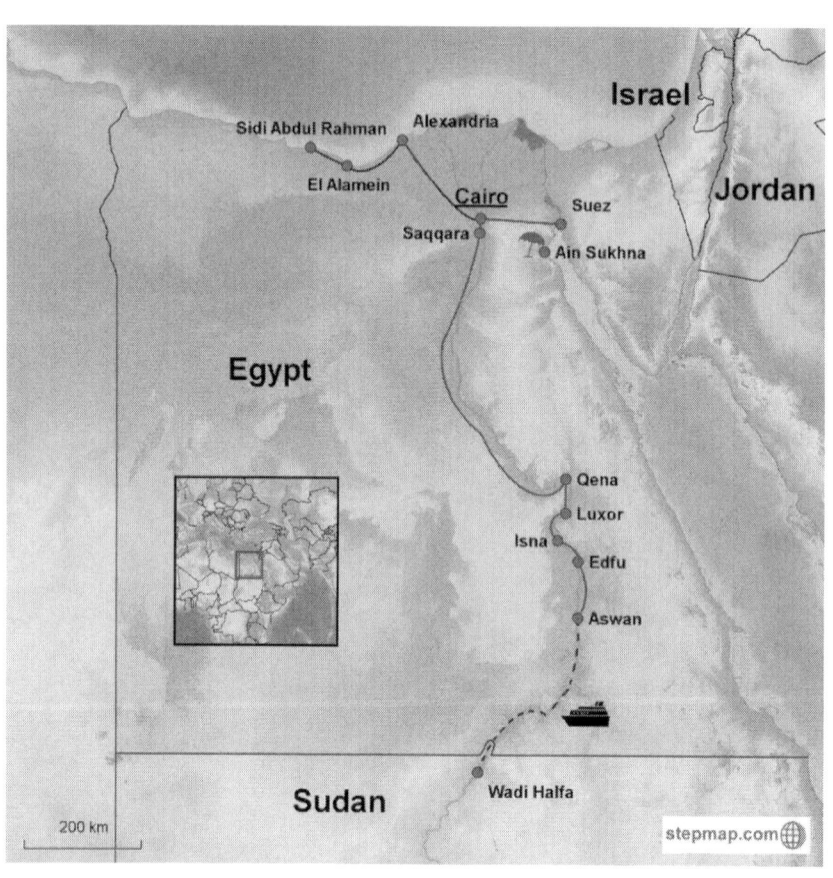

# Chapter 12 – Egypt

Wednesday 15th October to Sunday 9th November 1980

Journey days 26 to 51

We drove away from the docks and into Suez. Mike and Daphne must have been wondering if accepting a lift with us had been such a good idea after all. Nevertheless they insisted on paying for a meal so we managed to find a decent looking restaurant and relaxed over some welcome food, beer and wine before heading out towards Cairo and stopping for the night about 30 kilometres down the road.

To finish the day off Dawn opened the 'fridge door and discovered that a carton of milk had turned rancid and leaked all over the bottom of it. It promptly poured out of the door and onto (and into) the carpet.

Having arrived in the dark it was interesting the next morning to find ourselves camped just outside a busy stone quarry and we were awoken by a constant stream of heavy trucks driving in and out and the workers shouting cheerfully to us. All around was just flat brown desert with some low hills rising behind us where the quarry was situated.

Breakfast with Mike and Daphne

It was nice to have company for breakfast and I think that Mike and Daphne appreciated our facilities as compared to their own frugal equipment. We tucked into boiled eggs, toast and coffee and then set off for Cairo, some 100 kilometres away. The road was the usual strip of tarmac across the barren desert and every now and then a large, friendly sign advised us that 'Foreigners are Forbidden to Leave the Main Road'. This sign was to be a common sight throughout Egypt and would cause us problems when it came to camping.

As in Jordan we were constantly reminded of the delicate Middle East situation by the presence of vast military camps and training areas with endless lines of trucks and tanks and guns. It was along this road that the Israelis advanced in 1967, and a monument only a few kilometres outside the Cairo suburb of Heliopolis marked the eventual cease-fire line.

Heliopolis rose from the desert in the shape of countless multi-storey residential blocks, and suddenly we were back into the hustle, bustle and aggressive traffic of big city life. Mike and Daphne were to leave us here and catch a tram into the centre of Cairo, whilst we went in search of more friends working on yet another BAC defence contract. Most of this support team lived in a large block of flats in an area of Heliopolis known as 'Merryland', which eventually turned out to be a large fenced off leisure park. As usual we had only vague directions based on a small map which was a photocopy of just part of a complete map of Heliopolis. The main feature marked was a group of 'unfinished, multi-storey flats'. As the map was obviously not recent, these could, of course, now be 'finished, multi-storey flats' of which there seemed to be an abundance. We plunged deeper into the concrete and our hesitant moves at traffic lights and junctions brought us to the attention of a local man in his car who waved us down and enquired of our destination. With his directions we set off again with an optimism which gradually faded as neither 'unfinished blocks' nor Merryland appeared. Once more our deliberations at junctions attracted the attention of another local and this one kindly led us to Merryland in his car and, yes, at one end of the park was a *very* unfinished, multi-storey block, easily the biggest block we had come across.

The BAC flats proved to be an impressive block situated in a quiet road and overlooking ornamental gardens at the back of Merryland. A perusal of the names on the doorbells in the main entrance didn't enlighten us at all so we picked an English sounding name and tried that, with the result that we were invited up to their flat by Chris and Maurice, who we had never met before. Maurice was a member of the support team and over a welcome cup of tea explained that due to a current Moslem holiday many of the people that I knew had flown out to Cyprus for a few days break. However, in one of the ground floor flats an ex colleague of mine from Oman was still in residence and a quick telephone call brought Dave to the door where he greeted us effusively - despite the fact that he hadn't met Dawn before. With typical expat hospitality he declared his flat to be at our disposal for as long as we wanted and led us downstairs to meet his wife Irene and eight year old daughter Rachael, who was immediately and unceremoniously turfed out of her bedroom to make way for us.

So began an unexpectedly long stay in Cairo.

By now we had decided that we would head through Egypt to Sudan, possibly to go to Kenya but with no firm decision on that. Unfortunately, due to the public holiday, all government offices were closed and it was therefore impossible to do anything about applying for Sudanese visas. Not to worry. Cairo had lots of tourist attractions and we settled back quite happily to enjoy our stay.

Yet again Dawn had 'been and done' Cairo before but it was all new to me. Our tourist schedule started with the Pyramids, situated at Giza on the opposite side of Cairo to Heliopolis. There was a decent road system around the city which spared us some of the traffic horrors of the centre and in fact the road from Heliopolis was initially a wide, pleasant dual carriageway leading from the modern, spacious areas of the relatively new suburbs and winding gracefully into the eastern outskirts of the city. It cut through, and slightly above, the silent, deserted and foreboding City of the Dead, a huge city within a city consisting of streets and streets of house-like tombs and mausoleums. It never failed to send a bit of a shiver down my spine, especially on the one or two occasions that we drove past at night. Street lights were dim and few and far between and I found it all very creepy.

The rather eerie City of the Dead

91

It was a relief to leave the City of the Dead behind and be awed by the magnificence of the Mohammed Ali mosque and the adjacent Citadel, but then to be stunned by the sight of some absolutely dreadful blocks of flats. We were told that these were legacies of Russian aid in earlier years. They showed evidence of very poor construction and an appalling lack of maintenance, all overlaid with filth and rubbish. From windows and sagging balconies hung all manner of clothing and airing mattresses and it looked as if the accepted method of garbage disposal was simply to throw it out the window, where it collected in festering heaps. The mind boggled at the thought of what the insides were like.

Past these modern slums the road reduced to a single carriageway, curving into the centre of Cairo through crowded *old* slums, teeming with people picking their way around rickety stalls selling vegetables and cooked food. Ancient, wobbly horse drawn carts meandered amongst huge trucks belching clouds of blue fumes and overloaded with all types of goods. The road was potholed and lumpy and oil stained and traffic and pedestrians wandered all over it. To us there was an overall air of poverty and resignation but these people presumably just lived and existed to different standards than ours and perhaps it was unfair to measure their way of life against what we thought of as normality.

A set of traffic lights, enforced by a dusty looking policeman, controlled our tide of traffic as it merged with the main stream of vehicles heading out towards Giza. As ever it was every man for himself, the object always to be just ahead of the next car, taxi, bus or truck, squeezing into impossible gaps, hand on horn and having no consideration whatsoever for the consequences. Everything just crawled along in a spasmodic fashion with no chance of any steady progress because of the constant blockages caused by the ridiculous driving standards.

We slowly made our way out of the city, caught up and carried along like a piece of flotsam in a storm drain, surrounded by lots more floating, bobbing rubbish and eventually washing up in the vicinity of the pyramids. Here the road was lined with neatly cropped bushes and shrubs to provide a more pleasing environment for the tourists, and the local shops and emporiums had been superseded by garish restaurants, discos and casinos.

The pyramids were situated right on the borderline of Cairo where it met the desert, with the teeming suburb of Giza to the north and open desert for some distance to the south. Apart from a brief glimpse of their summits, and despite their size, the pyramids remained completely hidden from view until the road climbed up past the Mina House Hotel, and the last resting places of Cheops, Chephren and Mycernus were suddenly revealed.

Until this moment my mental image of the pyramids had been one based on childhood encyclopaedia pictures which always depicted them rising majestically from picturesque, rolling sand dunes. I expected to see waving green palm trees and sun baked courtyards of white stone slabs, everything clean and spotlessly tidy.

I was wrong.

From the Mina House side there were no golden sands and no palm trees, just lots of brown earth and rubble and dust. It looked as if the original site had never been cleared up once the building was completed. The sharp, clean lines of the pyramids that I seemed to remember from my childhood were no more. Except for the very crown of Cheops the original granite facings had been stripped hundreds of years ago to be carted back to the city to use in the construction of the Mohammed Ali mosque – not so much recycling as out and out vandalism. The exposed stone blocks beneath rose in steps and had been eroded and misshapen by wind and weather and no doubt the passage of many thousands of pairs of scrambling feet before climbing was banned. Every ledge was covered in rubble.

The immediate surroundings, far from my imagined stone courtyards, were rocky and gritty and uneven. Palm trees? I don't think so. Areas around the pyramids had been excavated to a depth of twenty feet or so to reveal many small burial chambers which, far from being carefully preserved for presentation to visitors, now took on the duty of toilets, unfortunately with no plumbing or facilities. If there is one everlasting memory of Cairo it is the acrid stink of urine.

For a fee of about $3.00 each we were allowed inside the pyramids. Despite the lack of external care, there can be no denying the awesome size and workmanship once you are walking in the inner passageways. The battered exteriors hide incredible stonework with precise joints between huge individual blocks. Small wonder that Egyptologists still scratch their heads when trying to explain how this work could have been carried out.

The entrance to the pyramid of Cheops initially sloped down steeply at about forty degrees through a low rectangular passage, and then opening into a high, spacious cavern. At the end, the way lead through another low, square tunnel to the final burial chamber where the granite sarcophagus lay open and empty. Being Egypt, the lighting was very dim and the room echoed to the voices of our fellow tourists. When I say dim I mean frugal as opposed to moody. We waited until they had all left in order to experience the loneliness and isolation of this chamber of the dead but somehow the expected atmosphere wasn't there, presumably lost to the over-riding influence of both exploitation and neglect.

*The best side of the pyramids*

We left the pyramid of Cheops and strolled over those of Chephren and Mycernus to take a quick look inside, but I guess that once you have seen one pyramid you have seen all three, and very few people bothered to go further than Cheops.

We found the whole experience somewhat underwhelming. The overall shabbiness was depressing and sad and one wonders why more was not done to preserve and clean and present what is, after all, one of the Seven Wonders. The huge numbers of visitors must raise massive amounts of money but there was absolutely no evidence that any of it was invested in maintenance or upkeep. We walked around and were quite startled when, from right behind us, a cheery, upper class English voice cried "Tally ho!". We turned to find a grinning, be-robed Arab perched high on the back of a haughty camel. He was one of many touting for business to carry tourists around the site. Americans were greeted with "Hiyo, Silver" and no doubt there were practiced salutes for other nationalities. As usual, we were not in the business of spending money on such things and politely refused all offers.

"Tally ho, old chap!"

From the pyramids I looked around for the Sphinx and was surprised when Dawn pointed to a small lump of roughly rounded rock a short distance away. The bulk of the Sphinx was below ground level, having been carved out of the bedrock, so that only the back of the head was visible as we approached it from the rear. It was much smaller than I had been led to believe by my now not-so-trusty encyclopaedia. On reaching the actual site one looked down into a sort of quarry with the Sphinx sitting in the centre. From here the profile started to look more familiar but it wasn't until we had descended into the excavation that it took on its famous shape and was completely recognisable. The face, of course, had been much disfigured by pot shots taken at it, but it was still an impressive structure and the enigmatic smile remained inscrutable.

Some days later we returned to watch the spectacular Son et Lumiere show and, softly lit amidst the surrounding darkness, one could finally appreciate the wonder that must have been generated when these magnificent monuments were originally created. With the camels and hawkers gone and the squalor cloaked by the night, one was privileged to have a taste of the past and now it was easy to visualise the rolling sand dunes and palm trees of my boyhood imagination. It was as if thousands of years had never passed, seated beneath the same starry night sky that has always been there. Like an aging actress, on stage and rejuvenated back to her prime for a few precious hours by skilful make up and the warm glow of footlights, the pyramids and the Sphinx left us in awe us as they once again sat proud and majestic.

After visiting the pyramids we had a brief encounter with the local police. It was necessary for us to register ourselves in Egypt within a few days of arrival, and this was supposed to be at the nearest police station to where we were staying. The police at the Heliopolis station had at first denied all knowledge of this procedure but when pressed had moved onto the defensive and stated that the officer responsible was away for the holiday and would not be back until too late, anyway. Opposite the Mina House Hotel, near to the pyramids, was a small police post so we decided to try our luck there, it being a tourist area, after all. The two men in the front shed (I can only describe it as a shed) were obviously nonplussed by our request but when we persisted they reluctantly led us around the back to a much smarter office where we found two young officers immaculately dressed in spotless white uniforms. One of them spoke excellent English so we proceeded to explain our requirement again. At this point Dawn stepped in (I was too honest) and stated that, as we were staying at the Mina House then this must be the requisite closest police station to report to. With a Sphinx-like smile and a raised eyebrow the officer asked for our room number. I was about to admit defeat at this point but Dawn, without a moment's hesitation, calmly looked him in the eye and said "235". The smile grew a little quizzical and the eyebrow raised a little higher and our officer suggested that presumably, therefore, he could telephone the hotel and they would confirm our residence there? At this Dawn exploded indignantly - of course they would confirm it, why shouldn't they? It was now sink or swim and I managed to join in with a bit of affronted bluster of my own, though I don't think for one minute that we fooled anybody. Nevertheless, Dawn's righteousness won the day and we finally left with the necessary stamps in our passports and the feeling that we had been lucky to come across an official with a sense of humour.

A couple of days after visiting the Cairo pyramids we drove some fifty kilometres out of the south of Cairo to visit the Stepped Pyramids of Saqqara. The road ran alongside an irrigation canal and we had our first look at the irrigated land for which the Nile area is so famous. Straight from my childhood schooldays there was the shaduff, the Archimedes screw and the ox driven water wheel. Occasionally a diesel driven pump could be seen but predominantly the technology remained the same as when Cleopatra passed this way.

We found the Saqqara site to be cleaner and pleasanter than the one at Giza. There were no pestering guides, no cries of "Tally ho" – and it was cheaper. Built as the tomb of King Djoser in the 3rd Dynasty, the Stepped Pyramid was older than the Giza pyramids and, as its name implied, looked like a series of flat, square grey boxes piled on top of each other, each one reducing in size to form the classic pyramid shape. The steps were each about thirty feet high and crumbled and rounded with age. Other buildings on the site had been carefully renovated but the pyramid remained untouched. It was not possible to enter the tomb but some of the smaller surrounding tombs contained impressive examples of hieroglyphics. By this time, however, we were becoming a little tired of tombs and after a refreshing Pepsi we headed back to Cairo.

The stepped pyramid at Saqqara

Don't ask!

In the evening we were invited to accompany Dave, Irene and Rachael for a bite to eat with of one of Dave's Egyptian work colleagues. We were quite fortunate throughout our journey to have these opportunities to meet and be entertained by local people and we duly set off to visit Mamdoo and his family at their home. This was down a typical poor looking street. After being greeted at the front door we were led through a small dining area into an even smaller lounge area only about ten feet square. The walls were a familiar faded light blue which had obviously been applied many years before. The chairs, too, had once been upholstered in vividly coloured materials but these had also faded over many years. The hospitality, though, was impressive. We were introduced to, and shook hands with, numerous members of the family who stood silently grinning and apparently enjoying the novelty of our presence before disappearing after another round of handshakes. We sipped Pepsis and made small talk with Mamdoo – the only English speaker - and just before the conversation started to flag he produced a very old backgammon board and proceeded to demonstrate his skill and dexterity with it. It was so well used that the inlaid veneer triangles were almost invisible but he flicked the counters around at lightning speed and completed his moves before the thrown dice had completely settled. None of us were regular players but we managed to fumble our way through a couple of games, politely letting Mamdoo win. It was then time to eat. Due to, presumably, the space limitations and also their code of hospitality, only Mamdoo, his mother and three of his brothers sat down with us whilst the daughters and cousins slaved over a smokey hot stove behind a curtained doorway. The food was excellent with a large selection of fried meats, liver and meatballs plus stacks of French fries and salad. It was all very simple but so very genuine and served with such pride and generosity that a millionaire couldn't have treated us any better.

It wasn't a late evening and we left at about eight fifteen, back to Dave's and a welcome beer.

******

Whilst driving through Jordan I had been somewhat perturbed by the amount of blue oil smoke issuing from the engine breather pipe. Cairo was to be the last place for any serious maintenance and I had to decide whether or not to investigate the problem or just ignore it. It would have been irresponsible to set off into the unknown without everything in order and I certainly had the time as we were having to wait for the Sudanese embassy to reopen after the Eid el Kabir holiday. I therefore took the cylinder head off, looking for evidence of broken piston rings. The bore of cylinder 4 looked a bit scratched so, in for a penny, in for a pound, I crawled underneath, drained the oil and removed the sump and piston number four. It was a bit coked up which was causing the scratching but the rings were fine. I scraped off the deposits and put everything back together, changing the oil and oil filter at the same time. It still blew smoke just as much but I had set my mind at rest. I subsequently learnt that blowing oily vapour wasn't unusual and that later models of the Rover were, in fact, fitted with a closed system that fed the breather output back into the air intake.

Cylinder head and sump off for a quick piston check

99

All this took place in the road outside the flats, which were in a fairly high class residential area, and I received a few odd looks from passers-by.

The closure of the Sudanese embassy for several more days meant that we would be in Cairo for at least another week and we therefore had too much spare time on our hands. At weekends Dave and Irene and some of the rest of the team would head for the beach at Ain Sukhna on the Red Sea and we joined them one time for a swim and a barbecue. It was a two hour journey but would have been much longer if we hadn't made use of a military road which cut a large corner off the official route. Access to the road was by bribery with cigarettes of the guards on the barrier. Close up these were a very scruffy bunch of fellows. Rumour had it that a generous Russian government had provided the Egyptian army with thousands of pairs of size thirteen boots with no laces, hence many shuffling soldiers.

It was very pleasant down by the sea but with the public holiday there many more people with the same idea. A cool refreshing swim followed by a barbecue and beers was excellent, although for some reason Muggins ended up doing all the cooking. I wouldn't have claimed to be the most proficient barbecue chef but it turned out fine and Dawn took the whole thing in her stride and lay on the beach all day.

After 5 days in Cairo we were concerned that we were maybe outstaying our welcome and as the Sudanese embassy remained firmly closed we decided to take a trip to Alexandria and then to El Alamein, which I particularly wanted to see. The 1100 kilometre drive to Alexandria was uneventful. We took the desert road and found ourselves back in familiar bare countryside. At a rest house halfway, we met some French guys on motorcycles who had been held up by immigration for eight hours at the port of Alexandria. This was some consolation after our own Suez experience.

We entered Alexandria through the back door, I think, finding ourselves in a really rough and dirty docklands area. Turning west we navigated our way to the rather pleasant coast road and started to look for somewhere to stay for the night. All along the road, every few kilometres, was a road leading to a modern new village down by the sea. Surely we could find a quiet spot down one of these. Off we went down one of them but then came to a dead end with hardly a glimpse of the sea beyond the buildings. We tried to explain our needs to a group of local youngsters and were directed to a place called Homaville, further along the coast. Sure enough a large sign announced Homaville and we drove down the side road, around some building plots and down to an ideal quiet stretch of beach. We parked, stretched and yawned and meandered down to the water's edge. Perfect. By this time it was late afternoon and we seemed to have timed things really well. However, just as the sun sank on the horizon an army officer and a soldier strolled across from a sort of shack just near us. Despite the lack of a common language the message was clear – sorry, you can't stop here. Things became confused when it appeared that we would have to seek permission from the commandant – who is the commandant? – I am – well, can we stay for the night? – no, the commandant says that it is not possible – oh. We accepted that we would have to go but then discovered that the Rover was stuck in the sand. After an ignominious period of digging and revving and pushing we bumped out onto the road again. Gloom. The road continued through a large gateway, presumably into private property so we set off back to Homaville to seek local advice. One got exceedingly wary of asking for directions because it often resulted in an excited mob surrounding the vehicle with much shouting and thrusting of hands through open windows and very little else. The citizens of Homaville however, and this area generally, were somewhat more restrained and in response to our request for 'camping', one man jumped in his car to lead us to a suitable spot. The route took us back to the beach, through the aforementioned gateway and into the area beyond which revealed itself to be a small development of new residences, many of them unfinished. Our guide had a word with a man who was presumably the night watchman and who readily agreed that we could stay in the area. We ended up parked in the driveway of a nearly completed house and found the whole place to be very peaceful and quiet and if there were any residents we did not see them and they certainly took no notice of us. We sat back and relaxed and listened with astonishment to Radio Albania and its remarkable propaganda.

The British war cemetery at El Alamein

This was the start of what were to be three very enjoyable days on the north coast. From Homaville we motored to El Alamein along the main road following the white, rocky coastline and an incredibly bright blue sea. We stopped to visit the British war cemetery which is set in quiet isolation just off the road on the edge of the rolling desert. This was the site of the battlefield not so many years before. Surrounded by a wall the cemetery was entered through an impressive front entrance with steps up to a cloistered corridor with ledgers containing the names of all the graves. From the cloisters one looked out onto a gently undulating site with row after row of neatly engraved headstones with bright bougainvillea and other flowering shrubs lining the pathways. It was all very simple, very clean and very sad. At the far end was a small chapel. The sun was shining from a clear blue sky and the contrasts between the sky, the sandy brown walls, the white marble steps, the coloured plants and the regimental rows of headstones left a deep impression never to be forgotten.

Just down the road from the cemetery was El Alamein, hardly big enough to be described as even a village. Here was the Ministry of Defence 'Spoils Exhibition'. Outside were wrecked German, English and American fighting armoured vehicles and I was surprised to discover just how small so many of them were. The internal exhibition was a collection of military paraphernalia from the fighting there in the Second World War, together with displays of how the Egyptians had helped (?), all rounded off with layouts and information on their more recent conflicts with Israel.

An impressive relic at The Spoils Exhibition

Our Polyglot guide informed us that 25 kilometres beyond El Alamein was a beach resort called Sidi El Rahman with a hotel and an official campsite – one of only two that we found in Egypt. The road continued westwards along the picturesque coastline until the sea faded out of site to our right as it made way for a huge bulge in the coast. We took a right turn into this bulge and at the end was the hotel with some permanent tents belonging to it and beyond them an area of beach available for private camping at the very reasonable price of about $1.50 per night which included the use of some excellent clean showers and toilets. This was ideal but the catch was that we should have obtained permission to camp from the police at El Alamein. Protestations again and we managed to persuade the man on the gate to let us in for one night without the necessary police sanction. It really was a beautiful place. The colour of the sea varied from a bright emerald green to a deep royal blue and the gentle waves lapped lazily onto the almost white sand. Behind us rose steep sand dunes, sheltering the beach from a fresh offshore breeze. There were very few people there and once again our arrival was met with complete disinterest. I took the Rover to within a few feet of the water's edge and we spent the afternoon and the following morning in blissful relaxation.

We would have stayed longer but the gateman now adamantly refused to allow it without police permission. This placed us in somewhat of a quandary. El Alamein was 25 kilometres away and we had run short of Egyptian money. We had perhaps just enough petrol to reach Alexandria but certainly not enough to include a return trip to El Alamein. Food was not a problem. We walked to the hotel but they would not change traveller's cheques. We reluctantly left in the early afternoon, spent $3.00 of our remaining $4.00 on petrol and headed back to Homaville for the night.

The following day we headed into Alexandria, desperate for some money. There was a thriving foreign exchange black market in Egypt and dollar traveller's cheques were readily negotiable. We never had to use a bank and always managed to obtain a good rate. The black market would inevitably find *us* and a short stroll down a main street in the city soon attracted a loud whisper of "psst, want to change some money?" from the proprietor of a cigarette kiosk.

Money problem solved we drove along the sea shore which curved in a crescent along the Mediterranean. It was fronted by large, old and relatively new buildings which gave it the air of a somewhat run down seaside resort. The guide book referred to the old fort and the Ras El Tin palace as being open to visitors but at both places we were turned back by striped poles, armed soldiers and large signs proclaiming 'Military Area'. Times had obviously changed.

The sea front at Alexandria

The beach was very narrow at Alexandria and unlike the beautifully coloured waters of Sidi El Rahman, the water here was reminiscent of the grim grey of the North Sea. Rows of concrete beach chalets had been built all along the back of the beach but like everything else were in desperate need of some TLC and a coat of paint. There was not the dirt and filth of Cairo, however, and combined with the friendly, jostling crowds in the town we found it to be a really nice place. It was certainly very pleasant to be able to walk the streets and not be constantly accosted by touters and vendors. We drove back to Cairo in the late afternoon, arriving early evening at Dave and Irene's after a horrendous drive through the city's rush hour traffic.

We now had to tackle the business of Sudanese visas and Dave gave our passports to an Egyptian clerk at the factory to try and start the proceedings. Meanwhile Dawn caught up with the washing and I changed a universal joint on the rear propshaft. Ever since I had owned the Rover there had sometimes been a loud 'ting' when I pulled away. Whilst it sounded like something hitting the propshaft I had never discovered what it was until a few days previously when crawling under the chassis I had noticed that the universal joint at the back of the shaft was rusty and worn. I soon exchanged it for a serviceable one from my trusty spares stock. Dave returned in the evening with our passports unprocessed and the news that we would have to attend the embassy ourselves.

The following morning, and with deep sighs, we plunged once more into the maelstrom of Cairo traffic in order to locate the Sudanese embassy which was, unfortunately, on the other side of the city. Dave had lent us a company Peugeot which at least made the trip considerably easier than in the Rover, which was not designed for nipping about in heavy traffic. At the consulate we were yet again advised that we would need introductory letters from the British embassy. Fortunately this was only a short walk away and we returned half an hour later with the necessary letters and only ten dollars poorer. The visas would be ready the next day but we also had to submit forms to allow us to take in the Rover. Back in Oman we had collected some information about driving through Sudan and the regulations for the vehicle had looked forbidding, as they originally had for Egypt. Apparently it would be necessary to have it inspected at the Sudanese embassy in Cairo, to provide a full and detailed list of spares carried and also to furnish a certificate of roadworthiness. In addition to this we had learnt that we could not tow a trailer, must travel in convoy across desert areas and must not drive on the railway line. This last directive we found particularly amusing until we actually experienced first hand the Sudanese terrain. It would also be necessary to lodge a large sum of money with the authorities to cover the potential cost of mounting searches for us and our subsequent repatriation. This had all been a little alarming. I was confident that the spares we carried were adequate but any driver is apprehensive when it comes to inspections. I had managed to obtain a very impressive looking Certificate of Roadworthiness from a Brit working in Oman for the Oman Bus Company. He had gone to quite a bit of trouble to produce an official document covered in rubber stamps and stating that the Rover was in excellent condition – although, needless to say, he had not inspected it. The lodging of a sum of money could present a serious problem but our initial enquiries in Cairo had indicated that this would not be necessary. In the final outcome the whole list of formalities was casually bypassed and all that was necessary was to complete a form and in return we received a slip of paper for presentation to the Sudanese customs in Wadi Halfa (the border post) on which it was stated that the Rover would be loaded onto a flat bed railway wagon for transportation from there to Khartoum. The embassy man said that this would not be enforced but I managed to persuade him to add the rider 'unless accompanied by one or more vehicles in convoy'. So, we at last had our visas and vehicle clearance for entry into Sudan!

****

Our next stage, therefore, was to drive to Aswan and pick up the ferry across Lake Nasser to Sudan. On an Egyptian tourist pamphlet we had read that it was necessary to obtain permission to drive to Aswan so we braved the Cairo traffic once more to try and locate the Ministry of Tourism. This we achieved after the usual going around in circles and I nipped up the stairs of the typically shabby office building to enquire about the regulations. I was assured by an Egyptian lady that there were, in fact, no such regulations, but in these circumstances one always gets a niggly feeling that the person doesn't really know and that in order to avoid any effort they simply deny everything. It was therefore with some scepticism that I left the office, although subsequent events were to prove that the lady did, indeed, know what she was talking about and we did not need permission.

The last item on our list before departure was to obtain some information on the Lake Nasser ferry service. We had met some English tourists in Kenya earlier in the year who had driven from Egypt to Sudan and they had told us that it was cheaper to buy the tickets in Cairo as the agent in Aswan was rumoured to add some commission to the basic price (surely not?). It was Dawn's turn to investigate, so having approximately located the shipping office I remained in the Rover whilst she disappeared into the crowds. She eventually returned with the good news that we couldn't buy the tickets in Cairo but that there would be no problem conducting the business once we were in Aswan.

Well, at last we were clear to leave Cairo although there were just three more experiences worthy of note at this point.

All Arab towns and cities have their market areas and in Cairo this was a huge rabbit warren of tiny streets and alleyways called Khan el Khalili (the Turkish Bazaar). We drove there one morning with Irene and spent a couple of hours wandering around. The area is cut in two by a main road with fruit and vegetable stalls on one side, frequented mainly by the locals, and hardware shops and tourist traps on the other side. It is a colourful, bustling and fascinating place with all manner of attractive goods on display both inside and outside the tiny shops. Egypt was a particularly good place for leather goods and the prices of many items were astonishingly low, even before the obligatory haggling took place to reduce the price still further. In addition to leatherwork there were heaps of copper and silver items and lots of shops selling gold and gemstones. So tempting to take advantage of some bargains but both our budget and our lack of storage space precluded any serious shopping so we ended up with just a pair of leather flip flops for me and a set of Turkish coffee pots for Dawn.

The Egyptian museum was another tourist attraction that deserved attention and I made a brief visit one day after going into Cairo on the tram on my own, searching for better road maps (I failed). Despite the grandeur of the Tutankhamoun exhibition I found the whole place to be remarkably old fashioned, faded and shabby – in keeping with the rest of Egypt. The exhibits looked as if they hadn't been touched or dusted since they were first brought in and there was a serious lack of information with them. If there was a label to be found it was usually on a yellowing piece of card with crooked letters picked out using an ancient typewriter. Some rooms had piles of rubble where the plasterwork had crumbled but had not been cleaned up and the displays of mummies were frankly rather forlorn – there seemed to be little regard for the dignity and reverence that they deserved. I dragged myself around as I thought that I ought to try and do it justice but it was with some relief that I finally emerged into the sunlight after a couple of hours.

The final Cairo experience for me was a visit to the Arab British Dynamics missile factory just outside Heliopolis. Dave, along with Mamdoo, was responsible for the magazine area. I had been used to the Rapier anti-aircraft system where the missile is treated as just a round of ammunition stored in a sealed container until required for use. Both the launcher and target tracking units are substantial pieces of equipment and are subject to considerable routine testing and maintenance. The Swingfire anti-tank missile which was being manufactured under licence in Egypt was much smaller and less complex and apart from a relatively simple hand held firing and guidance unit, most of the technology was in the missile. I had not seen an assembly plant like this before and I was fascinated by the safety standards and anti-static precautions with the blast proof cubicles and conveyors designed to minimise damage and casualties in the event of an 'explosive incident'. A very interesting visit and all credit to Dave and Mamdoo for making it possible.

Our sojourn in Cairo was almost complete. It merely remained to load all our food and clothing back into the Rover and Dawn was busy ironing and packing everything. I had one final maintenance job to do. The aluminium roof rack that I had made and bolted to the rear of the Rover was not standing the strain too well. Its lateral rigidity was excellent but no matter how tight I made the nuts and bolts it soon developed a fore and aft looseness. I had come across a couple of pieces of aluminium section and bolting one diagonally on each side neatly solved the problem.

It was incredible but we had spent thirteen and a half days in Cairo, including our Alexandria excursion, out of a total of forty days since we had left Oman. It was most definitely time to be on the road again. Our last evening was spent in saying our goodbyes to the many friends that we had made and we stayed up drinking until two am. Consequently we were not at our brightest the next morning. Dawn had developed a rather bad cold and was not really very well at all.

We drove out of Cairo along the west bank of the Nile, heading for Luxor. These southern outskirts of Cairo were scruffy even by normal Egyptian standards, with many horses and carts, crumbling brick kilns, badly potholed roads and pretty grubby looking residents. A bit depressing. The road all the way south was densely populated. This was, of course, the rich Nile valley and there was intensive agriculture and irrigation all the way along it. Apparently, concern was being expressed about the long term impact of the Aswan High Dam, which had stopped the annual surge of water that used to bring fresh nutrients down from the heart of Africa every year. What was surprising was how narrow the fertile strip was, and it was only a relatively short distance from the river to where the green vegetation abruptly ended and bare sand dunes stretched away into the distance. It seemed that we were travelling alongside an irrigation canal running parallel with the main river and every ten kilometres or so a small bridge led over the river to the open fields on our left. At each bridge was a small village with hordes of running, shouting people – well, they all ran and shouted when *we* passed through. The crop at that time appeared to be Guinea Corn (said Dawn) and huge bundles of the long stalks were being moved about by donkeys and camels, looking like haystacks on four legs.

Poor Dawn spent the whole day lying on the bench seat in the back of the Rover, more asleep than awake. As the afternoon wore on I began to look for a suitable place to stop for the night, preferably before it got dark. Every few kilometres the familiar blue and white "Foreigners are Forbidden to Leave the Main Road" sign loomed, plus manned police posts at frequent intervals. We were not required to stop at these but I think that a note of our number was made each time we passed by. After the late night and relatively early morning I was starting to feel tired myself and finally decided to cross one of the bridges in the hope of finding a quiet corner of a field in which to spend the night. Some hopes! Within seconds of crossing the bridge the previously empty field was suddenly full of running, shouting people descending upon us from all directions. I stopped and the mob surrounded us, jabbering and gesticulating in a not particularly friendly manner. We had bought an Arabic phrase book and I attempted to politely ask the whereabouts of a suitable camp site. My stutterings had no effect on the crowd, the only reaction being a scornful scoff from Dawn in the back. After a minute or so of this chaos a man came running over who left us in no doubt as to his feelings on the matter. He ranted and shouted in a furious manner, pointing back over the bridge. By this time *we* were as anxious for us to leave as he was and I launched into an umpteen-point-turn on the narrow dirt road and nipped thankfully back out onto the main road without running anybody over. Obviously we still had the problem of where to stop and I was starting to feel really shattered but the road continued on and on with the canal on our left and a deep ditch on the right. As the sun sank and a dusty, red sunset spread across the sky the road started to fill with workers returning from their daily toil in the fields. There was nothing to do but keep going. As darkness at last fell the pedestrian traffic disappeared and all of a sudden there was a small road leading off to the right. I quickly turned down it and pulled onto the verge just a few metres from the main road, feeling completely exhausted, not least due to the stress caused by the local inhabitants along the way. I was also in a really foul mood. I just couldn't raise the energy or the inclination to move, and sat motionless at the wheel for hours, with Dawn still feeling like death in the back. Still we were not to be left in peace. Some local youths with a car and a motor bike stopped on the main road and surveyed us for about half an hour before driving off with a few shouts. They returned a few minutes later, threw something at us and then disappeared. Nice. This was the only time that we ever had any really aggressive trouble during the whole trip, which says a lot for Egypt....... I finally crawled into the back and we both then slept until six in the morning, having had nothing to eat since leaving Cairo.

Not unnaturally we were worried about further aggravation from the locals but in fact we had breakfast in peace, albeit with the curtains closed whilst groups of people passed by us but without apparent interest. As it was to turn out this was the start of a much better day generally. We were both refreshed and Dawn was feeling much better. The morning was sunny and cool and the traumas of the previous day were left behind and, fortunately, not repeated. It was nearly 700 kilometres from Cairo to Luxor and we had covered 400 of those so just 300 to go and a nice early start for once. A few kilometres down the road we passed a grey Land Rover Carawagon, obviously foreign, parked just past one of the police posts. It would appear that it had spent the night there and in hindsight perhaps we, too, should have sought a similar sanctuary, always bearing in mind that your average Egyptian copper would be a far cry from your archetypal British bobby.

The villages became more infrequent although there were still plenty of people about. We passed through Qena, famous for its large, porous water pots or 'kullen' which cool the enclosed water by simple evaporation through the clay. All apparently made to the same identical size, many were also used in the construction of house walls and no doubt provided a considerable degree of thermal insulation. As we drove through the villages we found the children varied from friendly to cheeky. This road was obviously frequented by tourist buses and little boys would take great delight in lining up along the road then raising their djellabas and wiggling their little willies at the passing coaches – and us.

Pots in the walls at Qena

At one stage we were suddenly stopped by a man walking across in front of us with a chain which he hooked up to form a barrier. It was a railway crossing, and behind us one of these tourist buses pulled up. After the train had passed and the chain was being lowered, this bus roared up beside us and past us, cutting in very sharply. The rear end got closer and closer until with a thump it caught the front of the Rover and then accelerated away in a cloud of dust. I was furious, and without pausing to check the damage we set off in pursuit. We caught him up and it took me all my time to keep up with him with my foot hard down. There was no response to my urgent hooting and we thundered along until the coach started to indicate left to turn down a side road. I managed to overtake it as it slowed down for the corner and pulling in front I brought it to a halt. I leaped out, ran back and hauled open the door. The coach was full of somewhat startled tourists and I climbed in with my scruffy shorts and tee shirt and started shouting at the driver, who sat with a bland, innocent look on his face. The courier/guide came up and I declared hotly that their bus had hit my car and that I was consequently very annoyed. From the midst of the coach a strident, female American voice drawled "We din' hit yor core" which made me even madder. The fact that an American, supposed to be our ally in times of trouble, should side with an Egyptian idiot was the last straw. I hopped down to go and see what the damage was to the Rover and the coach immediately revved up, drove around us and set off down the road. Miserable coward. Anyway, in the event there wasn't a mark on the Rover but I had noticed that the rear fender of the bus had been badly pulled and bent when it caught our front bumper.

Land Rover 1, American tour bus 0.

Brick making by the Nile. Note the fellow hot footing it towards us, no doubt to demand money for taking the photograph.

We eventually arrived at Luxor late in the afternoon. I say '*at* Luxor' rather than '*in* Luxor' because much to our surprise we realised that we were still on the west bank of the river and Luxor was over the water on the eastern side. A hurried look at the map revealed that besides admiring the pots at Qena we should also have crossed over the Nile there. With no bridge at Luxor the next crossing would be at Isna. Both Qena and Isna were about 150 kilometres away, so popping to either and back to Luxor was patently out of the question. We had stopped in a small village of mud and brick houses, on a jetty that served a passenger ferry service that plied between here and Luxor about 300 metres away. As we sat scratching our heads at our predicament an Arab gentleman, dressed in his djellaba but speaking excellent English, appeared at the window having quickly weighed up our situation. He confirmed the lack of a bridge but offered to show us to a good camping spot near to his house. As always we were suspicious of such an offer, there surely being a link to money or carpets or something. Our fears were somewhat allayed, however, when he told us that he already had a Belgian gentleman staying with him, so we accepted the offer and followed him from the ferry terminal and down a narrow track half hidden in the grass. A sharp right turn brought us out on a vacant piece of land next to a white, two storey building. A great bough of a tree hung low enough to bar our way to the parking area so we crashed and bounced our way around to it through the long grass.

The white building was the house of our new friend Jabra, or to give him his full title, Gabar Aly Hussein. Turning off the engine we were immediately inundated with children, well, eight of them, all belonging to Jabra and who clustered shyly but excitedly at the back of the Rover. There was no sign of the expected camping Belgian but after some small talk Jabra went to his house and came back with a *very* old gentleman who reminded me a bit of Boris Karloff. This was no camper. Belgian, yes, and in fact it seemed that Constant de Wit was a bit of a celebrity in the Egyptology world and had published an authoritative book on hieroglyphs back in 1951. He was tall and thin and his face was deathly pale with a dry pallor that indicated a recent serious illness. His silver hair was brushed neatly straight back but his feeble movements and a slight distortion of his mouth pointed towards the aftermath of a stroke. He literally looked as if he had spent most of his life underground in tombs.

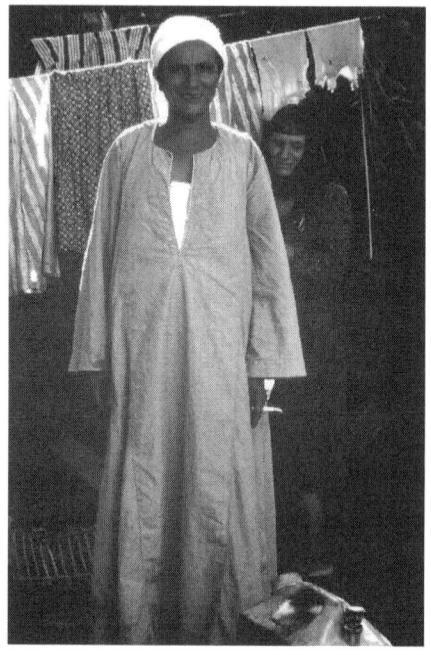

Our new friend Jabra

Constant had first come to Egypt in 1956 to explore at first hand the Egyptian Empire that he had been studying for many years back in Europe. He engaged Jabra and his donkey to guide him around the Valley of the Kings. Jabra must have been just a teenager then, doing his best to earn some money from the limited tourists at that time. A friendship formed between them and deepened over the years. Constant spent more and more time in Egypt and always employed Jabra when he was in Luxor and Jabra was eventually able to afford to build a substantial house in which Constant could stay when in the area. The donkey had been superseded by a 7 seater Peugeot taxi and the whole arrangement seemed to have worked out well for all concerned. Jabra had even been to Belgium for a holiday. He now employed another man to drive the taxi for him and Constant was spending up to 11 months of the year with him in Luxor, surrounded by creaking bookshelves of dusty volumes devoted to the ancient Egyptians. There was no doubt that Jabra had been very lucky. He came across as a rather delightful rogue who obviously thought a lot of Constant. Even from the short time that we knew him it was evident that he enjoyed considerable status in the community and strolled around the village like the local squire.

We were invited into the house that evening for a meal, a not exactly ethnic offering of tinned meatballs and macaroni and afterwards we sat outside the Rover in our private little yard and marvelled at a very photogenic red sunset behind the black silhouette of a nearby palm tree. A huge difference from the stress of the previous night.

****

Our embarrassment at arriving on the wrong side of the river had been replaced with a feeling of smug satisfaction when we realised that we could now drive to all the sites in the Valley of Kings without recourse to local guides, taxis or official coach tours. Most of the archaeological sites were on our side of the river and we just had to drive to the ferry jetty where an office sold the necessary tickets for the various sites. Two ferries crossed the Nile, a luxury glassed-in model for the package tourists and a basic felucca for the locals – and proper travellers like us, of course.

The tomb of Tutankhamoun

The Valley of the Kings was tucked away in the desert mountains about 8 kilometres from the river. It was just a short valley, ending abruptly at high cliff faces and baked unmercifully by the sun. We were only able to go inside 4 of the tombs and found the wall carvings and decorations to be much superior to anything we had seen in Cairo. The tomb of Tutankhamon (you can take your pick of various spellings) was obviously the centrepiece and it had been well preserved for presentation to visitors although all the treasures found in it were displayed in the Cairo museum. From the Valley of the Kings we drove to the Ramesseum, a huge ruined temple with massive carved columns that once supported an equally massive roof. I found this interesting but Dawn did not. Opposite the Ramesseum were the Tombs of the Nobles, hundreds of them. These were simple rectangular tombs cut into the hillside and decorated with paintings rather than carvings. The colours remained remarkably bright and fresh despite 4000 years having passed since they were painted. These tombs were ingeniously and economically lit by a local chap sitting cross legged outside and reflecting the sunlight in with a large mirror. This was also, of course, an ideal source of natural light to best display the paintings.

The temple of Queen Hatshepsut

After a quick look at the Valley of the Queens – nothing sexist but by this time we were getting a bit bored with tombs – we were heading back to the campsite via the Colossi of Memnon when who should we nearly run over, cycling gaily down the road, but Mike and Daphne. They had travelled to Luxor by train and were staying in a small hotel there. After a brief exchange of experiences we arranged to meet them later. Back at our camp we invited Constant to take tea with us in the garden and then had more inside with Jabra.

Mike and Daphne were staying at the Nefertiti Hotel and late in the afternoon we crossed the Nile (on the local ferry) to meet them there. Like Alexandria, we found Luxor to be very amenable and, despite being a major tourist destination, we were able to stroll around without any hassling. After a quiet orange juice sitting outside a little drinks shop we invited our friends back for dinner at the Rover Restaurant. Dawn cooked a super curry and Mike produced a bottle of wine, a real luxury. Jabra's sons watched in amazement as this hot food was produced from inside the Rover, and they rushed home to fetch chairs for our guests. Jabra joined us for a glass of wine and then later, after our meal, he returned to take us down the road to witness a neighbour firing bricks for his new house. We had passed many of these smoking kilns along the river and were glad of the opportunity to see one close up. The bricks were formed from local raw clay and, presumably after drying in the sun, they were stacked in a big twelve foot square, about eight feet high. On one side three arches had been constructed which gave access right inside the stack. Into these holes bundles of guinea corn stalks were burnt with the ferocity and heat of burning straw. No doubt post-harvest time was big brick making time with an abundance of stalks to be used. Each archway section contained seven thousand bricks so the complete stack or kiln produced twenty one thousand bricks. The occasion seemed to create a bit of a party atmosphere and about a dozen people were squatting and chatting and helping with the constant stoking process. The flames lit up the night like a scene from Dante's Inferno and already the lower portion of the kiln was starting to glow a deep red. This firing would go on all through the night and during the next day until the whole thing was incandescent. These fired bricks were used only for the lower courses of the house construction. Above them were just simple, and cheap, sun dried mud bricks.

Jabra gave us all a lift to the ferry in his taxi and we bade goodnight to Mike and Daphne. Back at the camp Jabra and his sons went through a ritual of covering up the car with immense rugs and blankets. On top of everything slept Jabra's dog, a large, long haired Labrador sort of thing - albeit a bit motheaten – which tended to leap up at intervals throughout the night to join the rest of the village dogs in a frantic chorus of barking. On the top of Jabra's flat roof was erected a tent, in which he slept every night purportedly to keep an eye on his car. We never figured out the reason for this, car theft presumably being pretty rare in this area, but we couldn't figure out an ulterior motive either.

The following day was to be for our visit to the Luxor and Karnak temples. We crossed over on the ferry and walked the 3 kilometres along the riverside to Karnak. Dawn's cold had reared its ugly head again and she plodded gamely on in the heat, refusing to pay the high prices demanded by the many horse drawn carriages parked at the side of the road. Karnak must have been an awesome place when it was built, and it remained an amazing place despite the ravages of time. It covered a huge area and the massive stones, plinths, columns and obelisks were covered in fantastic carvings. Some restoration work was going on but I, personally, am not sure about detailed restoration and think that it always looks rather artificial. I would prefer things to be left as they are – although not allowed to deteriorate further. At the far end of the site is the Sacred Lake, a huge square pool of ultramarine water with a large, stone sacred scarab mounted on a plinth in one corner. The sheer size and beauty of the Karnak temple went some way to restoring my flagging interest in Egyptian temples and antiquities and I enjoyed our time there.

Karnak temple

The Sacred Lake at Karnak temple

We walked back to Luxor – carriage prices rose even higher for the return journey – gave the Luxor temple a quick once over from the outside and then joined Mike and Daphne in the Nefertiti for lunch. This might sound grand but the Nefertiti can only be described as a small, mean hotel with very basic fare. After lunch Dawn and I walked to the Luxor hotel, an area in front of which was reported to be a camping spot. Sure enough there were two or three campers there, one of which was the Carawagon that we had seen by the side of the road a couple of days before. Close up this was a magnificent looking vehicle. It had an enormous luggage rack over the bonnet which was bristling with jerry cans, lengths of aluminium sand track, storage boxes and a spare wheel. A giant engine air filter protruded from one of the front wings and a powerful looking winch lurked below the radiator. One side had a large outline map painted on it with a route in red and the title 'Trans Asian 1970/71', whilst the other side had another outline map but this time of Africa with the legend 'Trans Africa 1980/81'. Wow! We were *very* impressed and felt very much a pair of amateurs when faced with this undeniably impressive set up. I'm sure that if we had been wearing caps we would have doffed them in respect as we shuffled over feeling awestruck to introduce ourselves to the owners, who turned out to be a Swiss couple a little older than us and their five year old daughter. Their English was not very good but certainly better than my rusty German so we conversed for a while and looked at maps. They were also heading down through Sudan and then into Uganda. We were eager to see if they would be catching the Lake Nasser ferry at the same time as us, as it would mean that we could fulfil the convoy requirement and be able to drive from Wadi Halfa. Despite the language barrier they would make ideal travelling companions and all that equipment and experience....wow again!

Unfortunately, however, it seemed that they would be catching a later ferry than us and that we were unlikely to see them again. Ha! If we had known then what we found out later we would have been *delighted* never to have seen them again.

Back at Jabra's we were invited in to eat again – corned beef and roast potatoes. The room that we ate in led off a small hallway which ran straight into Jabra's back yard where he had a couple of goats and a cow, some chickens, an old fashioned water pump and a large bread oven. After we had eaten, in state and alone, we were invited to watch television with the family and were led to the other side of the house and into a large family room with brown mud walls, an enormous cot against one wall and a black and white television set mounted inside a large orange crate. Jabra's wife and children seemed tickled pink by our presence and we sat and watched the news in English. When we rose to leave we were presented with two huge, round brown loaves which had been baked in the outside oven.

We left Luxor the next morning, saying a fond farewell to Jabra and his family. Jabra urged us to stay longer as he had planned to invite Mike and Daphne over for a meal as well. We felt quite guilty at leaving but there was no point in staying any longer in Luxor as we had seen everything that we wanted to see and had also arranged to give Mike and Daphne a lift to Aswan. We picked them up at the ferry, lashed their rucksacks on the roof and set off to find the bridge at Isna. The drive to Isna was atrocious. It was just a dirt road with undulations that made the Rover buck like a horse at any speed over 25 kilometres an hour. We lurched and crashed painfully onwards and finally reached Isna and found the elusive bridge to the other side of the Nile. We had decided to divert to see our last ruined temple on the way to Aswan, which necessitated a short diversion into Edfu to see the Temple of Horus. We were very pleased that we did because it was the best preserved temple that we had seen, complete with its original stone roof. Nevertheless we left it with a sigh of relief, being now well and truly 'templed out'.

*With Mike and Daphne at the temple of Horus in Edfu*

We celebrated with a picnic lunch outside the temple then headed to Aswan where we arrived at about four o'clock, the road being tarmac and consequently much faster. Right in the town and near to the Nile was an official campsite, surrounded by a low wall and bushes and neatly laid out with car parking spaces and a grassy area for tents. There was fresh water from a hose but the toilet facilities consisted of a small concrete shed with just one toilet, one wash basin and one shower. Never mind, at least there was something and all for just $1.00 per night. Mike and Daphne opted to use their tent and while they erected it Dawn and I surveyed the other site occupants for likely Nubian Desert crossers. In one corner, under a huge tree, was an enormous American RV, about thirty feet long but looking precariously balanced on just four ridiculously small wheels. It looked very resident and certainly totally unsuitable for off-road use. We subsequently learnt that it belonged to an American who was working locally. Next to us was a VW Combi and then a short wheel base Land Rover. The occupants of both were again Swiss and they had originally met somewhere on the continent and had travelled together since then. Now was to be the parting of the ways as the Land Rover couple were to continue into Sudan but the Combi would have to turn back. In fact, we subsequently met people in Khartoum who did cross the Nubian Desert in a Combi and with very little trouble. Anyway, it looked as if we had one vehicle to travel with until the next morning when they all came over to say that after much discussion they had decided that they really did not want to part company and that both vehicles would turn back. The couple with the VW were filled with enthusiasm for a Land Rover and the plan was to buy one and return the following year to venture into Sudan. We were obviously a little disappointed but I was somewhat mollified when they asked if they could make a sketch of the inside of my Rover so that they could reproduce it in their vehicle when they had bought it.

The remaining vehicle in the park was an old three ton Bedford four wheel drive truck with a one ton two wheel trailer. Both were painted shocking pink and the name TRAKS was emblazoned on the side of the truck. It was populated by an exuberant crowd of Kiwis and Aussis who seemed to be well established in the campsite. They seemed a very independent bunch and though we made no attempts to converse with them at that point, they were to become good travelling acquaintances over the next few weeks as the natural course of events conspired to continually bring us into contact with them.

****

We spent three days in Aswan. Arriving on the Monday, we discovered that the ferry left for Wadi Halfa every Monday and Friday. The Monday boat did not take vehicles so the forthcoming Friday sailing would be ideal for us. We spent a day on household matters, Dawn inevitably tackling the washing while I moved the roof rack from the back of the roof to the front. The Rover had always looked low at the back and high at the front and I had been planning the move for some time. Up until this time we had not carried much weight on the rack but the journey into Sudan would necessitate carrying a considerable amount of petrol out of Egypt and I wanted to get the load shared more evenly between the two axles. We purchased an additional twenty litre plastic jerry can and this brought our carrying capacity to some two hundred litres, enough to take us about 1,100 kilometres at our current consumption. Our calculations indicated that the distance to Khartoum was just over 1000 kilometres.

The problem was that my system of strapping items onto the flat roof rack also utilised the two sand ladders as supports and if we had to use the ladders it would necessitate unloading everything to access them.

The Nile at Aswan is very wide and the water flows very gently down from the two dams. The area is dotted with obstructions varying from large rocks to inhabited islands served by a local felucca ferry service. Elephantine Island had a tourist hotel and what looked to be a sizeable resident population. We took the ferry across and I was somewhat taken aback when a local lady, dressed in her all-encompassing black chador, calmly picked up a shiny tin can, dipped it in the Nile and had a thirst quenching drink. Obviously this must be normal for millions of people but so totally at odds with our own fixation with clean drinking water and I just had never seen it happen before – or since.

From Elephantine Island we crossed to Kitchener Island which was smaller and devoted entirely to a neatly laid out botanical garden. The crossing was made in a small rowing boat for a strictly and carefully regulated fee. A very pretty and peaceful place.

We also took a drive to see the two famous dams. The original, built in 1902, was quite small and unimpressive, spanning a relatively narrow stretch of the river and supporting just a narrow roadway across the top. About 7 kilometres further south, the High Dam, completed in 1971, dwarfed the original, a conical earth and concrete barrier stretching nearly 5 kilometres and holding back the 600 kilometre length of Lake Nasser. Next to the dam an impressive – but decidedly Soviet looking – monument was dedicated to the Russian workers who had carried out the task.

Over the dam we drove to the site of an ancient quarry where 'The Unfinished Obelisk' is an intriguing tourist attraction. About five or six feet square and twenty five feet long, the obelisk had been hewn out of the granite on three sides but still lay in a horizontal position anchored to the bedrock. Clearly visible grooves had been cut beneath it into which wooden wedges would have been driven and then soaked in water. The enormous forces generated by the expanding wood would have then neatly split the rock and released the obelisk in one gigantic piece. Apparently this one had a flaw in it and was therefore abandoned thousands of years ago when the Quality Inspector gave it the thumbs down. Nevertheless it was still mind boggling to consider how massive lumps of rock like this would have been moved to a barge and floated downstream to a temple construction site somewhere down the Nile.

We sat down one night and reviewed our financial situation. We had travelled nearly 7000 kilometres and including the cost of the boat into Sudan had spent about a third of our money. This was over a period of forty six days. The cost of the air fare to Jordan contributed disproportionately to this figure and we therefore felt quite satisfied with our overall progress.

On the final evening, Thursday, we had planned to have a farewell meal with Mike and Daphne who were going to catch the Monday ferry. Dawn was to cook chilli con carne and on the Wednesday evening put the red kidney beans on to soak. Feeling a bit peckish I nibbled two or three of them like nuts before we went for an evening stroll around Aswan market. After about an hour I suddenly began to feel extremely nauseous and ended up being uncontrollably and violently sick. We headed back to the Rover and despite continuing spasms of vomiting I felt worse and worse. I can remember sitting for a long time with my mind in a weird confused whirl, hardly knowing where I was and feeling absolutely dreadful until I finally curled up in bed and virtually passed out. The following morning I awoke feeling perfectly well again and the episode remained a mystery until many months later when we were watching a tv programme which pointed out the dangers of eating uncooked red kidney beans which are highly toxic in their raw state. I believe that people actually died after the raw beans were included in a wedding reception salad. Just as well that I had limited my intake.

Relaxing in Aswan

****

All week the inhabitants of the camp site had been fluctuating continuously. The two Swiss couples had left, some older Germans in a camper and a car had come and gone, but three vehicles had arrived which looked to be in the same situation as us. The Swiss couple with the Carawagon from Luxor had decided to move on earlier than planned and a second Land Rover with two Danish guys had rolled in. Finally there was a short wheel base Landcruiser with a couple of Japanese. The Landcruiser had a huge roof rack stretching from the back of the vehicle to over the front bumper and was packed with aluminium cases of photographic equipment. One of the Japanese had published a book of photographs of the Sahara and was now repeating the exercise with the Nile.

We soon made friends with the two Danes. Jan was a professor specialising in the study of animal diseases, and dissatisfied and disillusioned with his life in Denmark he had travelled to England, bought a second hand Rover direct from a farmer, thrown a mattress in the back, emptied his food cupboards into cardboard boxes and set off to drive to Kenya where he planned to settle and work. A truly delightful character. Jan was probably the same age as me, perhaps a little older but his travelling companion, Bjorn, was much younger. Somewhat immature and nervous, Bjorn was trying to find his role in life since leaving college and had sought expression in a travelling children's puppet show. Both of them spoke fluent English but with that pleasing Scandinavian accent and interpretation that can so often enhance a common, everyday English phrase. They were to be excellent friends over the next weeks and we were to spend many pleasant evenings sitting around engaged in far ranging discussions.

With the Swiss Carawagon and the Danish Rover we were now assured of a 'convoy' of three Land Rovers across the Nubian Desert, thus hopefully satisfying the requirements of the Sudanese authorities. The Traks lorry was, understandably, going to travel independently and the Japanese would be following the longer course of the Nile. The Nile loops out to the west and back again but we were going to follow the more direct north/south route of the railway line. At this point we were, I must admit, a little unsure about Jan and his complete lack of preparation for long distance desert travel, apart from the ideal vehicle, of course, which had the same rear pickup body pan as mine but with just a windowless solid top as would be found on a sheep farmer's version. He had set out with no more preparation than one would make for a trip to the local market, carried very few spares and had zero mechanical aptitude, much in the same mould as our friends Jack and Jacqui when they left Oman for the UK, I suppose. He had spent most of his time at Aswan buying and filling eight huge plastic containers with petrol which he packed into the back of his Rover and which were to ultimately split and leak and convert the whole thing into a potential fire bomb. Up the scale from Jan were Dawn and I with our purpose designed and fitted-out camper and then top of the scale appeared to be Bruno and his wife Elizabeth with the formidable Carawagon. In the final outcome the reliability and capabilities of the respective vehicles were to be the opposite of my expectations. Bruno was to suffer major front axle and gearbox damage, due mainly to colossal overloading and we were to have our share of much less serious problems. Jan, however, eventually reached Kenya without exploding in a ball of flame and with no more hiccups than a couple of punctures and the occasional top-up of oil and water. If he had had any regrets about his lack of equipment then top of the list would have been a couple of folding camp chairs. It was to become a feature of our time together that if either Dawn or myself stood up, even quite briefly, Jan could immediately be found sitting in the vacant chair contentedly puffing a cigarette through his copious beard, his eyes half closed and revelling in the comfort – and needing some heavy hints before moving out.

So early on the Friday morning there was an air of subdued excitement and last minute activity in the campsite as gear was packed away, clothes lines and washing taken down, water tanks topped up and final preparations completed. One by one engines started up, passengers climbed aboard, doors slammed and the heavily loaded vehicles creaked and ground out and onto the road for the 30 minute drive to the ferry dock. On arrival we joined a long queue of taxis and pickups all overloaded with bulging bundles containing aluminium cooking pots, plastic containers of all shapes, sizes and colours, sacks of onions and rice and an overall cornucopia of tradable goods. All along the narrow, dusty road swarmed hundreds of Egyptians and Sudanese, shouting and gesticulating and presenting the most amazing spectacle of orderly chaos which only the Third World can produce. At this time we all had our personal tickets but no tickets for the vehicles, which was a bit worrying. Neither the lake nor the ferry could be seen and the volume of foot passengers and their luggage gave us no little concern as to our chances of getting on board. Further vehicle movement was blocked by a barrier across the road and in vain we tried to find out what was going on.

It was necessary in fact, if not easy, in situations like this to have some faith in 'the system' despite the apparent lack of organisation, time and a common language in which to communicate. It was probably not knowing if one's paperwork was in order or not which caused the most worry right up to the last minute.

After about an hour the barrier was raised and we all eased into the yard beyond. Here we were segregated from the taxis and the pickups and parked to one side whilst they disgorged their contents at the milling passenger terminal. We now met two more groups with vehicles planning to cross with us. About 10 American missionary kids were riding in a cumbersome, cream Daf truck with an enormous cab and a canvas covered back. It had only two wheel drive and was certainly going to need some divine assistance if it was to traverse the Nubian Desert. Nevertheless there was a quiet air of excited confidence about the group and we half expected a chorus of 'Rock of Ages' to break out to complete the pioneering image created by the covered wagon. Our contingent was to be completed by a small, red four wheel drive Lada driven by a quiet Frenchman and his young wife. He spoke fluent Arabic, and was obviously used to the area and they kept themselves to themselves for the whole trip.

We could now purchase our vehicle tickets and the cost of the crossing came to just $130. This allocated us an area of deck space for the Rover plus access to the toilets and was certainly much better value than the Jordan/Egypt ferry. We waited another hour or so then had to tackle the customs and carnet formalities. Customs charged a flat rate of $10 for the privilege of leaving Egypt. Apparently this was only $6 on any other day but Friday. Here, too, we surrendered our battered Egyptian number plates. At last we moved through the final barrier and caught our first sight of the ferry. Whatever we might have expected it certainly wasn't this. By the wharf was tied a long, blunt nosed barge with a wheelhouse at the bow and a low engine room at the stern. The centre section was a deep, bare hold with huge sliding metal hatch covers which were not completely closed, leaving gaps for the unwary to fall through. I suppose that the whole thing was about 60 feet long and 20 feet wide. Behind this were two similar sized barges moored side by side but these were double decked. One just had two open decks with a simple roof and the other one had a row of cabins on both decks. All three looked pretty old and in desperate need of some paint.

The foot passengers were scurrying back and forth like ants, sweating and struggling under great bundles of luggage as they unloaded it from the line of pick-up trucks and carried it into the two rear barges. This went on for a further 2 hours and the amount of stuff loaded was colossal. During this time, and along with the other vehicle owners, we were eyeing the flat top barge with some trepidation as it was pretty obvious now how we were going to be transported. In fact it wasn't flat topped as each hatch cover sloped up from both sides at about 10 degrees and met in a ridge at the top.

The hectic activity of the foot passengers gradually slackened, the last bundles were hoisted aboard and their owners gathered at the deck rails to watch the finale of the embarkation process – us. A couple of sturdy ramps were produced and manhandled into position to bridge the 5 foot gap between the quay and each hatch cover. First to go was the big Daf truck and we watched with bated breath as, after several roaring attempts, it lurched precariously over the ramps and came to a rocking halt astride its hatch cover – to a relieved and ragged cheer from the rest of us. This was certainly the stuff to unite people in a common cause! The ramps were slid along and the Traks truck revved and waddled its way on. The trailer was not so easy. Disconnected from the truck it sat on its two road wheels and a small jockey wheel at the front. Fortunately its handbrake was good and with a group of giggling girls standing on the back to balance it, the rest of us pushed and pulled it across the gap and into position. Our turn next and we were allocated an individual cover which left us with about 2 feet either side before the drop into the hold.

A careful drive onto the barge

And so it went on. Jan was next, then the Japanese and finally Bruno. The Lada was squeezed onto the bottom deck of the open double-deck barge and was pushed and bounced about until parked to the satisfaction of the captain - a dirty Egyptian rogue indistinguishable from the rest of his grubby crew.

Well, we were on, and after lashing the vehicles to eyebolts in the deck we sat back and breathed a sigh of relief and took stock of our surroundings. Like Bruno and Elizabeth we had the luxury of our normal beds to sleep in. Everybody else prepared to sleep on the bare metal decks. It was cool and pleasant enough but the following morning tales of huge rats roaming about saw most people somehow cramming into their vehicles for the second night.

There now followed a manoeuvre whereby the two double deck barges were pushed apart and our barge slid between them. All three were then lashed together and the whole unwieldy conglomerate set off majestically down the lake.

And so we said farewell to Egypt, and not without considerable relief. I sum up our feelings and close the chapter with a heartfelt quotation from a diary entry made by Dawn – '....everything so totally disorganised – people lethargic, apathetic, unscrupulous and without any integrity or morals whatsoever'.

Goodbye Egypt

\*\*\*\*

Distance across Egypt – 2193 km

Total distance – 6901 km

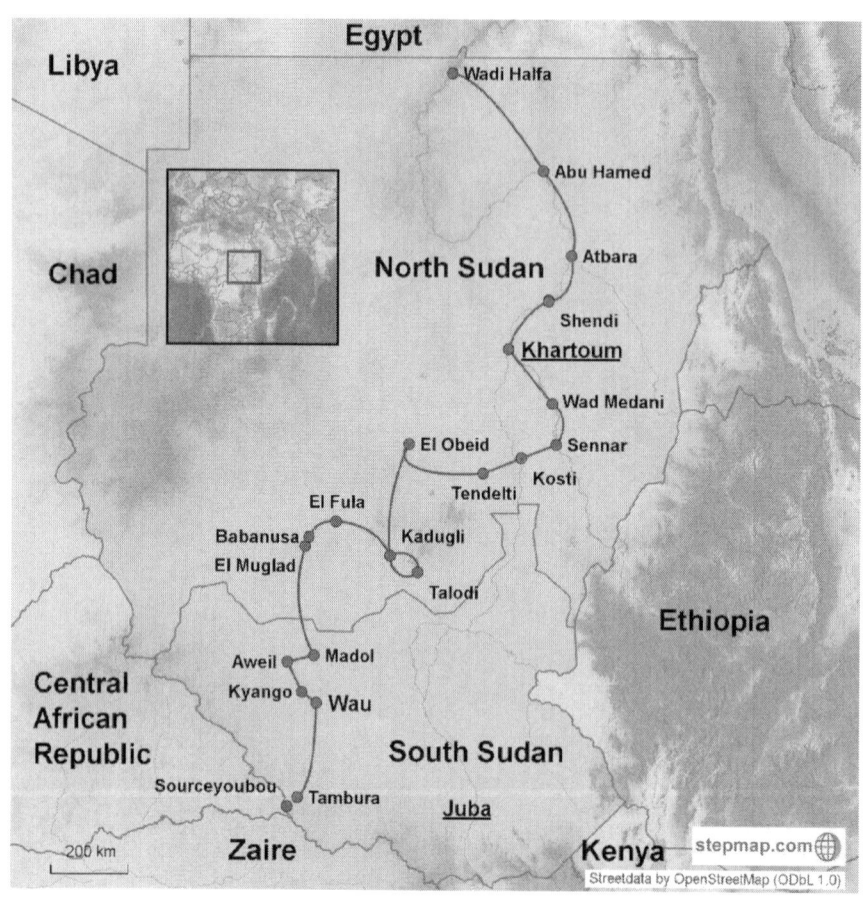

# Chapter 13 – Sudan

Sunday 9th November to Monday 22nd December 1980

Journey days 51 to 94

It was by now three o'clock in the afternoon. Lake Nasser stretched before us, a narrow, winding stretch of water nearly 150 kilometres long. It was completely calm and the sandy brown hills rose on either side to meet the blue sky. The local foot passengers were a friendly, unobtrusive crowd although they and their belongings soon overflowed onto our barge and by late evening the Rover was an island in the midst of bags and sacks and sleeping bodies, making access rather difficult. We realised that the flat top of the engine room and the narrow deck around it were not used by anybody else and we therefore spent many happy hours at the back of the boat sitting in our camp chairs reading or chatting to Jan, Björn and various occupants of the Traks truck.

A character on the Traks truck was Harvey, an anxious lad of oriental descent who was always spotlessly clean and impeccably dressed, albeit casually. What he was doing on a trip like this was beyond our understanding, surrounded as he was by the usual hippylike, happy-go-lucky crowd of young people usually associated with this type of rough and ready travel. Thoroughly shattered by his experiences he eventually jumped ship in Khartoum and flew off in much more appropriate style. He spent virtually all the time on the boat sitting bolt upright in his seat in the back of the lorry looking down with horror at the scenes all around him. Whether or not he ever braved a visit to the toilets I don't know.

We also met 'Enry Cooper, an English Character with a capital C, whose facial features and London accent earned him his apt title. 'Enry was a professional roamer and traveller. He was about thirty three years old I should think, and claimed to be the oldest student in the business, flourishing his fake student's card acquired in Amsterdam which entitled him to cheap fares and lodgings. He seemed to make his way through life by buying cheap and selling at a profit. He approached us one time with a big box of brand new Swiss army penknives at £10.00 each. He was usually to be found squatting amongst a crowd of Sudanese on the top deck of the cabined barge. This spot was next to the 'kitchen' which served up a foul-looking soup and nothing much else and which 'Enry described as "really good, mate, why don't yer 'ave some?".

It was an uneventful trip apart from when a New Zealand girl sat in one of our chairs and ripped it in half, which gave Dawn something to do, patching it together with material from an old pair of JVC's brown, corduroy trousers which had been used to wrap up some gearbox spares.

Each night when it became too dark to navigate, the ferry was gently nudged into the rocky bank and moored for a few hours. We passed the temple of Abu Simbel at about 9.30 on the second evening but saw nothing in the darkness. This was also the day of the New Zealand girl's birthday and the Traks lorry was be-decked with balloons and some bottles of wine appeared from somewhere. There was a very good atmosphere on the boat and it was most enjoyable and relaxing.

Coming into the international port of Wadi Halfa

At 11.30 on the morning of the third day we came in sight of Wadi Halfa – a bit of a shock. No teeming port with surrounding city, just a couple of small wooden buildings and a permanently moored barge similar to ours, with two huts on the deck and the familiar bare, brown hills rising from the shoreline. And that was it, a border post of the largest country in Africa. We gently moved in beside the moored barge and all the foot passengers prepared to leave. All the heaps of cargo from the outermost barge were moved to the innermost and all over ours in the middle. We watched this from the rear of the barge and were quite unable to get back to the Rover due to the mass of people and goods. Some Sudanese officials came aboard and fumigated everywhere and then all the passengers except us whites were lined up and inoculated. First off was a small group of white foot passengers who disappeared over a low hill to our right. Some of them took advantage of the armada of taxis, Land Rovers, Land Cruisers and trucks that had gathered for the arrival of the ferry and the rest plodded resolutely on their own two feet. At last the locals and their loads were allowed off, passing through the customs hut where their huge bundles were pulled apart for minute examination. As they started to emerge onto the shore we began to understand how the system worked. The trucks and lorries belonged to the local Sudanese traders and wholesalers who appeared to have their regular suppliers on the boat. The sandy shore became a market place with black headed figures in white robes surrounded by sacks and bundles of goods that were displayed, haggled over and sold. Still there were dozens of people and mountains of goods to be disembarked but it appeared that, by the end of the afternoon, all deals had been sealed, everything had been sold and both hardware and people slowly lumbered over the hill and out of our sight on swaying, overloaded vehicles.

Wadi Halfa 'Goods In'

Pop-up market, Wadi Halfa style

131

At about 3 o'clock we overlanders were approached by a very courteous Sudanese in order to start the process of customs and immigration. Our carnet would not apply in Sudan, and there was a quaint system whereby an official form was filled in and, depending upon the value of your vehicle, a figure was stated which had to be lodged with the authorities, pending your eventual departure from the country. For the Rover this figure was about £600.00. Another form was then filled in which waived this payment, and with the appropriate stamps and signatures one was free to drive into the country. Unfortunately by this time it was four o'clock and although customs had not finished with everybody it was time for them to knock off. We stood in amazement as we were untied and propelled some distance back into the lake where we were anchored for a third night 'at sea'.

The difference from the previous nights was amazing. It was very, very quiet with just the two dozen or so of us left there. The great piles of litter left by the departing passengers had been swept away, there was plenty of room to walk about and it was all rather nice. One of the crew and one of the Japanese produced fishing rods and whilst the Japanese managed to catch a couple of nice sized fish with his technical equipment, the crew member hauled them out continuously with a piece of stick, a length of string and a huge, crude float and hook.

After a good night's sleep we were up and raring to go the following morning. We returned to the shore, customs formalities were finally completed and then the polite customs official, accompanied by the Egyptian captain, came to the Rover and explained, with an apologetic smile, that the captain wanted about £6.00 from each vehicle in order for his men to manoeuvre the ramps necessary for our transfer to the land and to help us get off. Dawn and I didn't think much of this blatant attempt to extort more money from us and promptly went to inform everybody else of the situation, the outcome of which was a universal agreement not to pay, apart, that is, for the Frenchman and his Lada who presumably coughed up because the barge moved into position, the crew moved the ramps and he bounced off and drove avec aplomb over the horizon in the direction taken by the rest of the ex-passengers.

Meanwhile the rest of us continued to argue with the captain until he eventually unlashed and pushed out the double deck barge between us and the customs barge so that our vessel could at least be moved to the dockside. He still refused to move the necessary ramps without the demanded payment. This was no problem as there were more than enough of us able bodied men and girls to move them and we happily set to work. One pair of ramps had to be placed from our barge to the moored barge and then another pair from the moored barge to the shore. Our barge was then moved back and forth to align each vehicle with the narrow gap between the huts on the deck. It all looked rather hairy.

First off was Bruno who very gently and nervously eased across and down to terra firma. Swaying precariously with its large roof rack, the Land Cruiser followed and then Jan. Meanwhile I was frantically trying to start the Rover. The days in Aswan and the nights on the ferry had taken their toll on the battery and by this time it was as flat as the proverbial pancake. I cranked and cranked on the handle but to no avail. It was our turn to disembark and I'm afraid that we had to suffer the ignominy of being pushed off, which I think was more frightening than being under power. The drop to the water from the top of the second, steep pair of ramps was about 10 feet but suddenly there I was safe and sound on the sand and being pushed up the slope to a flat area.

*Crossed fingers and no engine*

Now it was all hands to deal with the Traks trailer. Because of the central front jockey wheel we had to fetch two more ramps to run it on. Once again a few girls hung onto the back as a counterbalance, we attached some ropes to the front to assist with the braking and one brave young fellow squatted on the drawbar grasping the handbrake. To his cries of "Brakes off!" and Brakes on!" we commenced a lurching progression off the hatch cover and across the first pair of ramps. Arriving safely and triumphantly on the customs barge we continued to the shore ramps which were very steep. Suddenly, after a couple of "Brakes on!" and 'Brakes off!", there was a terrified "Brakes offffffffff........!", everybody leapt out of the way and trailer and brakeman hurtled wildly down the remaining slope and onto the sand, arriving safe but not a little shaken.

Finally the two trucks. The Bedford had battery problems, too, and could not be started. We added additional supports in the form of two 40 gallon drums on their sides under the ramps between the two barges and heaved the truck forward. Off the hatch cover, and then, with the front wheels halfway across the ramps, the idiot of a driver tried to bump start it in four wheel drive. Both front wheels immediately locked up and one ramp was pushed forward and off the barge, ending up supported on just one of the rusty oil drums and with a two feet gap between it and the barge and the back wheel which was, of course still on the hatch cover. The truck had immediately stopped and we looked on in horror as it loomed above us. If the oil drum gave way the truck would simply tip over on its side. Nothing moved and after we had frantically inserted some lengths of timber to bridge the gap, the truck was able to inch its way to the ground without further mishap whilst we all stood well clear.

The Traks truck coming down with the Daf truck visible behind it

Six down, one to go. I stood on the bank to watch this one, along with a battery of photographers including Dawn, who had been gleefully recording the heart stopping incidents from a safe distance. I don't think that I had ever seen such a rigid, terrified look on anybody's face like the one the driver wore as the Daf came down towards us. He apparently decided that he had better get it all over and done with before his nerve broke completely and he lurched down to dry land to the delighted cheers of us onlookers.

Back at the Rover I jump started the engine from Jan's battery and we all set off for the town of Wadi Halfa, some 2 kilometres away. This was a relatively new town, the original having been swallowed by the rising waters of Lake Nasser. Not surprisingly it didn't look new and was just a cluster of shabby, single storey buildings of the usual classic shoebox design with no tarmac roads, all looking very dusty and poor. There was a mean looking hotel, a ramshackle bank – where we managed to change some money – and a handful of mostly empty shops. Dawn managed to buy some stale bread, lemons and onions but there appeared to be very little else apart from the inevitable tins of sardines and tomato paste that always seemed to be present and which somehow came to epitomise the grinding poverty in so many towns and villages that we were to pass through.

*Our permit to drive through Sudan*

We drove out to the police station where we had to present our vehicle permit and notify them of our intention to drive to Khartoum. Wadi Halfa is both a port and a rail head and is simply the staging post between the ferry from the north and the train to the south. There is nothing else and no other reason for it to be there. We entered the police station ready to show our permits and to explain all the preparations we had made in accordance with the information from Cairo. With a mixture of surprise and relief we encountered a very casual reception, tinged with a sort of "why have you bothered to come in here?" attitude. They were not interested in whether or not we travelled singly or in convoy but did thoughtfully warn us that it required a good, strong vehicle like a Land Rover to survive the rigours of the desert.

The missionary kids had originally planned to put their truck onto a flatbed rail car but now discussed the matter again and with no objections from the police they decided to try and drive and therefore wanted to travel with our three Land Rovers. We were not particularly happy at this as the Daf looked more suited to urban delivery work rather than a desert crossing. It was finally agreed that we would all start together, with the Daf at the rear, and that should they become stuck they would immediately abandon the attempt and return to Wadi Halfa to await the train. We had not seen the Traks truck since leaving the ferry and we assumed that they were by now some two or three hours ahead of us.

So we set off, leaving the police station, crossing the rail track over to the eastern side of it and heading south alongside it. The plan was to follow the railway line and the row of telegraph poles alongside it, there being no road as such, only the meandering tracks of previous travellers, and even these could be obliterated within a couple of days by the drifting sand. Almost immediately after leaving Wadi Halfa we encountered some high sand dunes coming right down to the railway line and we were straight into 4 wheel drive. Bruno got stuck and the Daf truck promptly aborted its mission, turning with some difficulty back to the town and this was the last we saw of them. A blessing in disguise for all concerned and pretty good proof that there is a God caring for us all.

We were in the lead and after about half an hour had to stop to wait for Jan and Bruno. Jan had experienced no trouble but Bruno was looking a little worried. He was apparently quite shocked when his Rover ground to a halt and Jan and I kept going. By now I had had the opportunity to study Bruno's vehicle more closely and my original feeling of inferiority in Luxor had changed to one of incredulity. I could now see that the Carawagon had what appeared to be quite serious potential problems. Land Rover stipulated that the front axle and suspension should only carry the additional weight of a spare wheel and a winch, and that additional loads should be carried on a roof rack which concentrated them over the rear axle. Even this load should be minimal and could, in fact, be exceeded by the weight of a sturdy roof rack on its own. In the case of the Carawagon it was impossible to mount a rack at the rear because of the raising roof, and therefore a front rack stretching from the cab to supports from the front bumper bar had been fitted, a quite enormous area which invited lots of luggage. I now saw that on the roof rack were fourteen (full) jerry cans, a large aluminium storage box, a spare wheel and six lengths of aluminium sand track. Into the cab roof over the front seats Bruno had built an integral one hundred litre water tank and I calculated that all this, plus the spare wheel on the bonnet and the winch, amounted to a load over the front axle which must have been at least one thousand three hundred pounds! In the back it was rumoured that he had a vast stock of heavy, tinned food. To assist the normal road springs he had fitted Land Rover approved, thick rubber doughnuts between the chassis and the axles and the whole vehicle was actually sitting on these, not on the springs, which were completely compressed. I had been very conscious of the loading on my Rover, with all the fitting out I had done, and had always kept an anxious eye on the springs as we had loaded in our possessions and the fuel cans etc. With Bruno's Rover, once the doughnuts had been used he could happily continue to add weight without, of course, any apparent effect on the vehicle. It must have had all the suspension capability and flexibility of a roller skate and must have been terrible to ride in. This was presumably his first foray into soft sand since leaving Switzerland.

Digging Bruno out again

On our first stop I tried to persuade him to let some air out of his tyres but he was very wary of this and vented just a few psi. He also mentioned an odd grating noise from the gearbox when in low ratio. He took me for a short drive and there was no doubt that something was amiss, but here was no place to do anything about it other than cross our fingers and carry on.

After that initial soft sand the going became much firmer and we were able to make good speed and Bruno only had to use his sand tracks a couple of times. At one time we were really moving across an open plain but hidden ruts could cause sudden and unavoidable heavy jarring and bouncing. On one occasion Bruno was running alongside us at about 80 kilometres an hour and I definitely saw his front wheels rise nearly two feet off the ground on one such rut, coming back down to earth again with a bone crunching wallop – all 1,300 pounds of overload under gravitational force. Meanwhile we motored happily on and the worst thing to happen to us was a gallon oil can bouncing off the roof rack, onto the bonnet and onto the sand.

The Rover in its element and still looking very smart

We had left Wadi Halfa at 1.45 and stopped for the night at 5, having covered just 118 kilometres. We were on a vast, flat, sandy plain, with low hills on the horizon. We were at last into Sudan which we saw as one of the major stretches of our journey and we gathered together that night with a satisfying feeling of achievement, laughing at memories of the ferry and looking forward to the challenges of the desert the following day.

The next day we covered 250 kilometres but found that, together with Jan, we were spending more and more time coaxing Bruno out of soft patches using his sand tracking. Fortunately it was lightweight aluminium in 5 foot lengths and was reasonably easy to move, but over stretches of 75 feet or so it called for good teamwork to keep hauling it up and running with it to the front of his

Rover to maintain the momentum. When he occasionally slipped off it needed strenuous digging and repositioning of the track to get him on the move again.

Our sand ladders remained firmly strapped on to our roof rack and we assumed that they were second rate compared to Bruno's professional tracking (we were to learn differently in the Sahara). We found that once Bruno had sunk a few inches into the sand and stopped it was very difficult to get the track under his wheels without digging a lot of sand away to bring the track down to the level of the bottom of the wheels otherwise it just would not climb up onto the tracks which tended to rear up at forty five degrees. Bruno continued to deny the failure of his vehicle and many times tried to accelerate off the tracks, after much sweat and labour to get him on them, and make a dive for solid ground. This invariably led to him immediately bogging down again and the whole process had to be repeated. The situation wasn't helped when it became obvious that the digging out process was usually performed by everybody except Bruno and his wife. Bruno would climb wearily from his cab and squat in the shade with a puzzled look on his face whilst Elizabeth fluttered about wringing her hands in anguish. With Bruno's demeanour it was pointless trying to reason with him so the rest of us just stoically got back to work with our simple shovel and our bare hands.

By mid-afternoon we had reached Abu Hamed, where the Nile rejoined the railway line after its saunter far to the west, and stopped in the police compound for the night. Bruno performed a grand finale by getting stuck just outside the compound, much to the amusement of the locals.

A stroll around Abu Hamed revealed once again a pitiful shortage of supplies. No bread, no vegetables except onions and no petrol – just tins of sardines and tomato paste together with some aerosol cans of Piff Paff fly killer. We couldn't even buy bottles of fizzy lemonade, only home-made mango drinks in Coke bottles with no caps, which we decided to give a miss. This lack of foodstuffs in the shops was to become sadly very familiar and we never did find out just what the locals survived on.

The next day proved to be a pretty disastrous one. We managed to buy some bread early in the morning and then set off beside the railway once more. We came into an area of low, rocky ridges, at right angles to our route and covered in loose, sharp stones. Between each ridge was a low area with very soft sand and Bruno ground to a halt in every one of them. We were in the lead and Jan was in the rear. It became routine that we would cross a sandy patch, stop on the next ridge and trudge back to where Bruno would inevitably be sitting immobile in the sand. Jan and Björn would leave their Rover on the preceding ridge and trudge forward to meet up with us for the digging and track laying process.

It appeared on Bruno's Michelin map that there was a main road marked further east and there was much discussion as to whether or not to try and find it. I was very sceptical about any sort of decent road in the area and preferred to stick to the railway. Dawn and I just had another Bartholomew's map, "Africa North East", which was a little small in scale but, in fact, had all the towns and villages marked on it. It, too, showed a nice red line somewhere in the area. We held a vote and, as only I was sure that no road would be found, we set off to find it. Accordingly the other two vehicles set off in a south easterly direction but we hung back a bit and when the 'road' still did not appear, they circled back and we continued close to the railway. By 12.30 the sun was very, very hot and we gratefully stopped for lunch. We had found that hot, sweet lemon tea was the most refreshing drink in these circumstances, and that first one after the long morning was like pure nectar, sitting in the shade and puffing on an equally welcome cigarette. Looking across at Bruno we realised that he was not well and that his periods of sitting with his head in his hands (whilst we were digging him out) had been a prelude to a total collapse. He lay motionless as Elizabeth laid cool, wet cloths over his forehead. It looked like a classic case of salt deficiency so we gave him some tablets to take and sat back to await his recovery. Jan and Björn were also feeling the strain and the heat and were also glad of a long break. The years that Dawn and I had spent in a similar hot, dry climate seemed to have left us more resilient to the situation and we found these long rest periods most frustrating.

Three and a half hours later (!) Bruno declared that he was ready to press on but looked very pale and tired. Almost immediately he became stuck again and in the next one and a half hours we managed just 8 kilometres, digging and using sand track most of the way. At 5.30 Bruno sank in a huge sea of sand and this time I decided to try and tow him out. He had a long length of cable on the winch and we paid it out for about 30 metres to our Rover and then with both engines in low ratio attempted to dislodge him. Nothing happened other than my clutch started to smell as it overheated so we abandoned that very quickly. We then tried with just the winch but the only result was me being dragged towards Bruno, who remained as immobile as a concrete building. We decided to abandon our efforts until the next day, so dug and manoeuvred Bruno up onto his sand tracks so that he was a least level for the night and then returned tight lipped to our own vehicles parked some distance away on firm ground. We had travelled just 71 kilometres that day and were very disappointed in Bruno's attitude to everything. He was seriously holding us up, had done nothing to help himself and hadn't even managed a single word of thanks or apology. It was a glum bunch that sat around that evening.

My right hand fuel tank had sprung a small leak, but an application of Araldite had made a temporary seal.

Before we moved off the next day, Jan had a quiet word with Bruno about the situation and the result was a sharing of his load. We took four full jerry cans and put them on our roof rack and Jan took a similar number. After sand tracking him 35 metres from his night time rest spot to firmer ground the reduction in weight certainly seemed to help, and he negotiated stretches that he would not have done the day before. He still ground to a halt a dismaying number of times, though, and his front wheels were showing a definite tendency to lean inwards, defying the rigid logic of the axle.

And so the day went on, climbing over rocky ridges and clawing through the sandy patches in between with the telegraph poles, the railway line and the green banks of the Nile at varying distances to our right, the low and mysterious hills of the Nubian desert lying far to our left and the unrelenting sun beating down from above.

We reached Berber in the late afternoon, having finally encountered short stretches of a discernible track, albeit just pairs of vehicle ruts in the sand, and having covered just 160 kilometres. Berber was yet another town of no tarmac roads, low brown mud buildings and a depressing overall air of bare subsistence and grinding poverty. We enquired the whereabouts of the police station which we perceived as a hospitable and safe haven in each town. A local who spoke some English invited us into the 'garden' of his brick and mud dwelling for water and lemon drinks before leading us on his scooter to the police station – yet another example of the selfless generosity of the poor, although obviously the ownership of a motor scooter must have meant that, despite outward appearances, he was perhaps the local bank manager or something. At the police station we were directed around to the rear where a large walled garden offered an ideal overnight haven – just a pity that access was through a low archway and I had to take everything off the roof rack in order to negotiate it. Dawn headed off to the market but found the usual dusty, empty shelves and lack of foodstuffs. A very nice campsite, though, with plenty of water for clothes washing and the sound of drums and singing in the evening after a very tasty nasi goreng with tinned tuna.

*The desolation of the Nubian desert*

Early mornings now followed a predictable but somewhat frustrating routine. Jan and Björn, Bruno and Elizabeth would be up and about at least an hour before Dawn and I awoke and emerged. Dawn and I would then have a leisurely breakfast and still be packed and ready to go long before the others. This particular morning it was three and a half hours after they had first arisen before our companions were ready to leave. We initially drove to the local petrol station, a remarkably modern Shell complex, only to be rationed to two gallons each because of the critical shortage. Whilst not desperate at this stage, neither we nor Jan had sufficient fuel to reach Khartoum after all the high consumption desert travel, and we wanted to obtain petrol at any opportunity. Bruno, presumably, had plenty of the stuff but there was never any hint of his sharing it in an emergency. We returned to the police station to see if there was any way in which we could be allocated more fuel but after wasting a lot of time we discovered that the official who could authorise it was away (a familiar tale). We left Berber and after a short time came to Atbara, so far the largest town that we had encountered and which even had short stretches of tarmac road and sturdily built brick houses. Atbara lay at the railway junction where the line branched off north east to Port Sudan, and was therefore an important place where we were more optimistic of finding fuel. Once again we reported to the police station and explained our predicament to a sympathetic sergeant who apparently had not been confronted with such a request before. He made a couple of telephone calls, however, the result of which were directions to the Shell depot and a promise of assistance. Bruno remained at the police station and Jan and I set off for the depot where we were met by a Sudanese gentleman who appeared to be highly placed in the Shell administration and who had interrupted his Friday holiday to come along and open up for us. Another example of the helpful attitude of the Sudanese. Not only that but he happily sold us 32 gallons of petrol at a very reasonable price.

With the late start and the time spent obtaining fuel it was after lunch before we left Atbara, leaving behind our brief encounter with tarmac and ploughing on in twin, sandy vehicle ruts. These were very, very rough and the going was incredibly slow and it took one and a half hours to cover just 50 kilometres. We had entered a different type of landscape now, less open and flat and quite densely covered in high green bushes which we threaded our way between. At 4.30 Bruno became very deeply embedded and by the time we had extricated him it was dusk. Though apparently miles from anywhere, a local casually strolled up and indicated that there was a better route about a kilometre to the east, with a railway station and market only 2 kilometres ahead. Full of optimism we followed his directions and, sure enough, found a much better route which was still very soft but obviously much used by other traffic. Stopping to discuss our estimates of the remaining distance to the aforementioned market, Bruno adamantly refused to go any further. He had enough food so why should he try and reach the market? The fact that we would have been in Khartoum by now if it wasn't for him didn't seem to enter his head. More disgruntled than ever with his attitude we nevertheless had little choice but to stay there with him and Björn and I left the others and drove on to find the market. It was the usual poor place in a small hamlet next to the railway line. Most of the shops and stalls were closed as dusk was falling but we managed to buy some fruit which we called lemoranges because of their round shape, green colour and sweet, lemon taste. Whilst negotiating our purchases and sipping a glass of complimentary tea, a huge truck rumbled up in a cloud of dust and we were introduced to our first enormous sweet grapefruit. Up to 6 inches in diameter these yellow/red fruits with their delicious juicy pink insides were to become a common part of our diet throughout Sudan. The driver of the lorry jumped down and offered us these 'grapes' as he called them. Björn and I imagined standard bunches of grapes and were open mouthed with amazement when we were presented with half a dozen of these football like objects. After grinding our way back to camp we had the satisfaction of seeing the embarrassment on Bruno's face when we gave him two of the magnificent fruit. He had the decency to refuse at first, but accepted them when we explained that they were free.

Apart from the mechanical problems of Bruno, our vehicles were taking the strain extremely well. Jan had trouble with petrol and foodstuffs spilling into a jumble in the back of his Rover and we had lost one twenty litre plastic water can due to it splitting open. Two of my vertical roof rack supports had fractured and were now in 'splints'. Bruno's roof rack was actually starting to bend and droop.

The next day was our sixth since leaving Wadi Halfa and we were determined to reach Khartoum. We set off a little earlier than usual and reaching the market of the night before found only a little bread worth buying. After this the route led over low, firm hills interspersed with the inevitable soft sand patches. It was an overcast day with a strong wind blowing the sand high in the air. At one stage the route became a mass of criss-crossing tracks disappearing into the scattered bushes and the dusty murk. It was all rather eerie and we struggled on in roaring low ratio to defeat the never ending effort of the sand to drag us to a halt. We eventually emerged onto firmer ground and, needless to say, had to wait about half an hour for Bruno who by this time we tended to leave to his own devices when he got stuck and only very reluctantly returned to help him.

We arrived in Shendi mid-morning and were very surprised to find a bustling market area abounding with fresh fruit and vegetables. Dawn had a great time stocking up on all those things that we been unable to buy since leaving Aswan nine days before.

The afternoon drive into Khartoum became faster and faster as the terrain improved and we were soon weaving and careering in line abreast on hard sand through sparse bushes, exuberant in having conquered the Nubian desert and occasionally being raced and overtaken by huge, modified and enlarged British Leyland lorries, known as Souk Lorries, each one driven by an equally huge, ebony black, grinning Sudanese driver under the watchful eye of his white robed Arab boss and truck owner sitting next to him enthroned amidst a mass of brightly coloured cushions. About 40 kilometres before Khartoum we encountered our second stretch of tarmac in Sudan and at last drove into North Khartoum at about six o'clock to the bright lights of street stalls, milling crowds and heavy traffic, a startling contrast to our week of solitude, peace and quiet. We crawled along the main road and soaked up the noisy, colourful atmosphere. Bruno had a travel book that stated that overnight camping was allowed at the German Club (this being his one and only useful contribution to the expedition) and we threaded our way through the traffic to cross the Blue Nile into Khartoum proper. This was much quieter than North Khartoum and we found ourselves in broad deserted streets actually lit by electric lighting. We stopped and I set off on foot to try and find someone to ask for directions. I soon came across a young policeman who spoke not a word of English but who, with a big smile, led me down a street to his station. The sergeant here spoke passable English and I enquired the way to the German Club. After a few moments of thought and discussion he spoke emphatically to the original policeman and then sent me off with him. Relocating the vehicles we set off with our guide pointing out the way. We came at last to an impressive building and our guide sat back triumphantly. Unfortunately it was the German Cultural Centre not the German Club, and after some additional advice from a gentleman there we set off once more. After yet another false lead we eventually ran the German Club to ground in a quiet back street near the airport. For a temporary membership fee of about £1.00 each we were told that we could use the club facilities including the bar, restaurant and swimming pool and we could spend maybe one night in the car park. It was quite late by this time and we were relieved to have found somewhere decent to spend the night in a strange city, and thoughts of a shower, a swim and a beer were icing on the cake. Our policeman was very pleased with himself for having led us to our destination but had the problem of how to return to his station, now some considerable distance away. Our offer to pay for a taxi was met with a horrified refusal. I finally persuaded him to accept a lift and he reluctantly agreed to me inconveniencing myself. He directed me back to the station and I took careful note of the route for the return trip. However, on arrival at the station he motioned for me to wait, ran inside and emerged a few seconds later waving a bunch of keys. He trotted over to a parked police Land Rover, jumped in and led me back to the club. What a tremendous introduction to Khartoum.

So began another long stopover on our journey. Petrol was to be no easier to buy in Khartoum than anywhere else in Sudan and it was to be nine days before we were able to hit the road again. Sudan and the Sudanese were so friendly, however, that it was all too easy to relax and forget the necessity to push on. Khartoum was nothing like I had expected. I had visions of low, blindingly white buildings scattered around the confluence of the Nile and surrounded by rolling sandy hills – a picture presumably generated from images of General Gordon facing the Mahdi's warriors nearly one hundred years previously. In fact Khartoum was a mass of old and not-so-old buildings, the Nile was only visible when right next to it and the surrounding countryside was rather flat and cultivated in various shades of green. The city itself consisted of three segments created by the confluence of the White Nile and the Blue Nile, which formed an upside down letter Y. In the upper north east segment was North Khartoum, in the upper north west segment was the old capital of Omdurman and in the bottom segment was Khartoum.

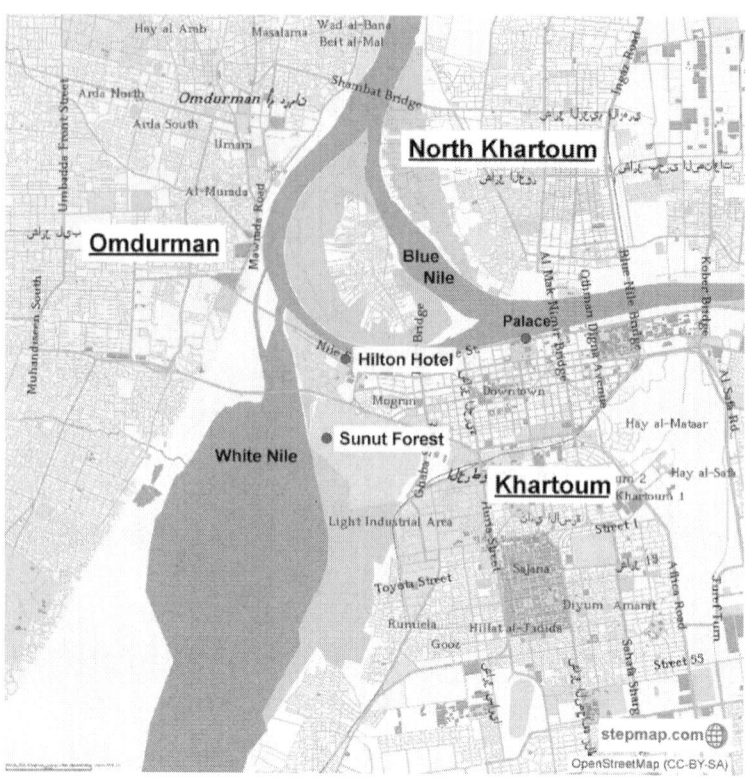

*Khartoum and the confluence of the Nile*

We saw little of North Khartoum apart from the scenes when we first arrived but Omdurman we visited to wander around the souk which we found to be a delightful place selling all manner of hardware, fruit, vegetables, textiles and spices. Most of our time was spent in Khartoum proper which was by far the most modern of the three areas with many modern multi-storey blocks. The centrepiece was the Presidential Palace situated on a tree-lined boulevard alongside the Blue Nile. It was guarded by coal black Nubian soldiers in smart red and white uniforms. Opposite the palace was an area of ornamental lawns and gardens and beyond them the main shopping centre. Adjacent to the palace were several large red brick buildings housing a large part of the Sudanese bureaucracy and where we had to register as aliens and also seek permission to travel to the south. The waterfront boulevard led north to a bridge over the river and into Omdurman. Along the road was the National Museum, which sadly we never found time to visit, and then behind another garden area was the Hilton Hotel, apparently the most modern building in the city at that time and fashioned in a typical commercial manner to create the

146

maximum number of bedrooms with the minimum consideration of the traditional style and architecture if its surroundings.

Behind the Hilton and effectively on the south bank of the White Nile was a large wooded area called the Sunut Forest and it was here that with Jan and Björn we found ourselves at the end of the second day. The German Club was not prepared to accept long term camping so Dawn and I had investigated the Sudan Club, finding it to be a very colonial British establishment, welcoming enough but with no camping facilities. We also approached the British Embassy for advice and of course it was its usual obliging self when asked for assistance in such matters. One sometimes wonders if the staff ever leave their cosy compounds and duty free cocktails to experience real life outside. It might help them to understand the needs of temporary visitors.

As it happened we bumped into several of our friends from the Traks lorry which, it transpired, had arrived in Khartoum just an hour before we did, despite leaving Wadi Halfa before us and being unencumbered with a Bruno. We swapped experiences over a soft drink and learned of their eventful journey. On leaving Wadi Halfa their driver had apparently circled around and ended up heading north rather than south. It was only when one of the passengers remarked how unusual it was that the sun was setting in the east that the error was discovered and they turned back. Having then located the railway track their problems became mechanical, a universal joint on the front prop shaft being broken and leaving them with rear wheel drive only. With the added drag of the trailer it would appear that their cross-country capability was, in fact, probably less than that of dear Bruno and little better than that of the ill-fated Daf. They had therefore resorted to the illegal practice of driving on the railway line, but at each of the ten stations along the way had had to divert off onto the sand before they were seen and each time they did this they immediately become stuck. Each station proved to be a 2 kilometre diversion of sweat and toil with muscle and sand track. By the time they reached Khartoum the group were pretty cheesed off with the whole thing and only their Antipodean resilience and good humour had saved the driver from a lynching. Anyway, they were now settled in the Sunut Forest behind the Hilton which apparently was the recognised rendezvous and camping area for overlanders. We found it to be a sparsely wooded area with ample room between the trees and a lack of heavy undergrowth which made for ideal camping and privacy. The interlacing branches overhead formed a dappled sunshade and we found it to be a very satisfactory place to stay with water 'borrowed' from a hose in the Hilton gardens and toilets being the good old shovel-behind-a-tree job. Let's face it, this was usually preferable to any public toilets that we were likely to encounter. The only drawback was between about five and six o'clock in the evening as dusk fell, millions of mosquitoes appeared from nowhere and descended on anything human in an attempt to pierce every square inch of exposed flesh. To be out then was excruciatingly uncomfortable but fortunately there was no residual itching although at the time one was compelled to perform a sort of St Vitus' dance accompanied by much swiping and slapping. Best to hide in the Rover until they disappeared as suddenly as they had arrived. All in all it was peaceful and quiet with a nice feeling of camaraderie with the other occupants. Over our time there these varied but included three Bedford trucks, four Mercedes Unimogs, a large Fiat camper and our three Land Rovers.

Next to Jan in the Sunut forest

Bruno had remained at the German Club for a couple more nights before appearing in the forest and camping several hundred yards away from us. To our relief there was never any suggestion of his continuing to travel with us. Most of his time seemed to be spent in taking his Rover to a garage where his gearbox was stripped and repaired, his apparently broken front axle was repaired and various welding modifications performed to strengthen his sagging roof rack. They kept themselves to themselves and we had very little to do with them.

Meanwhile our preoccupation was with the search for petrol, which led us around in a seemingly endless journey from building to building and office to office all over Khartoum until Jan eventually discovered the correct place to go. Petrol for local inhabitants was strictly rationed and each filling station had long queues of silent vehicles where drivers would patiently wait for hours to get their two gallon allocation. Travellers like ourselves had to make an application at the Petroleum Office which resulted in a letter to take to one of the depots and which surprisingly entitled us to as many forty four gallon drums as we wanted and at the fixed government price of about fifty pence a gallon. Having obtained the necessary permission we then had to find suitable containers to put it in. Both Jan and ourselves had calculated that our current capacities were insufficient for the journey ahead and we spent a frustrating morning driving around trying to buy jerry cans. For a country that seemed to be inundated with plastic goods of all sizes and lurid colours it seemed incredible that there were no suitable containers available anywhere. In the end we reluctantly settled for square twenty litre plastic containers that had originally been used for vegetable cooking oil and which were sold uncleaned in market shops. We paid about £1.50 each for six of these and Jan bought eight. Back in the forest we spent an afternoon trying to clean them up a bit and fashioning decent rubber seals to stop the caps leaking, using the remains of the nitrile rubber that I had acquired in Qatar. Despite my misgivings about their strength and durability they were to perform admirably over the coming weeks, surviving not only the bumping and jolting but also the daily cycle when they would go from being rounded and bloated in the intense heat of the day to semi-collapsed in the cold of the night. Stowage of these extra containers called for some modifications to the Rover.

The author writing up the log, Jan studying a water container and Dawn............doing some washing

My roof rack supports were now broken beyond use and I spent a fascinating afternoon in a noisy back alleyway of North Khartoum having a new angle iron frame welded up to support the rack directly over the Rover cab. I don't think that there was a hacksaw or a drill in the place and all lengths were cut with a hammer and chisel and all holes were made with a hammer and a punch. It was also here that I saw the modifications being applied to the Austin and Morris lorry chassis' in order to convert them to Souk Lorries. These basic chassis were apparently now manufactured in Japan and were of a rather dated design not seen any longer on British roads. They were imported as just a bare chassis, axles, engine and transmission plus the bonnet, dashboard and windscreen. The whole rear end was extended by a few feet by fitting large girders along the two back chassis members and relocating the back axle further to the rear. The cabs were simple square additions made of angle iron and sheet metal riveted together. There were no proper doors, just tiny half doors again riveted together from angle iron and sheet steel and secured with simple gate latches and bolts. The rear body was also constructed in angle iron and steel and the overall result was an outsize, square shaped vehicle in natural steel grey with shiny silver rivet heads and a rounded gleaming white British Leyland bonnet sitting incongruously at the front. The cab seat was a hard wooden bench and the upholstery was a pile of cushions as previously mentioned. The whole thing was very effectively completed with a pair of oversize rear wheels fitted with huge balloon tyres. Only two wheel drive, these clever modifications produced a unique vehicle perfectly suited to cope with the Sudanese conditions of no tarmac and lots of soft sand.

The modification of my roof rack brought it further forward again and also six inches lower so that stability would be improved in addition to evening out the load on the axles. Back at the forest I then manufactured brackets on the front bumper in order to carry two jerry cans tucked snugly against the inner sides of the protruding front wings, securely strapped in place with ex-Rapier straps. All in all a neat and secure modification programme which brought our total fuel carrying capacity to seventy four gallons – twenty in the twin tanks, nine in the two jerry cans on the front bumper, nine in the two rear inboard jerry cans and thirty six in assorted containers on the roof rack. Unfortunately I couldn't manage to repair the slight leak in the right hand tank so avoided using it unless it could all be used up in a single day with minimum loss.

Thus equipped with our assorted cans and containers Jan and I finally set off for the fuel depot. Here we encountered the next problem in that we had to purchase in quantities of forty four gallon drums and not fractions thereof. Our combined required amount of one hundred and five gallons therefore had to be reduced to eighty eight as there was no way that we could cope with three drums and a total of a hundred and thirty two gallons! Another shock awaited us at the pumps as the system operated on a metered two inch pipe delivery system. This would fill a forty four gallon drum in about twenty five seconds. This translated into about two and a half seconds to fill a four and a half gallon jerry can and the control valve seemed to be either fully on or fully off despite the efforts of the man operating it. We probably only lost a couple of gallons by the end of it all, most of it all over me, and headed back to the forest like a couple of mini petrol tankers.

The subject of fuel had been discussed at length with other overlanders. We had failed to ascertain what the supply situation was like in southern Sudan and whilst some people left Khartoum carrying sufficient to reach Kenya – a colossal amount – others decided to avoid the problem by shipping their vehicles by boat up the Nile. After leaving Khartoum the next place where we felt confident of finding petrol was Wau, 2,200 kilometres away and our maximum load of seventy four gallons would only take us 1,500 kilometres at the most, depending upon driving conditions. As it was, with the reduction in quantity from the depot we had to set off with only sixty gallons, knowing that somehow we would have to find fuel well before reaching Wau.

Besides foraging for petrol we were also kept busy acquiring some necessary Sudanese stamps in our passports and in obtaining permission to actually travel to the south. We had finally decided that we would not go to Kenya but would instead head west through the Central African Republic and though we obtained the necessary visas without difficulty or delay we could not get visas for Nigeria, our enquiries being met with a blank refusal. We checked at the British Embassy for advice but the explanation of our predicament fell on the usual deaf ears. We just had to hope for a more sympathetic attitude at the Nigerian embassy in the CAR.

We met up with Mike and Daphne through a friend of theirs at the British Council and learnt of their interesting experiences with local transport following the Nile route from Wadi Halfa. At the British Council we also collected mail from our respective mothers, the first contact since leaving Oman two months previously.

Our remaining supply task was to find some cooking gas. After days of fruitless searching we eventually found a store that would fill our bottles, one of which was empty and the other nearly so. Camping gas was proving not to be as ideal as I had expected, mainly because our bottles were too small and also because we had expected it to be more readily available.

Whilst in the forest we had been approached by a Danish family in a nearly new Safari Land Rover. Pallé, his wife Elizabeth and sons Klaus (sixteen) and Michael (ten) had left Denmark many weeks before, setting out on their dream trip to Africa. Both Pallé and Elizabeth were schoolteachers and had obtained permission to take a year off with their jobs held open for them on their return. They felt that both sons were of a suitable age to remove from formal education for a year and had therefore sunk part of their savings into a new vehicle and the rest was available for the cost of the trip. Pallé was a short, quietly spoken, almost apologetic sort of man, very cautious and a most unlikely character to have packed his family off on such an adventure. I have to say that after our experience with Bruno, both Dawn and I were somewhat reluctant to take on a third vehicle, having got on tremendously well with Jan and Björn and looked forward to continuing an amicable journey with them. Jan, however, was more sympathetic and despite having similar reservations, there was obviously a nationalistic bond between them and Jan also pointed out that they had already been waiting for 4 weeks for suitable travellers with whom to venture on the southern trail. Well, we could hardly say 'no', so we added them to our little convoy and I'm very happy to say that they proved to be excellent travelling companions.

So, yet again we were ready to move on into the unknown. Dawn and I would, in fact, have liked a couple more days in Khartoum to indulge in some basic sightseeing but the other two groups were anxious to be on their way so we bowed to the majority decision. Before we left, however, we caught the latest saga of the ill-fated Traks group. They had camped in the Sunut Forest for several days whilst their driver/mechanic repaired the front universal joint and restored their 4 wheel drive capability. They had at last lurched away with jubilant cries and shouts of farewell and we were quite sorry to see them go. Only a few hours later, however, a very subdued lorry load came rumbling back. The new universal joint had failed even before they had left the city confines and to add to their woes the driver drove into a tree to knock it down for firewood but succeeded only in bending the front bumper and springing a leak in the radiator. The tree remained unperturbed.

Pallé and his family had been staying at the Khartoum Youth Hostel which was in the vicinity of the German Club, a very nice suburban area. They had been camping in the garden with two young English couples who were virtually penniless and who were trying to sell their old VW Combi in order to raise enough money to be able to continue their journey to Kenya on public transport. One continually meets really likeable people in these sorts of situations and it is easy to strike up comfortable friendships. They usually last only as happy memories of the moment, however, as individuals go their separate ways with never a serious intent to meet or correspond in the future.

So it was with Pallé's family and the English couples, as they said fond but reluctant farewells when we arrived to collect them after leaving the Sunut for the last time. As it happened we were quite happy for a delay as it gave us time to grab a welcome shower and shampoo at the hostel.

It was the twenty fourth of November. We left the Youth Hostel at about eleven o'clock and travelled due south for nearly 350 kilometres on good tarmac until it ran out just before we stopped for the night. Our route took us down through Wad Madani, following the Blue Nile, and then sharp right and west towards Kosti, an uneventful journey during which we found the tarmac very boring. This was always to be the case. You crash and bounce for endless miles on rough tracks – or no tracks – praying for some tarmac but then, once you are on it, within five minutes you are bored.

Well, we weren't bored the next day and slowly rattled our way along a very corrugated road, over a rather splendid bridge spanning the White Nile and down into Kosti. We found the bustling souk which was well supplied with fresh fruit and vegetables. The sky was a glorious blue, the temperature was perfect and we strolled around without attracting undue attention and enjoying the miscellany of brightly coloured stalls, each proudly manned by a grinning, black Nubian. I say undue attention but at one time Dawn had her bottom grabbed by a local looney and the good hearted crowd seemed to be as indignant as we were. We bought fresh fruit and vegetables and some pitta bread and were treated to some tiny glasses of hot, sweet tea. A delightful experience after the empty markets and abject poverty we had found further north.

From Kosti we were to head to El Obeid, a large town according to our maps. The track ran alongside a railway line and the twin ruts were atrocious. We were forced to keep to this track due to the densely bushed country to our right. Driving so close to the railway embankment led to some alarming angles of tilt and in places more level alternative routes just had to be found through the undergrowth. We were in the lead and after some time lost sight of the others. We stopped to wait for them but it later transpired that Jan decided to try for one of these alternative routes and ended up bypassing us about a kilometre away. Meanwhile we waited in vain for about an hour before reluctantly turning around and setting off back to look for both him and Pallé. We eventually drove all the way back to Kosti, our concern turning to annoyance when we realised what must have happened. Turning around again we retraced our route, accepting the fact that we probably wouldn't see them until we reached El Obeid, two days journey away. In fact we came across them in a small village where they had discovered that we had not passed through and they had thus been waiting for several hours. Everybody blamed everybody else but fortunately anger was tempered by not inconsiderable relief at finding each other and, after all, apart from wasting precious fuel no harm was done and it was a valuable lesson in not losing contact whilst on the move.

We carried on along a deteriorating track, which soon became just two huge ruts in soft, deep sand – the result of the massive back wheels of the Souk Lorries which would be the usual traffic. Unfortunately the spacing of these lorry-made ruts was much wider than the track of the Land Rovers and progress was made in a permanently lopsided manner with two wheels down in a rut and the other two scrabbling up in the soft sand mound between the ruts. On either side was a line of bushes and trees which prevented us from diverting into the adjacent fields, which looked as if they had been recently harvested of a cereal crop. The country stretched ahead in long rolling hills and we ground our way through the valleys in between in four wheel drive and often low ratio, leaning first to the left and then to the right.

Thus we made our painfully slow, grinding way towards El Obeid. There were frequent settlements and the flavour was becoming more African with round, thatched mud huts in small villages between the more Arabic, square concrete houses in the towns. Most of that second day and the next we struggled through continuous soft sand, stopping at Tendelti and Umm Ruwaba to buy bread and vegetables. Not until the fourth day after leaving Khartoum did we have some occasional respite from the soft ground but still it was mostly four wheel drive. We stopped at El Rahad on this fourth morning for water and a cup of tea, then took a track out of the town and got really bogged down though we never actually stopped. It soon became apparent that this was not the right way and that we were on no more than a donkey track through the fields. We eventually came upon a lone young man and his donkey and asked him for 'sharia khabir' or 'big road'. With no more ado, and certainly without considering the inconvenience to himself, he tied up his donkey and jumped into the Rover with us and directed us until we came in sight of what he indicated to be the sharia khabir. With this, and much handshaking and smiling of thanks, he cheerfully set off back to his beast which was now about three kilometres away.

The 'big road' revealed itself to be just a broad expanse of criss-crossing tracks in the sand but there was no doubt that this was the highway to El Obeid. We were now seeing our first Boabab trees, with their contorted, leafless branches stretching rigidly up to the sky and looking for all the world as if they had been planted upside down by some confused gardener. The land was much flatter with scattered thorny bushes. At one time we were startled as we wound between some small trees and great clouds of locusts (or crickets or something) emerged explosively and clattered around in annoyance until we had passed. Several became disorientated and careered through the open Rover windows, much to our consternation as they flipped about until they sat on the dashboard staring indignantly at us as if to say "What the bloody hell do you think you are playing at?".

At last the ground became firmer and we made better time on our final run into El Obeid. Here we found rough tarmac roads and Jan and ourselves pulled over to wait for Pallé, still some distance behind. The sudden peace and quiet after the continuous noise of the ride was broken by the chattering of an inquisitive horde of children and the steady hiss of air from one of Jan's front wheels as it gently deflated in an apparent sigh of relief after all its exertions. There followed an hour of glorious entertainment for a seething mass of both young and old onlookers as Jan, Pallé and myself struggled to undo the five wheel nuts (obviously tightened with a steam hammer), dig out the spare wheel from under the usual tumbled miscellany in the back of Jan's Rover and prepare him for the road again.

During this time a statuesque local woman had appeared from a nearby house and invited us all in for tea. Pallé had therefore drifted off with everyone else, including Björn who had remained in the Rover writing a letter throughout the proceedings. Jan and I found ourselves to be the only ones left at the vehicles and now made our way to where everybody else was being entertained in the garden of the lady's house. Our hostess was a very handsome Sudanese lady, remarkably slim for her age of about 40, with flashing gold teeth and jet black hair drawn tightly from her face. Her skin was a smooth dark brown and she had a fine pair of sparkling eyes and a ready laugh. Wrapped in black she looked splendid. Apart from our few words of Arabic we had no common language but it is amazing how well one can communicate with international facial expressions and sign language. After the Arab lands where women were rarely to be seen, and certainly not heard, we were pleasantly surprised by the emancipation of these women that we met in El Obeid. Whilst her husband sat smiling but silent in the background, our hostess prepared tea in a tiny pot over a charcoal fire. She was initially assisted by her daughters but as word of our arrival spread around the neighbourhood a succession of enormous women just happened to call in for a chat. They were a great bunch, chain smoking, laughing and obviously passing ribald comments about us. Focus inevitably centred on Jan and Björn when it was discovered that they were unmarried and big eyes were flashed and large bosoms provocatively wiggled at them until the whole assembly collapsed in hysterical laughter.

We reluctantly left (Jan and Björn with relief) at about four thirty and drove off to find the police station. We were now experienced at this and headed for the tall radio mast which was a feature of each town and below which could always be found the local constabulary. Because of the many districts that we passed through it was always necessary to report our presence to the authorities. Jan had met somebody in Khartoum who had asked him to deliver a letter to a teacher at the Catholic school in El Obeid and had also suggested that we might be able to camp there. Sure enough we were welcomed into the large grounds of the Comboni Boys School and allocated a comfortable corner of a grassy courtyard lined with trees and with the use of toilets and showers in the staff quarters. The following day was Friday and we looked forward to a restful day. It turned very cold that night. After our meal we sat talking for a long time to a young English teacher at the school. Apparently there had been considerable unrest in El Obeid due to a shortage of flour for bread, and four weeks previously there had been protest riots which culminated in shots being fired by the police and several people had been killed. This sort of shortage was not necessarily due to unavailability but was all too often the result of unscrupulous merchants withholding stocks to force a price rise. It was so sad that these normally kind and gentle townsfolk should be driven to such extreme measures simply to obtain a daily supply of bread which was such a vital part of their meagre diet.

*Some welcome R and R at the Comboni school in El Obeid*

The sourcing and purchase of bread was a daily chore for us. It was baked very early in the villages and the hot, round pitta breads were absolutely delicious when fresh. Unfortunately it kept for little longer than two days at the most by which time it would be dry and stale. Butter, if it could be found, could not be kept in the hot weather. The Rover refrigerator was of little use as we rarely travelled fast enough to generate enough electricity to power it, and we were not prepared to spare any of our precious supply of cooking gas to run it in its alternative mode. Hence our butter substitute was soft cheese portions, round boxes of which were usually available in the shops. Therefore breakfast consisted typically of bread, cheese and Marmite, or Dawn would have a boiled egg if we had some. Mid-morning we would stop for a cup of tea and our first cigarette – rationed now due to their cost. Lunch would be more bread and cheese with perhaps tomatoes or cucumber and then our evening meal would be a vegetable stew, vegetable curry or the occasional meatless spaghetti bolognese. No matter what the fresh food shortages, Dawn always managed to produce a substantial, nourishing and tasty meal. We didn't eat meat during most of the trip, the sights and flies at the open air butchers being rather off-putting. We were eating very simply but quite adequately. As our shopping had to be done daily it gave us the opportunity to wander around village markets and 'meet the people' as it were, but with our three different groups heading in different directions we started to find that it was taking up to two hours each day to pick up a few items, just one of the frustrations of travelling in company.

As promised, the Friday passed as a day of rest. This day our daily pitta bread was replaced with some excellent white bread rolls baked by the nuns. In the afternoon Dawn and I went for a stroll into town. On our way we passed a small stadium, defined as such by a pitch, a couple of small grandstands and four low, wooden floodlight towers which had obviously never been fitted with lights. Behind the stadium was the Catholic church, built as recently as 1961 and against the small surrounding buildings it looked as big as a cathedral but close up and inside it was the typical two storey height of any modern English church. It was constructed of large concrete blocks, painted white and brick red and was most imposing.

After our second night at the school the menfolk of our group rose early and we set off into town in search of the elusive bread supply. The flour situation had eased somewhat and we obtained hot bread without too much difficulty. After breakfast Jan and I went on another search, this time for petrol and our request at the police station was met, much to our surprise, with no comment and the necessary authorisation. After our experience in Khartoum we had calculated our fuel needs on multiples of forty four gallon drums and had requested, therefore eighty eight gallons. On finding the petrol station on the way out of town, however, we discovered normal petrol pumps and realised that we could have had the exact amount that we wanted. The unfortunate result was that once again we left with less fuel than we could have carried.

From El Obeid we were to make a diversion from the north/south route. Jan had two beautiful books of photographs taken by Leni Rufensthal, usually better known for her association with Adolf Hitler. A brilliant professional photographer and documentary film maker, she had paid several visits to Sudan and had actually discovered two groups of people who had remained virtually unchanged for centuries. Her books, 'The Last of the Nuba' and 'The People of Kau', were large, coffee table volumes published in 1973 and 1976 and filled with breathtaking colour pictures of these people and their way of life at that time. It was Jan's ambition to visit the Nuba area if at all possible on his way to Kenya and his enthusiasm inspired us all with the same object. Obviously we would not be the first travellers to do this and we were to find it prudent not to mention Ms Rufenstahl or her books. There was now some resentment from the Sudanese government over the apparent exploitation of their primitive tribes and embarrassment that people still lived there naked despite the strides that had been made to modernise the country.

From El Obeid, therefore, we headed off southwards to Kadugli, some 300 kilometres away. Once more it was rough going, with very little opportunity for fourth gear and following the inevitable wide lorry tracks. We barely made 70 kilometres that day before stopping for the night. In the morning of the next day, however, and just some 30 kilometres further on, we crossed a railway line and bounced up onto a tarmac road which was, in fact, indicated on Jan's Michelin map. We were now in flat country with much more vegetation and open wooded areas. We saw our first (and last!) wild monkeys along this stretch of road and stopped to watch a dozen of them scampering about a short distance away from us. Just after this we had our first puncture, in the front left hand wheel.

Kadugli, on the edge of the Nuba Mountains area, was a clean and tidy town consisting mainly of buildings strung along the tarmac road, which abruptly expired at the end of the town and returned to its usual bumpy state. Despite its small size and remote location, Kadugli was remarkably advanced and we were to subsequently meet some young English people teaching in the area and also some Brits assisting with some farming projects. Our first call was again the Catholic church where we hoped to glean more information about the locations of the Kau and Nuba tribes, but after awaiting the return of one of the priests we left little the wiser. Knowing that we would have to obtain permission to visit the mountains we drove to the outskirts of the town for the night before tackling the issue the next day.

Faced with the inevitable time consuming paperwork, Jan and Björn were left at the police station whilst the rest of us went shopping for provisions. In a large hardware store we came across the Syrian owner who arranged for our puncture to be repaired whilst he gave us tea and we discussed the road from Kadugli back to the main north/south route.

Leaving Kadugli at eleven o'clock we plunged into an area of eight foot high grass and almost immediately came across our first 'real African' with loincloth, tattoos and body paint. The transition was unbelievable and as we came to the first humps of the mountains rising sharply from the flat plain there were picturesque clumps of tiny, round thatched mud huts clinging to their steep lower reaches. The track that we were on wound through these low, rolling hills and next to cultivated fields. The mountains, though small, were very spectacular with an overall covering of green grass, huge tumbled grey boulders, majestic baobabs and large bushes of bright red flowers – bushes with no greenery, just a mass of blooms. We were moving through Sudan on the heels of the rainy season and just a few weeks before this area would have been inaccessible due to the wet and the mud, but now we reaped the benefits of the rain with the luxurious, prolific growth in the mountains. In the dry season the mountains would be parched and brown and the grass blackened by fires lit by the villagers to drive out small animals for food.

This timing was yet another stroke of luck on our trip. When we had left Oman we had had no idea of the implications of the African rainy season and the fact that it could have held us up for weeks.

A Nuba village

Of course we stopped to photograph the houses and each time we would be rapidly surrounded by an excited crowd of women and children who materialised from their apparently deserted villages. Throughout this area we always had the feeling that the residents had an equal, if not greater, fascination with us than we had with them and that if they had had cameras it would have been us that would have been the subjects of keen photographers eager to record the unusual people in their midst.

The 'villages' were in scattered but frequent groups of six or eight dwellings and each dwelling consisted of three or four tiny round huts clustered tightly together. Each hut had a specific use such as kitchen, bedroom or grain store. The walls were reddish brown plastered mud and the roofs were conical thatches of long grass. The walls would often be decorated with childlike stick people and simple patterns painted on with a grey pigment.

The people that we met in these first encounters looked poor and thin. The bodies of the women were covered in decorative raised skin patterns, or scarification, resulting from incisions or from pinching the skin and piercing it with small sharp slivers of wood to leave raised welts that formed elaborate patterns. On the older women these welts appeared to have merged together and had formed ugly deformities looking like the aftermath of bad burns. On the young girls, however, the effect was certainly enhancing. Ears were decorated by blanket stitching the edges with cord or wire and lower lips were pierced to allow the insertion of decorative plugs. Noses were not forgotten and were also pierced and sewn. Children and tiny babies abounded though children over the age of about ten were not in evidence and were presumably out with the men working in the fields.

There was a rather odd incident when Jan indicated that he wanted to take a photograph of one of the babies and, though the mother nodded her ready agreement, she also made it clear that she expected some token in return. Jan returned to his Rover and came back with a banana, a fruit which we had found to be readily available so far in Sudan and which we had purchased in Kadugli, just 50 kilometres away. To our amazement the women regarded the banana with blank incomprehension. It seemed that they had not seen one before and Jan had to perform a pantomime act of peeling and eating it before it was suspiciously accepted and passed around for tentative nibbles. It eventually met with approval and rapidly disappeared.

National dress?

The mountains came down to the plains like knuckles from a hand, and in each steep valley we found groups of huts and curious natives. We finally stopped for the night in a field between two villages and climbed down to absorb the sheer beauty of our surroundings. The sun was to set gloriously over more low mountains several miles away, silhouetting the trees like black statues. Before this, however, to the "plinky, plonk, plank, plink" of crude four string banjo-type instruments the men and younger women returned from the fields and came over to us, accompanied by dozens of children. They may have been isolated from the world a few short years ago but they were not now fazed by the appearance of motorized vehicles and strange white people. They trooped into our camp area and stood around chattering and laughing. Jan's books referred to the total nakedness of the Nuba people but they had by now been encouraged or persuaded to be more modest and both men and women were dressed in an incongruous assortment of brightly coloured boxer shorts, worn slung low to just above the pubic area and halfway down at the back across the buttocks. They therefore reached down to knee level and gave the odd impression of very long bodies and short legs. Whilst the women went barefoot, the men wore sandals or lace-less trainers and around their ankles were rings of wool socks, the feet of which had been cut off. These knitted rings were also worn around the wrists but perhaps these were the remains of woollen gloves?? A status symbol, and definitely a very cool look, was attained by the wearing of heavy dark sunglasses, decorated with locally added white lines and zig zags. Leni Rufenstahl referred to the noble wrestlers of the Nuba and the fact that community life revolved around the training and nurture of these magnificent physical specimens, who ate only the best food, did the least work and adorned their bodies with white ash. Some of the men around us did, indeed, have excellent physiques and certainly all our visitors that night looked exceedingly healthy and had ash patterns traced on their bodies, but the Western clothes robbed them of their former elitism and stature and reduced them in our eyes to rather grotesque African punks. The four string banjo instruments were carried by some of the young men and apparently they composed their own individual 'tunes' which they played over and over again.

Coming home from work

We thought it sad that such beautiful people should have been reduced to such comic characters by the imposition of a so called civilisation, presumably by both Moslem and Christian meddlers, but who were we to think that they should be left in the Stone Age and denied the benefits of modern civilisation?

These Nuba people were a delightful and happy bunch, fit and apparently healthy and quite relaxed about us white people visiting them with our intrusive cameras. In fact I would like to think of them returning to their homes, tearing off their ridiculous Western clothes and sunglasses and laughing hysterically at the way they had fooled the strange white people in their odd, smelly metal boxes.

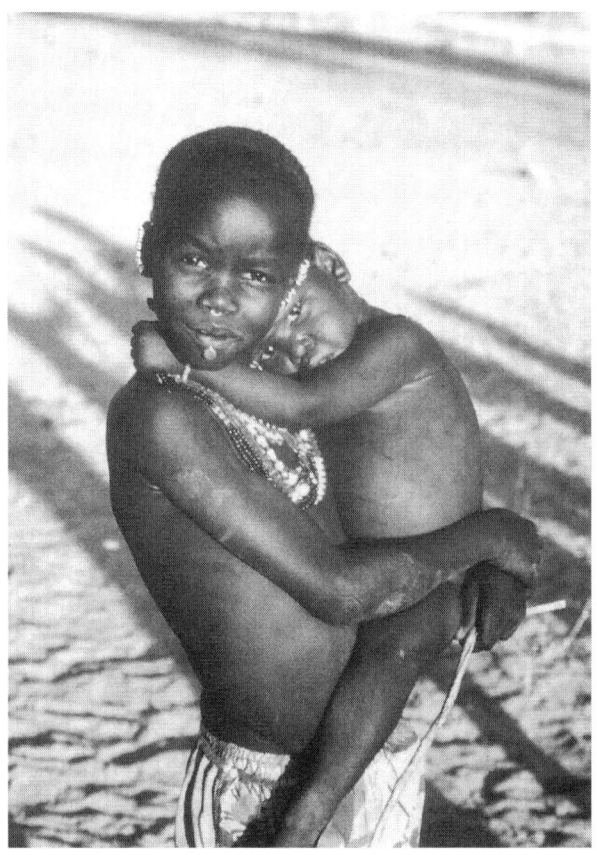

As the late afternoon wore on, the novelty of being surrounded by these primitive people gradually wore off, and as the sun set and we began to feel hungry we waited expectantly for them to return to their homes and their cooking fires. It would obviously not do for us to eat in front of them and we certainly could not entertain them all to dinner. The children were finally packed off and many of the adults followed them but a hard core of eight sat around amiably, sprawled in our picnic chairs and sipping mugs of tea that we had eventually felt obliged to provide. One fine young woman had seen Jan's meagre supply of cutlery and had gone into raptures over a dessert spoon. Jan was reluctant to part with it (none of us had excess equipment) and hung out for hours until we all joined the girl in her exhortations on the basis that once presented with the gift they would all go away. Jan reluctantly parted with the spoon but, alas, our friends stayed on – now presumably attracted by the wood fire which we had lit and which possibly hinted to them of cooked goodies to come. We all sat around with inane grins on our faces, by this time pretty much convinced that the only people being exploited round there were ourselves. Pallé and his family, who had remained a little distance away from our main group, eventually went into a quiet huddle and surreptitiously ate their dinner.

The eight guests reduced to three and then at seven thirty the three remaining stalwarts apparently abandoned hope of further refreshment and entertainment and strolled off home, no doubt not too late to partake of dinner there, and we all heaved sighs of relief and set to to produce our own meals.

After a hot and breezeless night, Dawn and I awoke at five thirty (not an hour that we were familiar with) to the subdued chattering of locals outside the Rover. A careful peek around the curtains revealed a couple of dozen or so of them hanging patiently about. Our travelling companions were already up and about, lacking the privacy that Dawn and I enjoyed in the Rover, and when we eventually emerged a while later it was to the astonishing sight of two queues of people, one to Jan and one to Pallé and Elizabeth, with individuals tendering a selection of wounds, sores and ailments for the ministrations of the white man's medicines. There seemed little doubt now that, despite their very recent awakening from thousands of years of no change, they were more than aware of the advantages of outside visitors with their offerings of food, clothing, medicines, polaroid photographs and glossy picture magazines. Very savvy people!

This impromptu and amateur clinic was somewhat over run. Jan was scrabbling about in his first aid bag with a harassed expression on his face, Pallé was nervously dabbing antiseptic onto some revolting looking ulcers and Elizabeth was trying to conduct a short course on hygiene to a group who were sporting new white bandages around various limbs.

Unfortunately neither Dawn nor Björn had any real interest in these unfortunate proceedings which had been thrust upon us but from deep within me there surfaced an urge to help and do my bit. With a bowl of water and Dettol and a container of antiseptic dusting powder I opened a third consulting room and went to work on a couple of leg ulcers. These puzzled us as they were quite common amongst our patients. At the time we assumed that they were infected insect bites but many months later a television programme about Sickle Cell Anaemia showed similar lesions on legs so perhaps that was what we were seeing.

With the casualty clinic over we turned our attentions to the more mundane complaints and solemnly doled out vitamin pills to cure headaches, backaches, tummy aches and all other internal complaints. No doubt many people would be horrified at our actions but we took care to be hygienic and I don't think that Dettol or vitamin pills ever did anybody any harm under similar circumstances. We didn't offer our services but they were clearly expected by the Nuba residents.

Finally putting away our Doctors and Nurses Kits we planned our activities for the rest of the day. Jan, Björn, Klaus and I wanted to climb into the hills, and set off with a local volunteer guide while Dawn and the rest of the group went to the nearby village to look around. The climb was splendid exercise and afforded us some spectacular views and afterwards our guide took us to the compound outside his house where he gave us peanuts and sesame seeds.

Camping in the Nuba mountains

Meanwhile Dawn was delving deeper into the way of life of these fascinating people and was shown into the hut of one of the young men, climbing through a small round entrance hole about twelve inches off the ground. Inside, his personal possessions were neatly displayed – more pairs of boxer shorts, a shirt and a pair of western trousers, gourds and charms to ward off evil spirits. Some magazine pictures bore testament to the presence of visiting travellers before us. It was interesting to note that the entrance holes to bedrooms were round, those to grain stores were oval and those to cooking facilities and food stores were a keyhole shape to allow the ingress of women with wide loads carried on their heads. Dawn was given peanuts and a type of yoghourt (origin unknown) and returned to the Rover with a bag of sesame seeds. She had also seen a couple of pigs, so the diet appeared not to be vegetarian. Water was drawn from a rather muddy waterhole and we were thankful of our own fresh supplies.

When we all returned to the vehicles it was to find them still surrounded by a milling crowd of interested visitors. Our campsite seemed to form a focal point for them that morning but they displayed no interest whatsoever in the Rovers. Dawn sat down amongst a group of the women and having gained their confidence she took some photographs of them before we all climbed back into our respective vehicles and went on our way. Despite the obvious disruption to their normal routine by our arrival, our departure met with only the odd wave and more generally a shrug of the shoulders as they sauntered back to their everyday lives until the arrival of the next batch of goggling visitors and their potential offerings of clothes, medicines and magazines….and spoons. Yet again I had the odd feeling that we were the objects of curiosity.

Continuing to skirt the southern edge of the mountains we wound our way past a few more kilometres of mud hut settlements and then suddenly we were back into Arab country populated with robed men and veiled women. The changes in the people were so sudden that I can only liken the experience to visiting film studios where one is transported all over the world and through history simply by stepping from one set to another. Admittedly the scenery remained the same but the style and size of both the individual huts and their grouped settlements were all now much larger. After about 35 kilometres we came to the town of Talodi, at the end of this particular mountain range, and found ourselves back in familiar surroundings of rough brick and concrete buildings, a central market square and noisy, overloaded lorries and a population of obviously Moslem Sudanese.

From Talodi we were to head back to Kadugli by taking a road through the mountains, running almost parallel to our outward route but a few kilometres to the north. This was the main route between Kadugli and Talodi, open all the year round and which contributed to the isolation of the Nuba people. The mountains were breathtakingly beautiful. They seemed so fresh and unspoilt and the huge outcrops of big, round, grey rocks prevented inundation by vegetation although determined baobab trees emerged from the most unlikely looking cracks and crannies. There were still many of the bright red-blossomed bushes, and their intermittent splashes of colour were like highlights added by an inspired artist to bring his canvas to life. We passed many more huts than we had expected to, and in the relatively short distance that we drove their styles changed from round to square, short to tall, smooth walled to those with foundations of large boulders and the circular thatched roofs varied in pitch and from layered thatch to plain thatch.

*A fascinating Baobab tree*

*Dried up river in the Nuba Mountains*

En route we stopped at the incredible sight of what appeared to be a complete village on the move and which headed towards us with a couple of hundred cattle and a few donkeys with household possessions including beds, mattresses and cooking pots carried on cattle and donkeys with their owners perched on the top. The procession shuffled past us in a cloud of dust and disappeared in the direction of Talodi. We thought at the time that this was a visit to the market to sell the cattle but in reality it was probably an annual move at the end of the wet season to find new grazing grounds.

After this we ran along a valley which had palm trees growing in it, yet another startling change. Just past these and near the village of Umdirah we stopped for a cup of tea and were approached by a tall native with a huge permanent grin showing a set of equally big teeth. After the usual polite greetings he urged us to join him and his friends at their thatched huts, a few hundred yards away. Always a little wary of local customs and expectations, Dawn and I, Jan and Björn nevertheless ambled over with him. His invitation had been accompanied by the apparently universal mime of tipping a glass to ones lips and I, for one, interpreted this to mean that alcohol of some kind was on offer and was naturally keen to investigate. We climbed up a low rise at the base of the mountains and were introduced to the most delightful, happy-go-lucky group of people ranging from grandma and grandad to sons and daughters, husbands and wives, aunts and uncles. Before us the mountains bulged up to the bright blue sky, to the left were some square mud huts, enclosed in their spotlessly clean yards by mud walls, and to the right was a grassy mound beneath the abundant shade of an enormous tree. Sprawled on the ground or seated on long benches our hosts were enjoying a blissful afternoon of bonhomie and relaxation. After cheerful greetings and handshakes I discovered that my instinct for alcohol had not let me down and that a significant contributing factor to the bonhomie lay visible in a large gourd bowl. The liquid in the gourd was thick and browny-orange and fermented from sorghum and dates and called Marissa. In the liquid floated a smaller gourd and we were invited to use this to take a taste. Not quite your traditional English ale, but an acquired taste that I quickly acquired and quaffed happily. Dawn, being more the gin and tonic type, politely declined any more after a first tentative sip. Bowls of unshelled peanuts materialised and members of the family busied themselves cracking them for us. Dawn was firmly adopted by an ancient old lady with a tremendous sense of humour and who cracked peanuts for her alone and refused point blank to help anybody else. One of the younger women came across. She was trying in vain to suckle her baby on a somewhat deflated breast. She eyed Dawn's attributes appreciatively then clearly indicated that perhaps she could assist with the feeding. Not an easy predicament to explain your way out of in sign language, particularly in a society where most young women would be either pregnant or nursing a baby most of the time. As ever, Dawn rose to the occasion and managed to convey her inability to oblige, resulting in puzzled looks and sympathetic head shaking from the womenfolk. The gourd rapidly emptied as it passed around the assemblage and a large white, galvanised bucketful took its place.

Well, it was very, very pleasant sitting there, but time, as ever, marched on and we reluctantly had to take our leave. Our original host and the grandfather accompanied us back to the vehicles, the latter bearing the dregs of Marissa in the bottom of the bucket. These we carefully poured into one of Jan's empty water containers. At this point the old man was seized by a succession of racking pains which he manfully overcame when we produced some 'magic pills' and he went happily away clutching the empty bucket and a selection of vitamin tablets.

A delightful interlude and we drove off with yet more vivid memories. I have often pondered on our interlude with the Nuba people. Whilst I have travelled a considerable amount around the world I have always felt a little uncomfortable when intruding upon the everyday lives of native people, particularly to take photographs and in obviously poor communities. Sometimes there are overt attempts to obtain money for photographs and sometimes there is annoyance at one's presence. One can be very aware of the huge difference in wealth, waving about a camera which may represent an unattainable small fortune to an Indian villager, for example. Nevertheless I never felt that the Nuba were in any way jealous of us or our possessions – except, of course, for Jan's spoon. They took no interest in our vehicles or of the contents thereof. They were happy to welcome us and show us where they lived but I always had the feeling that they were as interested in us as we were in them and that, far from being envious of us, they even felt a little sorry for these white people who lived in tiny, cramped metal boxes and wandered through their country like lost souls. No wonder they returned happily to their comfortable mud huts and their crops and their families and friends when we drove off.

We spent our final night in the Nuba region just outside Kadugli, and drove into the town the following day for food and fresh water. At the Catholic church this time we met Father John, a young, rotund Italian priest whom we found tremendously interesting to talk to and who knew a considerable amount about the local tribes. He had a very non-dogmatic attitude towards religion, presumably gained from his many years in the area. There is a haunting play written by Brian Friel called 'Dancing at Lughnasa', set in Northern Ireland in 1936. One of the characters is Father Jack, an elderly Catholic missionary who returns from Africa after many years there. It becomes apparent as the play progresses that not only has he become slightly mentally disturbed due to malaria but also that he has 'gone native' and that his religion has become a confused mix of Catholicism and African pagan beliefs complete with animal sacrifices. Without intending any disrespect, I thought that Father John was very reminiscent of Father Jack.

We left Kadugli for El Fula with a very noble looking, bearded African Moslem in Jan's Rover as a guide, which was just as well, as the departure point to El Fula from the tarmac road was almost invisible and the route thereafter none too clear. We were back on plains with short grass and scattered trees, very reminiscent of some English countryside. We dropped off our guide and came to the village of Lagowa where we found sugar and rice. This was the first rice that we had seen and also the first sugar for a very long time. Jan and Björn were nearly out of sugar and this was a most unlikely place to find it, being a very small village. The next surprise was when we came to purchase some and found that it was sold in pounds not kilograms. This tiny village was the only place that we found in the whole of Sudan that used imperial weights.

Friday the fifth of December 1980 started off as any other day on our journey but was to be probably the worst. The first thing to happen was the loss of our hosepipe. This was just a ten foot length which I used to fill our water tank and plastic containers from taps, and it was carried strapped inside the back door with the two camp chairs. On removing the chairs each day I put the pipe up on the roof, out of the way, and on this particular morning I forgot to retrieve it and stow it, only remembering some time later after it had fallen onto the track probably many kilometres before. We also lost our stiff hand brush which was the only thing to use to keep the carpet of the Rover clean and free from dirt and debris. Björn had taken to borrowing it and that morning left it lying at the camping spot, no doubt much to the joy of a local who later found it. Minor items but virtually impossible to replace en route and so important for our simple daily tasks.

Our convoy left the campsite and although we were scheduled to take the lead, Pallé surprised us all by volunteering for pole position and so we moved to the rear, which certainly sealed the fate of the hosepipe. It was another beautiful day and the track for once was wide, flat and firm and we were able to bomb along in fine style. We gradually lost sight of the others and lost more time when we stopped to photograph a particularly unusual group of baobabs. We were travelling fast and easily through an open area which turned gently to the left and into some trees. As the curve unfolded before us I looked in developing horror at the way the surface had become altered by previous traffic. The ground under the trees was soft and the continual passage of the big souk lorries with their widely spaced rear wheels had produced two deep ruts much wider than the Rover wheels. These ruts had become steeply banked as they turned and the gap between them was a significant and solid mound. Before I had time to brake, our right hand wheels had dropped into the right hand rut, only to hop out almost immediately as the left hand wheels pulled us over the mound and into the left hand rut, rocking the Rover in an alarming fashion. Our momentum and the deep grooves then threw us back to the right again and our progress became a chaotic bouncing zig zag from one side to another. The suspension was taking a real hammering and the rocking increased and increased until the inevitable end and we crashed onto our left side at forty five degrees across the track. I remember thinking that here was the end of the whole adventure and I let out an anguished cry of "Oh, Dawn!" just before we stopped and everything went very quiet. Immediately lessons learnt from reading Biggles books in my youth kicked in and I reached for the ignition and turned it off. There were about 30 gallons of petrol in cooking oil plastic containers on the roof – well, now on the side – and that first few seconds were spent in tensely listening and sniffing for any signs of leaking liquid. Silence.

I reached behind me for the fire extinguisher and then looked down at Dawn, who was buried under a blanket of red and blue air mail envelopes, maps and cassette tapes which had been thrown out of the storage box between the seats. Just her face was visible, looking anxiously up at me. It appeared that neither of us had been hurt so I turned my attention to getting out, pushing up the door and disentangling my feet from the pedals. The problem was that I had

171

nowhere to push my feet against. My first probings brought "Ouches" from Dawn as I inadvertently trampled on her. The storage box had partially collapsed and would not take my weight so it took a bit of scrabbling before I emerged and sat on the side of the Rover. Still no signs of fire so with a "Hang on, I'll let you out" I hopped down to the ground and rushed around to where the passenger door should have been and was, of course, confronted with the unfamiliar sight of the roof of the Rover. Collecting my thoughts a bit I retraced my steps and found Dawn's grinning face popping up out of the driver's door.

Realising that we were pretty helpless until aid arrived, we dug out cameras and cigarettes, took some photos and sat down for a very welcome smoke. An examination of the damage revealed nothing as bad as I had expected and it just looked as if the Old Girl had laid down gently for a nap. The roof rack was obviously a bit bent but the petrol containers were still securely strapped in place and not leaking. Swinging open the bonnet I removed the battery but then there was nothing more to be done until we were back upright on our wheels again. Our personal injuries amounted to very little, Dawn had a couple of grazes on her right elbow and left shoulder blade and a bruise on her left cheek. I had hit my head on one of the overhead switches resulting in a slight cut and a satisfying trickle of blood to add to the drama of the scene. I had never fitted seat belts to the Rover but doubt that they would have made much difference.

We had not seen Pallé or Jan for over an hour, and assumed that they must be way ahead and that it could be a couple of hours before they returned looking for us. In fact, Jan had overtaken Pallé and gone on ahead but Pallé was only about a kilometre in front of us and barely out of sight. He, too, had had a bad experience in the deep ruts, despite travelling at a much lower speed than us and he had had what can only be described as a premonition of our disaster and instead of doing the usual thing and just sitting and waiting for us to catch up, he turned around and came back to look for us. Quite remarkable. And so it was that within just five minutes or so of us coming to grief, Pallé rumbled into sight with a sense of timing that the US cavalry would have been proud of.

In no time at all we unloaded the gear on the roof rack and with our tow rope and chain looped around our chassis, Pallé easily pulled us back upright. Back on her wheels again the Rover looked a little bit lop-sided. The roof rack and the front left wing had both been pushed several inches to the right and, indeed, the whole top of the Rover had moved about half an inch to the right. In addition, the rear right hand wheel rim had been slightly buckled and the wheel had to be changed. Fortunately it seemed that little or no mechanical damage had been suffered. In fact, the worst effects of the incident were to be found when we opened the rear door and found that the catch on the door on the cupboard under the cooker had broken and the contents of the cupboard had cascaded down and out and over the sink unit. These contents were predominantly rice, flour, dried potato powder and custard powder and every packet or container had burst open to create an appalling mess. With a resigned sigh Dawn set to work to clean it all up, and it was then that the loss of the hand brush was discovered and I think that Dawn's anger towards Björn served to take her mind off things a bit!

173

*Chaos in the back*

Elizabeth and the boys helped Dawn with the cleaning up and I refitted the battery and hopefully tried starting the engine. It turned slightly then stopped immovably and I had to remove all the spark plugs and spin the engine to pump out the engine oil that had collected in the cylinders. With the plugs cleaned, dried and refitted the engine started first time and I turned my attention to the bodywork. By attaching the chain to, first, the left hand wing and then to the roof rack and tugging it with Pallé's Rover, I managed to straighten out the bent bodywork to a surprising degree, and with the roof rack re-loaded there was virtually no visible external evidence of our mishap. Internally things were looking much brighter, too, and once the front box was knocked back together and its contents re-packed, the only sign that something had happened was a stain of white powder and rice in the carpet. Dawn valiantly tackled it with a nailbrush and no doubt her thoughts of Björn became blacker and blacker.

Well, some four and a half hours after the accident we were ready to go. Pallé had kept us supplied with tea and cool drinks – it was very hot with little shade from the trees – and five local lorries had all kindly stopped to check if they could help. We set off rather cautiously but everything seemed to be fine, though I didn't go very fast and never did regain my confidence in the Rover's lateral stability on steep slopes. An hour and a half later we caught up with Jan just outside El Fula, who was suitably contrite, if not a little embarrassed, about his absence from the events. After all, he should have been between Pallé and us. Still, all was well that ended well, no serious damage was done and a good tale to tell in the future.

Not surprisingly, we felt exhausted and after our evening meal we had a welcome early night, only to be met the following morning by the sight of a very flat right hand rear tyre. This I replaced with our second spare so we now had two useless wheels, one with a puncture and the other with a bent rim. It was also obvious that the roof rack would need structural repair if it was to survive the conditions we were driving through. There was nothing to be done at the time and we had about 100 kilometres to go to reach Babanusa which was back on the main route to our destination of Wau. Hopefully Babanusa would have some facilities to enable work to be done. Once again we found ourselves by the side of the railway track, driving along a small embankment on one side. With the track to our left and a line of tall bushes and trees to our right just three metres from the track we had little choice of route. The other side of the track had an even steeper embankment and denser vegetation. Occasionally we could drive onto flatter ground away from the line but inevitably the undergrowth would push us back to the embankment. It was an unfortunate situation after our experience the previous day. Time after time we heeled over as we crawled along the bank and time after time we imagined the Rover tipping over again. At one particular spot, trapped tightly at a steep angle on the bank by the bushes and trees, I came to a halt, fearful to go either forward or back without tipping onto our side. Jan was ahead and had found a better route through the bushes. Pallé was behind and we ended up with Dawn driving the Rover and inching along with myself, Pallé, Elizabeth and Klaus walking alongside pushing on the roof to balance out the forces of gravity. Back on more level ground Pallé followed Jan's example and avoided this particular section.

With considerable relief we reached Babanusa at about three that afternoon. A typical small town again, situated at a major junction where the railway line ran off to Nyala in the west or turned south down to Wau. We found the market area and met several English travellers who were traversing Sudan by means of local transport. We also found a compound belonging to Geosource, an English oil service company who had also been in Oman and who were associated with the exploratory drilling for oil in that part of Sudan. We strolled over and introduced ourselves and though sympathetic they were not in a position to let us use their workshop facilities. Instead we were directed to a milk factory and a Doctor Dahi who would, they thought, be able to help us. It seemed a bit odd, a milk factory in such an arid area but, clutching a note from Geosource, we returned to our companions outside. At El Fula, Jan had once again taken a passenger on board, this time an Egyptian schoolteacher who wanted to get to El Muglad, 40 kilometres beyond Babanusa. We agreed, therefore, that Jan and Pallé should continue on to El Muglad whilst we remained in Babanusa, hopefully managing to carry out repairs to the Rover and then catching up with them the following afternoon. It seemed very strange saying goodbye and being left on our own again after all the time spent together, and I think that they felt much the same and left rather reluctantly.

Dawn and I headed for the intriguing sounding milk factory, which we found on the outskirts of the town, a tall, neglected looking cream building surrounded by equally neglected single storey buildings in a large fenced compound. Our enquiries at the gate led us to a house down the road where we ran to earth Dr Dahi. This fine gentleman was a well educated Sudanese who was the senior engineer at the factory. He quite happily agreed to help us and also satisfied our curiosity about the place. Apparently it was just one of several Russian aid projects in Southern Sudan, completed some years before and abandoned to local administration when the Russians left the country. The plan had been to utilise the milk from the large herds of cattle belonging to the nomadic Dinka tribesmen. The theory was that this would encourage the Dinka to increase the yields of their animals, thus making them more money, and the resulting milk would be processed and dried and distributed all over the region. A laudable and logical plan but unfortunately nobody thought to consult the actual tribesman who had little interest in finance and sought only to improve their standing in the community by owning more and more cattle with bigger and bigger horns. As long as he had sufficient milk to meet the needs of his family and a few others, why work harder to produce more? Certainly the sight of a gleaming new factory and the promise of cash returns failed to inspire them and after some initial vague interest they had shrugged their shoulders and drifted off on their nomadic way.

Sadly, the factory was therefore of little interest or use and had produced its best output back in the mid-seventies with just seventy tonnes of milk powder representing less than five percent of the its potential capacity. At the time of our visit it was limping along with a skeleton staff producing a little milk powder but its main product was Karkadeh or Karkadi which was manufactured from hibiscus flowers using a freeze drying process identical to that for milk powder. The resulting red powder was added to water to make a refreshing cold drink. The factory also processed some Gum Arabic, from the Acacia tree, which was a major export of Sudan.

As the years passed the Russian vehicles broke down and they were cannibalised for spares, the result being dozens of partially stripped jeeps and tanker lorries – but unfortunately no Land Rovers.

We encountered two similar white elephant projects during our travels in Sudan. In Wau the Belgians were building a brewery. At that time alcohol was available throughout Sudan but under some restriction. It could be bought in the hotels and clubs in Khartoum and we had purchased bottled beer and wine from a discreet outlet in the Khartoum market. Unfortunately, by the time that the Wau brewery was up and running the Moslem government had introduced Sharia Law in 1983 and refused to grant it a licence. The third odd factory we heard about was one for producing small, retail tins of tomato paste, despite there being no locally grown tomatoes and the fact that the paste would have to be imported in large cans and transferred into small ones. All the metal would be imported, too.

Next to the milk factory was a rest house which belonged to it, and which was looked after by a caretaker and used presumably for visitors as there were no suitable hotel facilities in the town. Like all the buildings it was very shabby. Dr Dahi said that we could camp in the grounds that night, which was ideal as we then had running water and toilet facilities. Once again we were glad of an early night, still feeling the emotional effects of the crash the day before.

Leaving Dawn with a huge pile of washing I set off for the factory at seven o'clock the next morning. Dr Dahi was as good as his word and assigned three men to help me. I removed the roof rack and with a sledge hammer and an anvil we made a credible job of straightening it. Some welding would have helped but there was no electricity, not an unusual situation in Babanusa, apparently. The sledgehammer also straightened the bent wheel rim and then my willing crew went to work on the punctured tyre using a variety of broken vehicle springs as tyre levers. I replaced the punctured tube with a brand new one and then we took the wheel to a massive Russian truck whose inbuilt compressor inflated it in about five seconds. In the compound were a pair of overgrown concrete ramps and I was able to drive up on them to inspect the underside of the Rover. All seemed well, just some worn rubbers on a front shock absorber. This shock absorber was not the right size, being about an inch too short and therefore causing extra stress and wear on the end mounting rubbers. I had expected it to fail before now, considering the rough tracks that we had negotiated. I therefore scoured the workshop for a suitable replacement but to no avail. Finally I borrowed an oil pump and topped up the gearboxes and axles. Having expressed my profound thanks to Dr Dahi and his men I returned to the rest house at midday where Dawn was struggling with a water supply that was never much more than a dribble.

With the vehicle now fully inspected and repaired, all our clothes clean and a couple of hours rest, we set off in the late afternoon for El Muglad feeling much happier. The route was along a dusty track, nice and flat and winding gently through bushes and trees. Along the way we saw many toucans, but none with a pint of Guiness on their beaks. Despite many attempts we failed to take a decent photograph of one.

We located our travelling companions camped in a yard at the rear of the government guest house. With no hotels in these poor towns the government had provided these small hostels where travellers could stay for a small sum, although you needed your own bedding. This particular place was a medium sized thatched building reminiscent of an old English farmhouse. The grounds of such places always provided us with an ideal campsite with rudimentary toilets and some running water.

The next day, after calling at a Chevron drilling camp for fresh water, we set off south for Wau, the next major milestone on our journey and some 500 kilometres away. From the flat plains we dropped slightly into a vast area which was obviously waterlogged in the wet season. Yet again it brought home to us just how lucky we were not to have arrived earlier, as it was obvious that it was only just dry enough to take us even in early December.

We were now in dense woodland with high grass and the narrow track winding like a switchback through the trees. The ruts could be very deep, formed in the soft mud and now baked hard and unyielding by the sun. Here we came across uncivilised-looking natives wearing just loincloths and with their heads shaved to leave a fuzzy tuft in the centre of the crown. Each man carried half a dozen slender spears, presumably not for decoration. We had the strong impression that these people were not familiar with white travellers and they regarded us warily – as we did them, with those spears. Regaining slightly higher ground the track took us through more open areas with the trees in scattered clumps. In the clearings were thatched huts built up on one metre wooden stilts to keep them clear of the waters in the wet season. This was probably as primitive an area as we had come across so far and the inhabitants looked destitute and ill-fed compared to the happy people in the Nuba mountains not so very far away.

This type of terrain continued the next day with some bad patches of dangerous ruts weaving through two metre high grass. Emerging from one particularly dense patch of forest we entered a small village and almost collided with a Toyota Hiace coming the other way. On the sides of this unlikely looking vehicle were various stickers advertising motoring accessories and large panels with Swaziland-London stencilled in bold, black letters. Inside, the back was packed with the most incredible jumble of boxes, food, sand tracks and clothes and in the front sat a very precisely spoken English colonialist type gentleman and a chatterbox of an American lady who was all teeth and spectacles. We spent an interesting fifteen minutes with them, exchanging information and being treated by this effervescent lady to a ceaseless and minute account of the route whilst surrounded by amazed and somewhat startled villagers. It was hard to imagine these two surviving the journey in their Hiace but people have travelled to the most unlikely places in the similar sized VW Combi, so who knows? It hadn't been unusual to struggle through a mountain pass in Oman, grinding up in the Rover in four wheel drive and low ratio only to be casually overtaken at the top by a Toyota taxi bouncing merrily along on its regular run between remote villages.

Soon after that we turned sharp right and drove 50 kilometres along a built up causeway, obviously constructed to provide access in the wet season. This was a fast section and we reached the magnificent speed of 40 kilometres an hour. At three thirty we reached the River Lol, which the American lady had told us was a difficult crossing. It was about three hundred feet across. During the wet season a manually operated ferry was in operation, but the water level had now dropped and the ferry was beached on a sandbank a little way downstream. Nevertheless the depth was still nearly three feet on our side of the river, shelving up to an easy exit on the far side. Obviously this would dry up completely in the coming weeks. The Swaziland Hiace couple had conceded defeat and paid a fee to the local villagers to haul them bodily across with a rope. We were assured that it was fine for Land Rovers, though. A little upstream was a railway bridge and only a couple of weeks before the river had been impassable by either ferry or ford and vehicles had been moved across on flat bed railway wagons. We were intrigued to hear that Bruno had passed this way three or four days earlier and had actually driven over the railway bridge, a kilometre or so hair raising experience, for despite the irregularity of the train service one did exist and who knew when one might come along. We were going to have to ford the river and Jan elected to go first, taking Dawn with him so that she could photograph me coming over. Together with a group of villagers we watched with bated breath as Jan eased steeply down into the water and then forged without mishap across and up onto the far bank despite a bow wave high up his radiator. I had experienced trouble back in Oman when driving along a wadi with just a few inches of water in it, when it had splashed up and wet the distributor, bringing me to a halt. A little voice now urged me to apply sticky tape to the distributor before attempting the crossing, a voice that I chose to ignore, and I headed into the water with my fingers crossed. Alas, only a few metres in, the engine spluttered and died and I stopped in about two feet of water, which meant that it was just up to the bottom of the front doors but not flowing inside. I hopped out and splashed round and opened the bonnet. I tried to dry the distributor but as soon as I turned the engine with the starter the fan dipped into the water and threw it back over the electrics again. I now noticed that the gentle flow of the river was slowly eroding the sand from around the wheels, causing it to sink with the result that the water level was rising, threatening to soak all the carpets. Meanwhile, back on the bank Pallé was doing sterling work haggling with the locals to agree a price for hauling me out. I floundered about helplessly. The water was by then an inch deep in the Rover cab and fast approaching the rear entry level. Pallé finally shook hands on a figure of about £5.00 and I unwound the tow rope ready for two dozen or so locals who waded in and pulled me ignominiously across with much shouting and chanting. Then Pallé drove uneventfully across – simply adding to my embarrassment.

Half the village muster to pull the Rover out of the river.
Jan leads the way with a distinct look of amusement.

Dawn had not been too well for the past two days and that plus the accident, followed by the failure in the river, left me feeling very despondent. We stopped for the night just beyond the river crossing and Dawn promptly fell asleep for a couple of hours.

Though we didn't know it at the time, the delay at the river was going to have repercussions far beyond the Rover breakdown. At the ferry village we had noticed a young boy of about nine years old who had a hideously swollen neck with long, open sores slashed across it. Through his cotton shift his heart could be seen beating very fast, and although on his feet and walking about, he looked very ill. The boy had TB, contracted from the unpasteurised milk that was drunk by all the people and a common complaint amongst the Dinka people. His condition was a secondary infection of the lymph glands.

After making camp Pallé sat very quietly for some time, and then had a long discussion with Elizabeth. He then approached the rest of us and declared that he wanted to try and help the boy by offering to take him to Wau, a sizeable looking town on the map where there must be a hospital capable of suitable treatment. He stated that he would only do so if the rest of us supported him. Wau was now only about 200 kilometres away and therefore we should easily get there the following day, so we all readily agreed, assuming that the boy and his family accepted, of course. Pallé immediately drove off alone to make contact with the boy and make his offer, returning an hour later to say that he had met the boy's father and that he was very willing to accept our help.

Thus it was that we were up and about early the next day, Dawn feeling back to normal. Pallé left and soon returned with the boy, whose name we discovered was Hassan, and his father, having politely refused the offer of a live goat in payment, and our convoy took to the road. We were on another raised causeway, in poor condition, and we bounced our way to Aweil just a few kilometres down the road. We stopped for shopping and passed a small medical centre on the way in. Elizabeth was looking a bit stressed and the smell from Hassan's sores was making her feel nauseous. Young Michael was also showing signs of strain so we transferred him to our Rover. I don't think that Elizabeth and the boys really wanted anything to do with the situation, an impression that strengthened in the following days, and it was a huge tribute to Pallé's unselfish and compassionate nature that he valiantly stuck to his promise to the boy despite upsetting his own family. For him it was to be a very difficult personal experience without the support of his wife and sons, and he was to sum it all up at the end when he said that despite his own misgivings and a rational instinct that told him not to get involved, he decided that for once in his life he was going to do something that was not rational but which he simply thought was right.

Having seen the small clinic at Aweil I suggested to Pallé that we seek the advice of the local clergy, evidence of which was a large and impressive red brick church a short distance away. This magnificent building was to be typical of many such examples we were to come across in Southern Sudan and which all bore testament to the stature and affluence of the Catholic Church there. We found vast complexes of churches, halls, seminaries and nunneries all built of the distinctive red bricks but which had all seen their heyday some years before, and the civil war and poverty had reduced these once proud institutions to struggling monuments of a bygone era.

Nevertheless, whilst the material wealth had diminished, spiritual wealth was abundant, albeit administered by probably just a fraction of the number of God's servants who had once worked here. In particular we met some inspiring nuns who were giving unstintingly of their lives in a continuous battle against poverty, illness, food shortages, politics and mounting religious oppression from the Moslem government in the north. In a tiny house next door to the Aweil church, Pallé and I met Sister Mary, a Ugandan nun who had fled her country under the Amin regime and who was now, with one other nun and a single priest, struggling to run a home for three hundred and fifty orphans of the civil war. Who were we, with our money and our Land Rovers, to ask for help from such an already overburdened community? Sister Mary explained that the hospital had no doctors and that only minor casualties could be cared for there, with virtually no trained staff, equipment or medicines. Very saddened by her tale, Pallé and I returned to the vehicles where the shoppers had collected having found little in the way of foodstuffs.

The Michelin map described the road from Aweil to Wau as being "improved and all weather". It was evident that much work had been done at some time to build up and grade the surface, but neglect had reduced it not to ruts and potholes but to kilometre upon kilometre of huge corrugations. We had been used to these corrugations in Oman but had never come across anything quite like these before. Formed by the outsize wheels of the souk lorries, these monster ripples rattled every piece of wood, metal and bone and I swear that there were times when my vision blurred as even my eyeballs vibrated. The noise was awful and the wheels banged from ridge to ridge as the suspension sought in vain to cope. Somewhere along this stretch the motor drive to the electric aerial disappeared without trace from under the left hand wing. Theoretically it was possible to accelerate to a speed where the ride, though noisy, was relatively smooth. We found that at 60 kilometres an hour we ironed out the worst of the ride but it was difficult to reach that speed with the wheels in mid-air half the time. Having reached that speed it was a case of hang on grimly and try and maintain some directional control. Cornering was like driving on ice and the Rover sort of floated and skated on even the slightest bends. In addition there were occasional potholes and other surface deformities which looked like suspension breakers and with no hope whatsoever of slowing down in time they had to be negotiated with tensed bodies and crossed fingers. Slowing from 60 to a stop was the worst, as everything went out of synchronisation and one seriously wondered how the vehicle could survive such an onslaught. The only option to driving at 60 was to drive very slowly, one ridge at a time. Jan decided to speed ride, Pallé took the 5 kilometres an hour slow ride and we alternated between the two, finding it difficult to reach the magic 60, anyway. I found the whole thing very frustrating and as a consequence my temper suffered and I became more and more irritated as we rattled along. By the road were dotted more small, stilted villages with their attendant spear toting inhabitants, and one wonders what they made of these white men hurtling past their huts raising huge clouds of dust with teeth clenched and fixed stares, accompanied by an ear shattering crescendo of rattling and banging.

******

Some 30 kilometres from Wau we bounced and shook to a halt next to Jan, who had stopped and waved us down. We were in a village and Jan led us to the shade of some trees where a group of locals was gathered. In the midst of them, lying propped up on one elbow, was a young teenage boy, a smart looking warrior with his hair set and styled with mud, his body decorated with raised skin patterns and wearing just a simple loincloth. His right knee was bent painfully at ninety degrees and Jan indicated an appalling fifteen inch long burn which ran on the outside from behind the knee and down the calf. The skin was shrivelled and singed and a deep half inch wide gash of raw red flesh was exposed. Apparently he had wrapped himself tightly in a blanket the previous night and lain down close to the fire to sleep. Whilst asleep he had rolled onto the fire and the result was before us. The local treatment had been to cover it with a sticky liquid – probably honey – but the group now looked silently to us and the White Man's Medicine which they realised was necessary.

Friends of the boy with the burnt leg.

The awful wound was patently beyond our limited capabilities but we still had no reason to doubt the existence of an adequate hospital at Wau and therefore offered to take the boy there. All this communication somehow took place without a single word of common language between us and the acceptance of our offer was quite clear. Michael was therefore transferred again and sat in with Jan and Björn and a group of the villagers lifted the boy and placed him in the back of our vehicle, sitting him on a piece of plastic sheet to keep the sticky stuff off the carpet.

And so we drove the last 30 kilometres to Wau, still on the bone-shattering corrugations and more like a fleet of ambulances than a group of overlanders. We entered Wau at about five o'clock and saw the wonderful sight of a tarmac road. Our relief was short lived when we drove onto this blacktop and found it to be just as jolting as the track, and we quickly abandoned it for the dirt again. Further into the town conditions improved and we found ourselves in what was now to us a typical dusty Sudanese town with one and two storey buildings and stores which were firmly closed as the sun went down. By amazing good luck we drove along until we came across a short driveway leading through an open double gate across the top of which was welded in steel letters the welcome words "Wau Civil Hospital". We entered a compound reminiscent of an army barracks block with long, single storey brick blocks with corrugated iron roofs. It all looked rather deserted and crossing the weed infested central yard we parked next to a pair of derelict Land Rover ambulances and set out to make contact with the Sudanese Health Service. We found the "Out Patients" clinic, a squalid, dimly lit building through the open doors of which could be discerned depressing green painted brick walls and grubby cream cabinets. The floor was bare concrete and covered with an accumulation of dirt and debris. A sad group of patients sat on benches in the twilight outside, their expressionless faces indicative of little hope in the facilities available. There was a marked absence of any staff , then or, in fact, on any subsequent visit no matter what time of day, but the appearance of Europeans soon resulted in a young orderly, who spoke good English, coming onto the scene to see what we wanted. We explained about our two patients and that we hoped that something could be done for them. We were informed that our boy must go to the police station to obtain a 'Form 8' to allow him admittance to the hospital. We had just struggled to help the lad out of the Rover and in vain I suggested that I go to the police on my own, so we heaved him back in again. It had been a long and taxing day and by this time I was starting to feel pretty tired and irritable. Two young men climbed in with us and directed me to the police station, just a short distance away, and the first thing I saw on entering the yard was Bruno's Land Rover parked in one corner. I assisted my wincing patient out once more and helped him hop up the steps to the office where the usual dirty bare walls, dim lighting and generally depressing atmosphere awaited. With the help of the two youths I explained the situation to the desk officer and then left them to fill in the paperwork whilst I went out to renew my acquaintance with Bruno and Elizabeth. To my surprise Elizabeth seemed overjoyed to hear that we were in town. I think that she was feeling the strain and loneliness of travelling on their own. Bruno was his usual rather reserved self but after a short exchange of news said that the police were quite happy for us to stay in their yard. Bruno had been there for three days trying to find petrol and was optimistic of getting away within the next couple of days. He painted a gloomy picture of the petrol situation. By this time we had emptied all our portable fuel containers and were down to just a few pints in the tank. My entourage appeared from the office so I took my leave of Bruno, stating that I expected that we would all be arriving soon to spend the night with them. As it turned out this didn't happen and this was to be the last I saw of our Swiss friends.

Back at the hospital I learned that Pallé's passengers had been admitted without formality and that the diagnosis of secondary TB had been confirmed. This would receive the standard treatment of a course of Streptomycin antibiotics and it was expected that the boy would make a full recovery. Excellent news. We had also learnt that our boy was called Ukele.

Ukele was apparently of the Jur tribe and was assigned to a casualty ward and Dawn and I helped him across to it. By now it was almost dark and the silence and gloom of the place was almost creepy. The ward was in one of the long barrack-like buildings, the entrance through a dirty rickety flyscreen and an unpainted door. Through a shadowy vestibule the ward stretched before us, barely lit by a couple of very low wattage bulbs. There were about ten beds down each side but only a handful of recumbent patients. Ukele was pointed to a bed just inside the door and we looked in shock at the filthy, soiled mattress on the equally dirty bed frame. There were no sheets, blankets or pillows. A grubby, rickety doorless wooden cabinet stood by the bed on top of which was a wooden frame with flyscreen panels presumably to protect food and drink from insects. In fact, it was holed and broken and useless. This was not what any of us had had in mind when we optimistically offered to bring the two boys to Wau. Our experience of medical facilities at home and overseas had completely failed to prepare us for the realities of a clinic in a poverty stricken Third World, still reeling from years of civil war and suffering under a white, Moslem Arab government totally unsympathetic to the needs of a huge part of its population which was black and either Christian or pagan African. By now feeling very unsure about the situation we had created we left Ukele looking bewildered, if not frightened, and emerged with some relief into the fresh air.

In our absence the others had been told of a government rest house where we could possibly camp. My impression of the police yard was not altogether good and so we followed the directions to this rest house. Like many places it had at one time been a rather fine building, two storeys with a pitched roof and open verandas on each floor. It was set behind a brick wall in a large area of open ground and a broad driveway swept through rusty metal gates. When we went inside it was to the now familiar atmosphere of an affluent time gone by, superseded by disuse, neglect and just a sheer lack of money for any kind of decent upkeep or maintenance. We unearthed the 'manager' and he agreed to let us camp in the grounds at the front, but no fees were discussed. We parked alongside a strip of grass running across the front like a long traffic island, over which a motley string of naked light bulbs intermittently shone as the town's electricity supply struggled to meet demand.

It had been an eventful day, but just a forerunner to the trials and tribulations that were to follow over the next seven days. With our two patients to worry about plus the problem of obtaining petrol plus the overall atmosphere of the place, Wau was to have quite an impact, both emotional and logistical, much more than anywhere else on our journey.

Wau itself was created in the nineteenth century as a centre for slave trading. The French fortified it as Fort Dessaix in 1889 but thereafter it was under British rule and governance from 1898 to 1956. It therefore evolved as a bit of a hotch potch without any dominant ethnic group, its roots being commercial rather than tribal or religious. By the time that we arrived in late 1980 the population was about fifty thousand.

On the eastern side of the town was the Jur river, running pretty much south to north on its way to drain into the White Nile, and the town was built on the rising land on its west bank. The souk was a collection of shanty huts and stalls down near the water's edge and was the bustling hub of the town with crude brick built shops and stores behind. From the souk stalls the locals sold fruit and vegetables and some cooked food. Also to be found were blacksmiths with their fires roaring from the blast of hand operated skin bellows. The blacksmiths themselves squatted at their anvils and skilfully wrought beautifully shaped knives and spear heads from old car springs. To the north of the market a couple of narrow streets housed the bakers, the tea shops, the hardware stores and the local traders with rice, flour and plastic containers of kerosene. To the south of the market was a small police station and next to it a bank. Continuing in a south easterly direction along a tree lined avenue took us past a suspicious looking zoo (which we decided not to investigate) and then to a large building that housed the local government offices on the banks of the Jur.

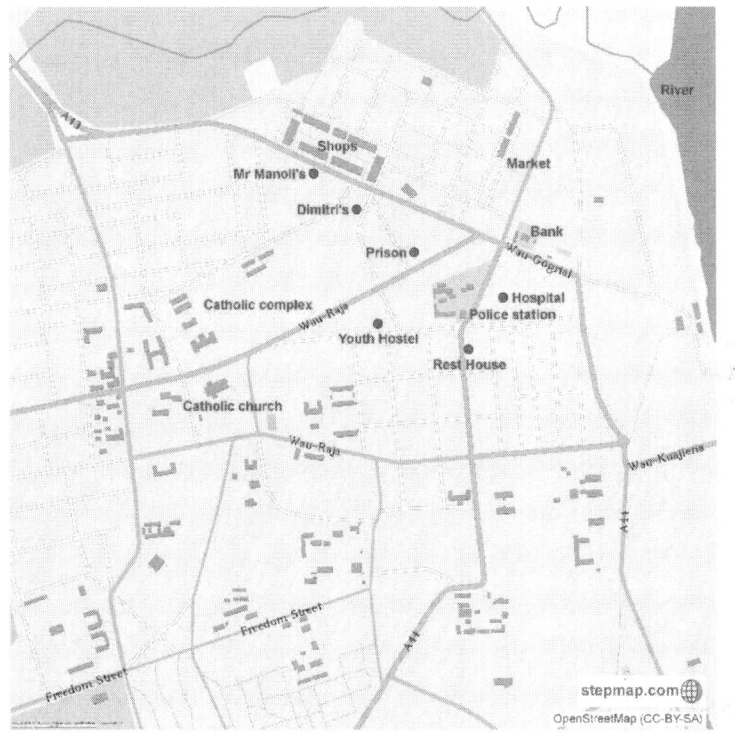

*Our landmarks in Wau*

Heading west from the market took us to what appeared to be the old garrison area. Immediately on the right was the town prison, a grim looking place surrounded by a twenty foot high, grey wall. Every evening at dusk, the top of the wall and the visible roofs inside became a roosting area for dozens of ugly black vultures that sat hunched and brooding like ranks of ornithological Grim Reapers. Beyond the prison the once military area had been built in neat squares of streets. The houses were single storey red brick with pitched corrugated roofs, looking quite English in style. Each bungalow had a walled garden backing onto a rear alley. At the bottom of each garden was a brick outhouse accessed by a short flight of steps and wherein was a lavatory, the output of which dropped straight down into the room below and a strategically placed bucket which could be removed through a door into the alley so that the waste could be discreetly carted away by the unfortunate individuals designated to the task. A typical arrangement for the living quarters of British officials overseas at that time. By 1980 the collection system had long been abandoned but some house occupiers obviously continued to use the facilities and the gaping access doors spewed forth revolting heaps of sewage covered in wriggling maggots and flies.

Beyond the houses, what presumably had been the headquarters buildings and parade ground now housed the regional police station. A little further on, our rest house appeared to have been the officer's mess, perhaps, including visitor's accommodation. In the grounds at the back were the remains of a small concrete stage, complete with wings and proscenium arch. One could imagine the scene from a film where the present day ruins fade across to the splendour of yesteryear with soldiers in dress uniforms, their ladies in tightly bodiced long dresses and perhaps 'The Importance of Being Earnest' being performed on the newly built stage. Even further along the road, past a large open sports area, was a magnificent red brick Catholic cathedral which had opened as recently as 1956. Over the road was a massive sprawling compound containing the Catholic mission with an amazing number of buildings and gardens, mostly hidden behind an eight foot high wall. The main civilian population of Wau lived in poorer, Arab style houses spread widely to the north of the garrison area. Throughout the old military area trees had been planted and were growing in abundance and in its heyday it must have been a not too unpleasant place to be posted to – a little bit of England in a far off foreign land. By 1980, however, only eight years since the end of the debilitating civil war, there was a depressing air of poverty, resignation and neglect about the place. The shops were incredibly poorly stocked and there were very few vehicles about. Nevertheless it had a haunting attraction to it, with the ghosts of better times still seeming to wander through the old streets.

Sadly we were to find that the place was also riddled with corruption, and that any wealth in the town was controlled by just a handful of powerful men. The government in Khartoum had little interest in their southern regions, an attitude unfortunately also held by the British governors in the nineteenth and twentieth centuries, the result being that the area had never received any serious investment. The only people to take interest were Christian missionaries and in addition to saving souls the Catholic Church, in particular, had brought much to the region with education and health care.

Only two years before, oil had been discovered in central Sudan, and we had been aware of the growing implications of this and the inevitable ownership politics that would accompany it. It seemed highly unlikely that Khartoum would allow the south access to the future oil bounty, and coupled with the incredibly complex tribal rivalries and jealousies that simmered just below the surface, there seemed to be little hope of any significant improvements for South Sudan in the near future.

We met many young English people who were in the Sudan as teachers. However, of some two hundred that had arrived that year, only ten had been assigned to the south. We heard stories of schools where the Sudanese staff were too drunk or too lazy to attend classes and that when an English teacher appeared eager pupils would crowd the classroom and stand outside at the windows in a desperate attempt to quench their thirst for education.

****

Our immediate, and we thought only, priorities in Wau were to register with the police, get our now expired visas renewed and to find petrol. By the time we had reached the rest house after leaving the hospital we were virtually running on the fumes in our empty tanks whilst Pallé and Jan had about six gallons between them. We were trapped in Wau until we resolved the fuel situation.

The morning after our arrival we all went over to the regional police headquarters and registered our presence. The question of the visas we decided to leave for the time being. Dawn and I cashed some travellers cheques at the bank and then whilst Dawn headed for the souk, Jan and I went to the regional commissioner's office just down the road to formally enquire about the petrol situation. If we had expected magical supplies for travellers we were to be disappointed. We were met with the bald statement that there was no petrol in Wau and that there was no forecast of when any might be coming. The commissioner was polite but firm and, after all, why should we expect help and sympathy when even a man in his position probably struggled to run his official car? With our optimistic hopes of official petrol dashed we returned to the rest house for a general discussion on where to go from here.

Dawn returned from the souk having met three English girls from Khartoum who had travelled to Wau with Mike and Daphne, who, unfortunately had now left. Dawn also brought disturbing news of recent rioting in the souk with one man being knifed and the police firing over the heads of the crowds.

We sat around and considered our position. Pallé had wandered around the town and learned of a certain Mr Dimitri who was rumoured to have stocks of black market petrol. In addition to this possible source, Jan had been given the name of a Mr Manoli whilst still in Khartoum. Dimitri turned out to be the local Shell agent. The plot started to thicken. My enquiries had revealed the presence of a British construction company which was building a new medical training centre on the outskirts of the town. We decided to follow up our respective leads and meet back at the rest house later. The construction site was about 4 kilometres away and I walked there along a road between thatched huts belonging to poor looking people. On arrival I discovered the company to be Mowlems and learnt that an Englishman and a Scotsman worked on site but not in the afternoons so I retraced my steps none the wiser as to the petrol situation. On the way back I came across the Wau Youth Hostel, another obviously ex-military building in a wired off compound. It was a small, low building with three rooms and a wide corridor also used for accommodation purposes. There were about eight young people there, English and American, quietly washing clothes in a stone sink outside the building or cooking tiny meals over charcoal stoves. There was sufficient space for us to park the three vehicles and as the manager of the rest house was now asking about £1.00 per head per night it looked like a more suitable alternative. Unfortunately the warden was not there and I returned to the rest house with little useful information from my afternoon's efforts.

Back at the rest house we compared notes. Mr Dimitri had offered Pallé three, forty gallon drums of a mixture of petrol and aviation fuel – supposedly resulting in a 'super grade' – at about £80.00 per drum (official government price being about £20.00 per drum in Khartoum). Jan had seen Mr Manoli who was apparently the biggest wheeler dealer in the district, but though sympathetic he could offer no petrol at that time but said that we should keep in contact with him as the situation could change on a daily basis. Dimitri's three drums was the minimum amount we needed but we baulked at the price and were also wary of the mixture. We decided to bide our time although Mr Manoli had hinted at prices of £140.00 per drum.

Dawn and Jan had been to the hospital and what they had to tell us confirmed our suspicions that our responsibilities to our two patients had not ended when we delivered them to the care of the local establishments. It appeared that drugs and medication were in very short supply and in order to perform even a blood test on Hassan, Dawn had had to buy a disposable syringe from a chemist. Ukele had had the sticky mess cleaned off his leg and been given some tablets and also a grimy blanket. Our enquiries the night before had led us to believe that he would be fed but it now transpired that this would be just a couple of pieces of bread each day and that he had yet to receive any. Dawn had therefore returned to the souk and bought food for him. She told us of the many cockroaches roaming around the ward and that she had seen little evidence of either staff or hygiene. Things weren't helped by the fact that nobody spoke the same language as Ukele. On the home front, Klaus had indications of a kidney infection, Michael had a sore throat and Jan had a badly swollen hand, presumably from an insect bite. All in all things could have been a lot better and the day was brought to a fitting close with the discovery that there was no water at the rest house.

We were now back in Christian territory and Sunday was the day of rest instead of the Moslem Friday. Therefore the next day being a Friday we were able to conduct business as usual. We went first to the regional police to sort out our visas and then Dawn and I went to the souk. There was no bread. Jan, Pallé and I had arranged to meet at Mr Manoli's office at 11 o'clock. This 'office' was a small back room behind a shop selling Kodak films and offering a processing service but which was totally devoid of any stock. As I walked there I was somewhat alarmed as people came hurrying from the direction of the town, talking excitedly and looking nervously back over their shoulders. One youth shouted something to me about a fight as he ran past but with what I told myself was British aplomb, I carried on against a fleeing tide of local residents. When I reached the first street in the town it was deserted except for shopkeepers frantically clearing their goods from the pavements and closing and bolting their shutters. It was strangely quiet and there was an almost tangible air of expectancy and tension. My aplomb was fading a little but I felt that I owed it to Jan and Pallé to turn up for our rendezvous. The main street was deserted when I reached it and all the shops securely boarded up. It was like a western movie just before the gunfight. When I arrived it was to find that there was nobody at Manoli's and I decided that it was now high time to exercise some caution and return to the rest house. There was not a soul to be seen although I expected a howling, bloodthirsty mob to erupt from the souk at any minute. Further out from the town I came across small, expectant groups of people in close proximity to the safety of their houses. There was still a deathly hush over everything and a sense of foreboding and I was relieved when I reached the theoretical safety of the rest house compound. Dawn had been to the police station to collect our visas but was ignored as the local constabulary grabbed guns and rifles and roared off into town in a couple of trucks. We waited apprehensively but, in fact, nothing happened and things slowly returned to normal. We learnt later that there had been a 'commotion' in the souk but that the police had quelled the trouble almost immediately, still being on the alert after the disturbance the previous week.

We were still no further forward with our search for petrol and Dawn, Jan and myself set off in Jan's Rover to the Mowlem construction site. Success this time and we met the cheerful and friendly character of Bill Smith, Site Manager. We had a lengthy chat about things in general before steering the conversation around to the subject of petrol, which Bill must have known was inevitable anyway. To our delight, he said that though he had none at that time, he was expecting a lorryload in four or five days time and he saw no reason not to sell us a couple of drums at standard pricing. This seemed excellent, and in order to demonstrate that we were all good chaps we arranged to meet him for a drink the next night at the Hotel Barbara – a drastic move considering our financial situation and the possible exorbitant fuel bill looming on the horizon. Bill also offered us more hope by suggesting that we visit the Marial Bai Ranch, an experimental farm about 15 kilometres away run by some English lads and where we might have some joy in finding petrol. We had to explore every avenue and therefore decided to invest more of Jan's dwindling petrol reserves in a visit.

It was a pleasant drive out to the ranch, although the road was heavily corrugated. We drove between small cultivated fields punctuated with tall palm trees and mud huts. At the Marial Bai we were met with the now usual sympathy and understanding but regretfully no petrol. Nevertheless Dawn, Jan and I spent a fascinating afternoon there.

The Marial Bai was home to a Project Development Unit (PDU) scheme sponsored by the World Bank. Its aim was to improve local farms and cattle stocks by the gentle introduction of simple techniques which didn't rely on sophisticated mechanical machinery or technology. Ruins of broken tractors bore testament to the failure of previous schemes designed to rudely drag the archaic agricultural system into the late twentieth century. A lack of training, understanding, experience and spares had soon rendered these vehicles useless.

Four young English lads were in charge of the activities. Kelvin and Willie were stockmen, Martin was a specialist in animal powered ploughing, and Andy was a mechanic. In a guided tour around the place we saw the cattle that were being improved by cross breeding and also by spraying them with insecticide to combat the debilitating effects of flies and ticks. They were having encouraging results and had increased milk yields by four or five times those of the Dinka cattle and the cows looked fit and healthy. They had lost a few to roaming lions and crocodiles in the river but were generally optimistic of the future although the Dinka herdsmen remained unimpressed by milk yields and stubbornly clung to their traditional aims of the more the merrier, the bigger the horns the better and never mind their condition.

Arable farming using a plough was a totally new innovation to this area, the historical method being simple broadcasting of seed. Farmers were now being shown the huge advantages of growing crops in straight lines having prepared the ground using a basic plough pulled by a pair of yoked cattle. One wonders who was most taken aback by this approach, the farmer or the cow. The training included how to carve the wooden yokes and we also saw men learning to control the animals by drawing a heavy log along in furrows, not an easy task, particularly the turning at the end of each row. All in all it was a fascinating visit and heart-warming to see these young lads prepared to live in such primitive conditions and be so enthusiastic and dedicated to improving the lives of these neglected Sudanese, whilst at the same time remaining totally sympathetic to their culture. The visit was rounded off by them sharing an excellent shepherd's pie dinner with us. A memorable and educational afternoon.

On our way back to the rest house we called in at the Youth Hostel and this time the warden was there. He was quite happy for us all to move in and at the standard rate of about £0.25 per head per night. This was fortunate, because on reaching the rest house we discovered that an official car had arrived during the afternoon and that an 'Idi Amin character' had ordered us all out in no uncertain terms. We therefore collected the Rover and headed for the Youth Hostel. Dawn and I went via the hospital to see how our patients were doing. This was a particularly depressing time of day to visit, as darkness fell and the only lights were the occasional dim glimmer inside the buildings. In the gloaming, small groups of visiting relatives squatted around little heaps of smouldering leaves from which curls of pungent smoke rose gently into the still evening air. This was presumably a tribal method of combatting airborne diseases. Whether effective or not they certainly added to the overall gloomy atmosphere. Hassan and his father were fine but poor Ukele had had just a couple of pieces of bread to eat. Obviously we would have to attend to this problem the next day.

We settled down for our first night at the Youth Hostel but were rudely awoken at about three o'clock by a burst of shouting and scrambled activity. Elizabeth had awoken and disturbed some thieves who had been going through our campsite. I should mention that whilst Dawn and I slept securely in the Rover, our companions slept in tents, their vehicles not being fitted out with beds. At the time we assumed that the object had been to steal petrol from us, but with just a few drops left this was a forlorn hope on the part of the thieves. Nevertheless they made off with our remaining twenty litre water container, Pallé lost a metal jerry can, a plastic one, a pair of trousers and two shirts whilst Jan also lost a water container and the cap off his remaining one. Not valuable losses but ones which would prove to be very inconvenient. We also later discovered that the cunning bastards had crawled under Jan's and Pallé's vehicles and cut a wedge out of the short piece of flexible hose connecting the external filler to the petrol tank. Through the hole thus created they could feed a length of tube in order to siphon out the contents of the tank, but it looked as if Elizabeth's cry of alarm had scattered them before they took much. Our twin tanks were filled from inside the vehicle by removing the front seat squabs so our couple of pints of fuel were quite safe from this sort of attack. It was an unsettling experience which put us on guard for the future, it being our first encounter with crime on our journey. The stolen items could not be replaced in Wau and in fact it was not until we reached Nigeria in forty days time that we were able to replace our water container. In the meantime we had to manage with limited drinking water from our small integral tank whilst water for washing was carried in a plastic jerry can previously used for petrol and which resisted all efforts to remove the residual taste of the fuel. The loss of Jan's container cap was also to prove to be a great nuisance to him.

In the morning we had a quick breakfast and then Dawn and I set off for the hospital with some food for Ukele – some Nasi Goreng put aside from our meal the night before. At the hospital we gathered that Ukele's mother had managed to make her way to Wau and was somewhere around. We also learned that Ukele needed anti-tetanus toxin and that, of course, the hospital had none. There was also a need for Gentian Violet antiseptic, but again, none in the hospital. We made a note to never complain about the NHS again. Apparently it was not uncommon for doctors to sell their drugs to the local pharmacists in order to supplement their meagre income.

We left and headed for the souk and on the way encountered a local woman who Dawn took to be Ukele's mother. She greeted her effusively and in Pidgin English and with broad gesticulations attempted to assure the woman of our concern and good intentions. The poor lady looked quite taken aback and bewildered and we suddenly thought that perhaps this wasn't Ukele's mum, after all. Mumbling her embarrassed apologies Dawn backed away and we scurried off to the souk. I admit that I pulled Dawn's leg quite a bit about this episode but, blow me, it later transpired that it was Ukele's mother, after all.

Back at the Youth Hostel, Jan reported that he had been given the tip to contact the Assistant Commissioner for the Rumbek region, who was in Wau to allocate some stocks of petrol. Having made the contact and spoken with this gentleman, Jan was hopeful of perhaps two drums and had submitted a written request. Pallé had seen Dimitri again and he was now offering us two drums of regular petrol for £85.00 each. After some discussion we agreed to stall for bit longer in the hope that we could obtain our supplies from either Bill Smith or the Rumbek Commissioner, both of which would be much cheaper and would also avoid us putting money into the Black Market. Pallé and I set off in his Rover to speak again with Mr Dimitri and try and string him along a bit just in case we needed his fuel after all. He, of course, was playing the supplier game and telling us that he only had the two drums and that it was a case of 'first come, first served'. Mr Dimitri was a swarthy, squint-eyed, piratical looking Greek dressed in dirty trousers and a grubby tee shirt who also ran the local off-licence in addition to his main claim to fame as the Shell agent. It would have been interesting to see the reaction of the staff in the Shell building in London if Mr Dimitri had strolled in and introduced himself.

Leaving Mr Dimitri's office, Pallé and I now set off to look for the UNICEF organisation which we had been told operated from a compound in Wau and where we wanted to enquire if they could help in any way with Hassan. With only vague directions to follow we failed to find the place and ended up on the edge of town where we were fortunate enough to come across a local lad who spoke some English and who hopped in to show us the way. We drove a confused route back into Wau and past the cathedral. Pallé and I were now convinced that our guide had about as much idea about where UNICEF was as we had. We were by this time back in sight of the Youth Hostel and decided to seek a second opinion. There was a tall, respectable looking Sudanese standing by the roadside, slightly familiar looking and who, with a puzzled expression, nodded confidently in response to our enquiry "UNICEF?". We dismissed our original guide, who had at least had a free ride into town, and replaced him with this other fellow and trundled down the hill past the Youth Hostel, where we hooted and waved to our companions in the compound. Our passenger looked even more perplexed and pointed frantically at the Youth Hostel. At this stage Pallé and I decided to abandon our quest for UNICEF, which had become just a wild goose chase, and we turned round and drove back to the hostel. As soon as we pulled up outside our passenger leapt out chanting "UNICEF, UNICEF" and pointing urgently at the sign by the gate which clearly proclaimed 'Wau Youth Hostel', albeit in faded letters. Obviously there was some confusion, although how UNICEF and the Youth Hostel came to be associated together we never found out. The whole debacle finally came to an embarrassing end when we realised why the Sudanese gentleman looked so familiar – he was the warden of the hostel! No wonder he had looked so puzzled at our enquiry. Well, with the lack of a common language it was impossible to explain things to him so Pallé and I resigned ourselves to him mentally filing us away as just two more examples of rather odd Europeans. During my absence Dawn had walked around all the pharmacies in town, four of them, but none of them had any anti-tetanus vaccine. She was really shocked by the lack of medical supplies. The question of our patients welfare was now taking up a lot of our time and as Dawn wrote in the log that night – '…it seems to have overtaken our own petrol problems as our major concern today'.

After the trials of the day, the evening was to be spent relaxing over a beer or two, the first alcohol since Khartoum, twenty two days previously, discounting the Marissa in the Nuba mountains. The usual trio – Dawn, Jan and myself – walked to the Hotel Barbara about 2 kilometres away in the older part of the town, an area we hadn't visited before. As a hotel it was a bit of a joke, but there was a pleasant courtyard with tables and chairs and here we found Bill with a young, black female companion who he introduced to us as Christine, the daughter of Uganda's Chief of Police during the infamous rule of Idi Amin. We spent a very amiable evening with Bill and Christine together with the boys from the Marial Bai Ranch who also turned up a little later. Three absolutely delicious cool, Amstel beers suffused me with a feeling of contentment and well-being.

Back to reality the next morning, and Pallé, Jan, Dawn and myself got together for a serious discussion about our two patients. By this time we had unfortunately split into two groups, our group of four being totally immersed in the hospital and petrol situations whilst Elizabeth, Björn, Klaus and Michael totally disassociated themselves from these fundamental problems that faced us. More than ever I felt sorry for Pallé in this predicament but despite the lack of support from his family he never once wavered in his objective of seeing Hassan on the road to recovery.

Despite everything, we still expected to leave Wau fairly soon, confident that we would obtain the necessary petrol from one of our potential sources. We were still very unhappy about the plight of Ukele, who remained lying on his filthy bed, his leg still untended and rigidly held bent at ninety degrees by the deep burn, whilst cockroaches roamed freely over any food left on his bedside cabinet. Despite Dawn's efforts to provide a suitable diet for him he had little interest in eating. The arrival of his mother had done little to help, and the pair of them just sat in the ward looking lost and nervous. We seriously began to wonder if we had done the right thing in bringing him to Wau where the medical facilities had turned out to be so appalling, almost non-existent and the likelihood of infection all too real. We all felt particularly guilty about Ukele at that time. Hassan and his father were in a better position. The TB ward, slightly cleaner than the casualty ward, housed a couple of dozen long term inmates who sat around disconsolately in their dirty surroundings during the day until their relatives arrived in the late afternoon with food which they cooked over charcoal fires in the yard outside. Our arrival was always greeted by warm smiles and many handshakes, as if we could conjure up some magic that would benefit them all. It left one feeling very inadequate and rather shallow when compared to the stoicism and cheerful resilience that these people had in the face of hardships that we still couldn't really come to terms with. One man in particular was a good friend to us. Samuel was a middle aged Sudanese who spoke reasonable English. He acted as interpreter for us with Hassan and his father and was therefore invaluable in helping us to explain our position and our future plans for them. In turn we learnt that Hassan had attended the hospital the previous year but that his father had removed him before his treatment was complete and hence his current condition. We hoped that our genuine concern, together with our faith in the medication he would receive, would convince the father to follow the full period of treatment this time, which was a month in the hospital plus a further eleven months of daily tablets. It was interesting as Hassan had become a bit of a celebrity in the ward, being by far the youngest patient and, of course, the focus of attention of these white people.

Our discussions with Jan and Pallé had included the problem of finances for these people. Ukele and his mother had no money at all but whilst we fed the boy we were given to understand that his mother had relations in the town who looked after her. Hassan and his father were also without cash and Pallé had been supplementing the food he took in with a little money now and then. Generally, however, we felt that handing over cash was not the best solution and we talked endlessly about what to do for them when we left. Hassan's case was perhaps the most straightforward and on the basis that he appeared to be a Christian we eventually decided that Dawn and I would contact the local Catholic organisation and appeal for their help. We hoped to find somebody who would continue to visit Hassan every day and continue to give him and his father the moral support that we had tried to introduce. We would also leave a sum of money with the church to be doled out to the father and which would last for the remainder of the month's treatment. We remained in a quandary about Ukele.

Dawn and I duly set off for the Catholic compound, a huge maze of mostly deserted, neglected buildings interspersed with quiet, overgrown gardens. We walked around aimlessly until directed to the priest's house. Here we found a young Sudanese lounging in a chair on the veranda, smoking a cigarette and listening to a church service on the radio. It was Sunday. To our surprise this chap turned out to be the priest and we patiently explained our predicament. I'm afraid that he didn't inspire us with any confidence and we felt that we were getting nowhere. He explained that he himself could do little to help but perhaps the nuns could be of assistance. This sounded much more promising and we followed him around and past more derelict buildings until we came to a delightful well-tended garden and house, tucked away in peace and solitude. The priest introduced us to Sister Mary, an Italian nun, and then left us. Here was another awe-inspiring, compassionate woman who had given her life to the welfare and care of others. We sat in the cool shade and listened to her heart-rending tale of the fight against poverty and disease. There was only herself and another Italian nun, who was now too old to leave the house, plus another Sudanese priest who was ill with malaria. Their primary concern was the seminary up the road but Sister Mary usually made a daily visit to the Civil Hospital, pedalling over there on her bicycle. She told us of the dire shortage of medicines and drugs and pointed to a large wooden crate which had been delivered several months before, full of date expired drugs that she refused to administer. Having bravely survived the bitter civil war and now left with insufficient money, insufficient staff and insufficient help of any kind, this handful of good and dedicated people had been forced more and more to retreat behind their red brick walls and struggle to train a handful of priests to attend to the spiritual needs of the people whilst unable to do anything much for their more earthly needs. And when some help arrived what was it? - a crate of date expired drugs that some other medical facility had thrown out.

We sat and listened to this tragic account of life in Wau, all too conscious that we were going to ask this already overworked lady to take on yet more responsibility whilst we ourselves happily trundled off to enjoy our travels. We eventually brought the conversation round to the reason for our visit and told her all about our encounters with Ukele and Hassan, and our hope that she could help with the care of Hassan after we had gone. Sister Mary listened carefully to everything and then said that, yes, she would do what she could and suggested that we meet her at the hospital the following morning and introduce her to Hassan and his father. This was wonderful news, and we left with the feeling of some weight having been removed from our shoulders.

We had still had no success in obtaining any anti-tetanus toxin for Ukele, but our enquiries had led to the suggestion that we might find some at a German sponsored leprosy hospital, some 10 kilometres out of Wau. Again the Gang of Four piled into Pallé's Rover and we headed for the highlands where the hospital was situated. On the way we passed by the infamous tomato canning factory and ugly dumps of rusting tins and coils of metal. The factory looked as active as the milk factory had done. The leprosy centre had been open for just a year and was situated in the wide open spaces on an airy plateau. It was an amazingly clean, bright and uplifting place after all the depressing medical facilities we had so far encountered. It was run by Karen, a young German lady who was the matron. She was a little suspicious of us at first and we received a cool reception. With the chronic lack of services, any foreign backed institution in South Sudan must have attracted many hopeful sick at the gates and it must have taken a firm course of action to control and restrict entry. This hospital was strictly for the treatment of leprosy and Karen was quite blunt in her refusal to become involved with other illnesses. To this end she explained that she no longer stocked anti-tetanus toxin, having tired of people coming from Wau in search of it. She nevertheless invited us into the common room and gave us cold drinks, and as we sat and talked her initial reservation disappeared. We had a long and amiable conversation which culminated in her showing us around the hospital where we saw and met victims of leprosy and Karen explained the treatments being given. To our surprise we discovered that it could be cured if diagnosed early enough, and that a long course of tablets was all that was needed. The problem was in convincing the sufferers the importance of the regular dosage. Some of the patients had already lost fingers and toes and they were being shown how to look after themselves and how to avoid the cuts, burns and lacerations to their numb flesh which could then so easily become dangerously infected. The hospital was very small with basically three single storey blocks around a square, central garden alive with brightly coloured bushes and flowers. There were perhaps six rooms in each building, each room with two beds. They were airy and spotlessly clean, a far cry from the conditions in Wau. In one room we found the one exception to Karen's adamant rule of 'lepers only' and I do believe that she was a little embarrassed that we had discovered this little chink in her armour. A young Sudanese mother had apparently walked for days to bring her tiny baby to the clinic. The poor child had fallen into a fire and its body was virtually a complete mass of raw, red flesh. It was a miracle that it had survived and Karen had taken the woman in and was showing her how to bathe and care for her child and was now prepared to keep her there for as long as was necessary.

We saw the laboratory, which particularly interested Jan, and then prepared to take our leave. It was now or never and someone managed to ask about petrol. It seemed almost like a betrayal, that Karen might think that we had used her and wasted her time for our own selfish ends. Fortunately I don't think that she did see it this way and regretfully informed us that they had barely enough for their own needs.

Petrol or no petrol it had been an absorbing and educational afternoon, and refreshing to be in such a clean and invigorating atmosphere. Having become accustomed to the deprivations of Wau Civil Hospital, though, this brief interlude only served to underline the horror of that establishment when we returned to it, and we were still no nearer finding the anti-tetanus for Ukele.

We arrived at the hospital the next morning and met Sister Mary as arranged. She spoke the native tongue and Hassan's father seemed more than pleased with our plan and we seemed to have reached the best solution under the circumstances, thanks to Sister Mary. We agreed a daily sum of money to feed Hassan's father for the one month that Hassan needed to stay in the hospital and Sister Mary would keep this and administer it to him on a daily basis, at the same time keeping a check on Hassan. No such progress with Ukele, and after a rather lazy day Dawn and I went to see him in the early evening, taking some food for him. As I've said before, this was always the worst time to visit, as the sun went down and the few dim lights were switched on in the wards. The leaves were falling from the trees, adding more starkness to an already sombre scene. It was always very quiet and still and apart from the odd patient or relative sitting around it always looked totally deserted and I used to find it unutterably depressing and sad.

We had still failed to communicate with Ukele and he would regard us blankly with no signs of emotion, friendly or hostile. This particular evening there was a young Sudanese orderly or male nurse in the ward and we asked him if he could speak English and also if he could converse with Ukele. Too late we discovered that he was reeling drunk, apparently a common occurrence with some of the staff, but our first experience of it. There followed a tedious half hour of drunken rambling. The bed next to Ukele had been occupied for the past two days by a young man who had been stabbed in the face and hand and consequently didn't look too happy. He had lain in the bloodstained clothes in which he had been admitted and had received very little attention. He was obviously in considerable pain but our 'orderly' pushed him roughly to one side in order to sit on his bed. We listened to a long tirade of nonsense, interspersed with the waving of a large key, which, we were informed, "Ish de key to de oberatin' teatre". We ended up as two very reluctant visitors to said 'operating theatre', our host insisting that we accompany him to see it. After fumbling to unlock the door he strode in and proudly indicated what to us looked like a rather Victorian set up, not helped by the usual inadequate lighting. Being very aware of the usual strict hygiene rules applied to such facilities we both felt awkward tramping about in there and at last managed to make our excuses and take our leave, but not before Dawn was presented with some anti-malarial tablets.

The next day was Tuesday the sixteenth of December. Despite there being no immediate solutions in sight to any of our various issues, we had decided that we should have a 'feast' to celebrate our travels together and to mark the imminent end to our association. Pallé, Elizabeth, Jan and Björn were heading for Juba and then down into Kenya, whereas Dawn and I had decided to cut across through the Central African Republic and start circling back to cross the Sahara and back up to Europe. The feast was to be barbecued chicken with suitable side dishes. We didn't usually eat meat due to its suspicious origins, and Dawn continued to turn out amazingly tasty and nutritious meals using stock cubes and vegetables. For the feast we would buy three live chickens, thus hopefully guaranteeing their freshness and freedom from disease. Dawn was to be responsible for the vegetables, Pallé and Elizabeth for the fruit and Jan and I had the dubious task of buying the chickens.

First, however, Jan and I headed for the hospital in a determined effort to sort out the Ukele situation. We had come across a pharmacist called John on one of our visits. A sober and personable young Sudanese, we hoped that he would be able to help us make some progress. John proved to be just the person we needed. He could converse with Ukele and his mother and we at last learnt that they were happy with our help, which was a huge relief to me, and, furthermore, we were able to agree to the sum of money that we would leave behind when we left in order for Ukele and his mother to feed themselves and survive. Also we were able to communicate our serious concern at the lack of treatment that Ukele had received, and John introduced a male nurse called Luka who was detailed to attend to the wound. It was early morning, the sun was shining into the ward and we left feeling much buoyed up by the first real progress we had made since committing poor Ukele to the tender mercy of the hospital.

From the hospital we went to see the Rumbek Commissioner about the petrol situation. To our surprise he quite unexpectedly announced that we could have two drums of forty gallons each. He wrote out an official authorisation for us to take to the local depot and we hastened there to confirm our luck. No problem, we were assured, and we could collect it at any time. All of a sudden things were starting to get better. Down in the souk Jan and I wandered around assessing the few scrawny chickens up for sale. I don't think that either of us were very comfortable with buying live birds and taking them back to the Youth Hostel but we finally settled on our prey and set off with them trussed together by their feet and hanging ignominiously upside down. The humble chicken is surely the most ill-used source of fresh meat in the world. It can be reared anywhere, takes up little space, eats scraps, is a convenient size, is easy to kill and cook and tastes nice. Unfortunately, it is also all too easy to transport stuffed into all manner of bags and containers or trussed and festooned upside down or simply tossed onto public transport to be kicked about the floors of buses and trains. Well, our three could at least look forward to a couple of hours of peace and quiet back at the Youth Hostel before their final journey to that big henhouse in the sky.

Having discharged our duties to the feast, Jan and I returned to the hospital where we found Ukele's leg had been stripped of the dead skin around the burn and was looking much better. I didn't like to think of the pain that he must have suffered, but Luka seemed to be a compassionate and capable young man and hopefully did his best to carry out the procedure with the minimum of pain. Nevertheless, Ukele had probably come through a trial that as a test of manhood his tribe would have approved of.

From the hospital Jan and I went out to the Mowlem site to see Bill Smith and to check on any news on the petrol front there. To our disappointment he informed us that he had taken delivery of fourteen drums of diesel fuel but no petrol. This effectively ended this line of enquiry so we went around to see Mr Manoli who said that he might get one drum and that we should check with him later. It was lunchtime so we went back to the Youth Hostel where the main course of the evening's feast was happily pecking about under our Rover, enjoying a few scraps optimistically given to fatten them up a bit. After lunch Jan and I continued our quest for petrol by going back to the depot to pay for the promised two drums from the Rumbek Commissioner, only to be told that now there was no petrol left. This was deflating news and we hastened to the Commissioner's office to clarify the situation. The Commissioner was very apologetic and explained that a quantity of three hundred and twenty four gallon drums had been lost due to evaporation, but that the next day he would personally come with us to get the petrol from another dealer. Whilst not as satisfactory as had been hoped this was nevertheless the best we could hope for under the circumstances and we were grateful to the Commissioner for his honesty and ongoing support.

We arrived back at the hostel to find that at least one major problem had been resolved whilst we had been away, how to dispatch the birds. With none of our party keen to do the dirty deed, the warden had been approached for his help and he had cheerfully emerged with a small chopper and swiftly decapitated them. Jan and I found them hanging on the clothes line. It was then all hands on deck for plucking and drawing, the latter task falling to poor Pallé while Jan and I went once again in search of Mr Manoli, who we failed to locate. Back to the Youth Hostel where John and Luka turned up and we had a cup of tea and a chat with them. They seemed to be a very genuine pair of lads and we felt reassured that Ukele was now receiving the best attention that was available, despite the absence of the anti-tetanus toxin or any decent antiseptic substance.

We had an excellent feast. The chicken was barbecued to succulent perfection and was accompanied by Dawn's mixed salad and yams, followed by fruit salad, coffee and cakes. We had also splashed out on a bottle of sherry and some beers and, despite the ongoing lack of petrol, we all retired to bed with a sense of well-being and a degree of optimism that at least our two patients seemed to be on the road to recovery.

First call the following day was on Mr Manoli, who now revealed that he had been hoping for a drum from Bill Smith, who was refusing to hand it over! Crossing Mr Manoli off our supplier list we set off in all three vehicles to meet the Rumbek Commissioner who would hopefully satisfy most of our requirements through the official route. We paid a very fair price of £75.00 for the two forty gallon drums and drove to the government depot to collect them. Here we discovered that all the drums had holes and leaks in them. From two of the best looking drums we proceeded to siphon the contents into our jerry cans, this being the best way to measure it, and then into the vehicle tanks. We estimated that we transferred seventy seven gallons of the purchased eighty, and felt that under the circumstances it would be churlish to complain. We now had to swallow our pride and accept the single drum offered by Mr Dimitri for £85.00, and having seen him and paid him we drove to his Shell depot and continued our siphoning operation. The end result was effectively a total of twenty seven jerry cans, shared as twelve (fifty four gallons) for us, seven for Jan and eight for Pallé, based on our individual calculations of the distances to be covered and our average consumptions. Jan and Pallé would have enough to reach Juba, just 650 kilometres away and we were carrying as much fuel as we could get our hands on under the assumption that our next opportunity to buy more would be in Bangassou, some 1000 kilometres away in the Central African Republic. Our average consumption through Sudan on the bad roads had been just twelve and a half miles or twenty kilometres to the gallon. We didn't expect any better road conditions in the CAR so our fifty four gallons equated optimistically to 1080 kilometres which meant that we would probably arrive in Bangassou driving on fumes again.

We had a last shower at the Youth Hostel and then packed up and moved to the police compound for our final night in Wau, where we would feel more secure with our priceless loads of petrol. We paid our last visit to the hospital. This was a sad occasion as we had by now formed quite a close association with the place, despite its awful conditions. Apart from the one drunken orderly, we had met some fine people there who were inspiring in their optimism and resilience when faced with such daunting and soul destroying obstacles. Our previous doubts about our actions were now considerably eased by the huge improvements in our patients and the knowledge that we had put things in place to continue their care if only for a very limited time. Ukele looked much happier now that John and Luka were taking an interest in him and little Hassan looked remarkably smart in a spotlessly clean white shirt and neat short trousers, courtesy of the amazing Sister Mary. People might criticise us for interfering in things that we didn't understand, but in hindsight I have no doubts at all that we had done the right thing under the circumstances.

We spent a final peaceful night in the police compound where we were made welcome by the polite and friendly constabulary though perhaps not quite so polite and friendly the next morning to an unfortunate inmate who had spent the night in one of the cells. He was obviously still drunk and was hanging onto the bars of the door when the police unlocked it and swung it open. The poor fellow swung out with the door with an inane grin on his face and then collapsed in an untidy heap on the ground, where he was casually left to sort himself out.

Dawn, Pallé, Elizabeth, Michael, Björn, Klaus and Jan

We made a last quick visit to the souk and then to Mowlems, where Bill had promised to accept our letters for posting in Khartoum and London when he went there for Christmas, then it was out on the open road again, heading for Busseri and then on to the border with the Central African Republic. It was only nine o'clock, the road – not tarmac, of course – was good and we started to adjust to being on our own again after the past five weeks or so of travelling in the company of the other two Rovers. It was certainly good to be on the move again. Our elation was short lived when we arrived at Busseri, just 20 kilometres out of Wau, and found that the ferry across the river was out of action. A heavily laden souk lorry had tipped off the boat and was lying on its side in the river and was blocking the movement of the ferry, which was now also half full of water.

We resigned ourselves to a considerable wait whilst people shouted and more vehicles arrived on both sides of the river. At one stage we were approached by an old chap pushing his ancient motorbike and looking for petrol. How do you refuse, when your vehicle is sprouting jerry cans all over it? We gave him a couple of pints, all too conscious that this could be the vital two pints that would leave us short of Bangassou some days hence.

Some time later a big, old bulldozer came clanking down the road from goodness knows where and the lorry was eventually righted and pulled out of the river. This left the ferry to be baled but at two thirty we were told that there would be no river crossing until the following day. This obviously wasn't part of our plans but a young Sudanese priest who was also waiting to use the ferry offered to take us back to the local Catholic mission for the night. This was an excellent offer so we followed him just a few kilometres back and off the road to where yet another huge and sprawling group of substantial buildings was to be found with its own large and impressive church in the centre. This was apparently another seminary plus a school for children where we chatted with Mary, another young English girl thousands of miles away from home who was teaching in the secondary school. Amazing.

The next day saw us arrive early at the ferry but it was still not in operation. By eleven thirty, however, it was finally in action and one or two trucks had been ferried over and I had seen, to my consternation, that the vessel could not reach the far bank due to the low water level, and that it ground to a halt in the shallows about thirty feet out into the river in perhaps two feet of water. Memories of our ignominious breakdown in the previous river crossing sprang immediately to mind, further emphasised when a Land Rover tried to reach the ferry from the far side and died in the attempt. Forewarned and more sensible this time, I tackled the vulnerable distributor with sticky tape in an attempt to waterproof it. Just before it was our turn, two different Rovers successfully negotiated the thirty feet gap from the other side, so I felt a little more encouraged but still extremely nervous. Dawn made the crossing first in a precarious looking little metal boat so that she could take some action photos, well, hopefully action photos. Onto the ferry via ramps, across the river as far as possible and then a deep breath as I plunged down into the water with a huge feeling of pessimism, but my fears proved absolutely groundless as the Rover pushed sedately through the water with a proud bow wave and then clambered up the bank and onto dry land. I just don't know what I was so worried about.....

At the ferry we had picked up a passenger, a local woman looking for a lift to Bazia, some 55 kilometres along the road. It was the usual appalling sort of track, and we bumped along and meandered around rocky outcrops. The constant bouncing resulted in a leak of our precious fuel from one of the plastic containers on the roof rack so we stopped and transferred it to the safety of the vehicle tank. At Bazia we dropped off our passenger and reported to the police in order to pass through a barrier across the road. We stopped for the night in the middle of nowhere with nobody in sight apart from a couple of locals who strolled past toting guns. We had made good progress from the ferry and all being well would be leaving Sudan the next day. We were both ready to leave and anxious to put some miles behind us.

We didn't manage to leave Sudan the next day after all. We reached the last major town, Tambura, about mid-afternoon but only after finally shearing off a front shock absorber mounting plate. As mentioned earlier, one shock absorber was too short and I was amazed that we had survived so long with the constant stress on it caused by the continuous bad roads. With the lower bracket now literally torn in half it was necessary to try and repair it before going any further. At the Tambura police station we were directed to the local hospital where we found a surprisingly modern, if small, and clean establishment run by three Italian nuns who were primarily running another leprosy clinic. Their Sudanese driver suggested that we try the Catholic mission at Mpoi, just a few kilometres further on. However, we were welcome to spend the night in the hospital grounds, and with clean showers and toilets we took advantage of the situation – and Dawn did some washing.

Mpoi was 25 kilometres away along a decent, red dirt track and through some very pretty woodland. At Mpoi we came across yet another huge Catholic church with associated schooling and resident nuns. Mpoi had been one of the first places to be set up by missionaries some eighty years before and had been developed as a religious and educational centre. Under the educational umbrella was a vocational training facility and here I found Brother Attorini and his remarkably well equipped workshop. He willingly fired up his diesel powered generator and I was able to quickly weld up the broken plate. Not only that but he had a pile of old Land Rover bits and pieces and amongst them I uncovered a shock absorber of the correct length so did a swap with him for my short one. It was a Sunday when we arrived and mass was just starting in the church. I sat at the back and was treated to a delightful service which included much melodic African singing accompanied by the rhythmic beating of drums.

By midday we were on our way back to Tambura where we managed to buy potatoes and huge bananas in the souk, but there was very little else. Finally, at about three thirty we arrived at our last town in Sudan, a small place called Sourceyoubou which was where the customs and immigration post was before we entered the Central African Republic. We spent the night behind the rest house and were somewhat alarmed when about twelve enormous souk lorries turned up, apparently also intending to cross the border the next day. Experience had shown that whilst we usually had few problems with border formalities – with the exception of Egypt, of course – local travellers were often targeted and submitted to long delays, so we didn't want to be at the back of such a queue. But, whatever transpired the following day, it looked as if we would be leaving Sudan, taking with us some very vivid memories of a very remarkable country.

****

Distance across Sudan  -  3,873 km

Total distance travelled from start – 10,774 km

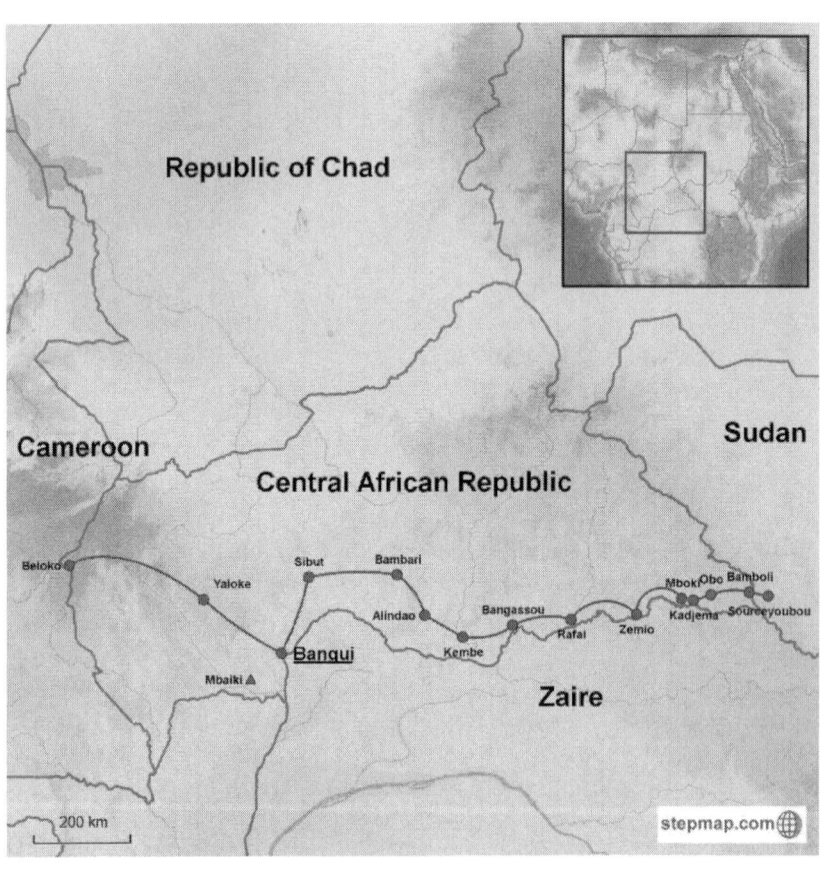

# Chapter 14 -Central African Republic

Monday 22<sup>nd</sup> December 1980 to Friday 16<sup>th</sup> January 1981

Journey days 94 to 119

Not wanting to be behind the souk lorries we were up before seven o'clock to beat them to the border post. We had been unable to obtain any CAR currency earlier in Sudan but now changed our remaining Sudanese pounds for CAR francs. Having completed these negotiations we discovered that we still needed some Sudanese pounds to pay a Customs charge. Hitch-hiking on one of the souk lorries was yet another young English teacher. We had fed him the previous evening and he now repaid our hospitality by changing some US dollars for Sudanese pounds so that we could settle our debt and be on our way.

At the border post we also met three young missionaries coming from the CAR into Sudan. They gravely warned us of the doom and gloom that we were about to encounter. Dreadful roads, no petrol and no banks until we reached the capital Bangui, way beyond our projected fuel range. As we didn't have any choice in the matter we filed all this information under 'Too Difficult to Deal With' and at last left Sudan at ten fifteen, heading into Deepest Darkest Africa.

The immediate shock was to discover that the awful roads and tracks of Sudan had nothing on those of the Central African Republic. It was only six kilometres across no-man's land to the border post at Bamboli but the track was so rutted and hazardous that Dawn got out and walked several times as the Rover pitched and yawed in a most alarming fashion. We crawled to the border where formalities were soon dealt with, the officials in their little hut evidently familiar with the carnet procedure.

Leaving the border we headed west along an apparently little used track hemmed in on both sides by dense jungle. Little used, maybe, but nevertheless the only road link between Sudan and the CAR. Once more we realised how lucky we had been to arrive after the summer rains. The state of the track bore evidence of the dreadfully muddy conditions which had prevailed until relatively recently. I had seen photographs of overland trucks being dug out of soft mud several feet deep, their passage resulting in mud gorges half the height of the vehicle and only slightly wider. We now came across these in their dry, rock hard state and gingerly eased our way through them. In the wet season, numerous streams carried water to the Bomu River, somewhere to the south of us. Crossing each stream entailed descending a steep bank, traversing a simple log bridge and clambering up the opposite bank. The bridges were just logs laid side by side with no cross pieces or planking. The only way to negotiate them was for Dawn to hop out in front and guide me so as to keep the wheels on the narrow wood and out of the gaps. It was a nerve-fraying experience and we saw no other vehicles all day. Presumably the souk lorries at the border didn't come this way after all.

The astonishing aftermath of the rainy season

We were aiming to reach Obo before nightfall and although the track improved slightly some 25 kilometres from there, and we therefore made slightly better time, it nevertheless took us over seven hours to cover 110 kilometres that day, arriving in Obo just before six in the evening. Obo was another sprawling town of mud huts and poorly stocked little stores. We found the Catholic mission from where we were directed to the American Evangelist mission. This turned out to be a very salubrious looking place with all mod cons, not the usual image of a missionary station. We introduced ourselves to an American called Don and chatted about the situation, eager to obtain information about our chances of survival. To my surprise, Don offered to sell us fifteen gallons of petrol – liquid gold in these parts. We decided to discuss this further the next day and returned to our camp site in the midst of orange and grapefruit trees, treating ourselves to a tin of corned beef for dinner.

Despite the appalling road conditions, our first impressions of the CAR were favourable. The contrast with Sudan was quite marked. Everywhere seemed much cleaner and the people looked healthier and happier and the language was French, which would have been a huge advantage to us if only our own French had been better. Nevertheless it did make communication much easier. The villages were all neat and tidy and the earth around the huts looked as if it was constantly swept to keep it so clean. Lots of fruit trees around the houses and some huge pineapple plants.

*A typical log bridge, of which there were many*

The next day we met with Don again and he now suggested that we simply buy some francs from him in order to purchase petrol nearer to Bangui, where it would be considerably cheaper than the £4.00 a gallon that he would have to charge us. This seemed pretty sensible and we were also glad of the opportunity to lay our hands on more local currency so we changed some cash dollars with him.

The mission was run on a very commercial basis and Don took us around to show us the rice mill and the tannery. The local people had access to the mill in order to process their rice and sell it for cash, and the leather from the tannery was used by the trainee pastors to make saleable products such as belts and bags and sandals in order to earn money to support themselves. It was all very impressive and a very different approach to things compared with our experience of the Catholic missions in Sudan. Don lived with his wife and two teenage sons so very different to the solitary and celibate lives of the Catholic priests and nuns. We bought a kilo of rice.

The visit to the mission facilities, followed by the obligatory visit to the police station to register our presence, meant that once again we were much later than we intended by the time we eventually left Obo at midday. The road was considerably better than the day before, albeit it with the occasional awkward section across dry streams. All went well until we reached Kadjema, where the use of a small, manual ferry was necessary to cross the river. We had been warned that the fee should not be more than about £1.25. The ferry was manned by three local youths, and as soon as we were in the middle of the river they brought it to a halt and demanded £7.00 to continue to the other side. Admittedly they were in a relatively strong position but we were in no particular hurry and had no intention of submitting to such blackmail, so we argued for a bit then calmly unfolded our camping chairs and settled down to read our books and await events, which we hoped would be another vehicle wanting to use the ferry.

Driving up to be hi-jacked!

The time passed in this uneasy stalemate until eventually, two and a half hours later, I think the boys also had to admit that the odds were increasing on another vehicle turning up and they finally capitulated for a fee of £1.25 plus some cigarettes. Sure enough, soon after driving off we met a UNICEF Land Rover heading for the crossing with some locals who agreed that £1.25 was good but certainly no more. I wonder how much *they* paid?

The late start and the ferry delay resulted in us covering just 80 kilometres before reaching Mboki for the night, where we camped in the village next to the church. The next day was Christmas Eve and we wanted to reach Zemio, about 150 kilometres away, for Christmas.

Yet again our plans for an early start were thwarted when a service started in the church and we politely waited for it to end before starting the Rover and driving off. As it happened, we thought that we had arisen at seven o'clock but later discovered that we had crossed a time zone and it was really only six o'clock, so we could have had another hour in bed. We called into the Mboki gendarmerie for the obligatory registration and collected a couple of letters from them to deliver to the police in Bangassou.

The road was gradually improving as we headed further west, no doubt because of the increased population and hence more traffic, but the only vehicle we encountered was an eastbound Land Rover with four Germans on board. From them we learnt that the petrol situation was not going to improve and that we still had some very rough country to negotiate.

Later we came to another small ferry much like the one that had caused us so much trouble the previous day. This time an older ferryman appeared after a twenty minute wait and took us across without incident. We happily paid him £1.25 and gave him a Dunhill hat as a tip.

We arrived in Zemio at about four o'clock and after registering with the police found our way to the Evangelist mission where we had been told there was a camping area for travellers. Here we were given a somewhat reserved welcome by the resident American pastor, Don Rickman. I suppose one could hardly blame him, his calling being to bring the word of God to the natives not to run a camping facility for happy-go-lucky travellers. Not only that but it was Christmas Eve and he was probably looking forward to a nice quiet family celebration. The camping area was beautiful, up on an escarpment overlooking endless miles of green landscape to the south. An ideal place for us to rest up for our own little Christmas and we had no intention of imposing on the Rickmans. Dawn cooked up a rather nice chicken stew and we sat nostalgically reflecting on Christmases past. We lit a fire as the temperature dropped and had just made a cup of coffee when Mrs Rickman (Lois) arrived with a large piece of sponge cake. She invited us to a film slide show in the church followed by 'moral sketches'. Our curiosity aroused, we went over and spent a pleasant if unusual evening being entertained by an enthusiastic and very amateur group of the local brethren. Lois also kindly invited us to share their Christmas meal the next day and we retired that night feeling content and relaxed and nicely into the spirit of Christmas.

Christmas morning and we had just one present to open, a soft parcel that had been handed to us by our friends Gordon and Barbara, and John and Gill, before we left Oman. This had been the subject of much speculation during our journey and it was with no little excitement that we ceremoniously removed the wrapping paper to reveal a couple of baseball caps and the instruction that we must wear them whilst eating our Christmas dinner. Under the circumstances we decided that this might not be appropriate social etiquette at the Rickman's table.

Christmas Day 1980 with the Congo in the distance

We had planned breakfast to be a veritable feast of fried potatoes, fried bread, ham and eggs but in the absence of any eggs and with the forthcoming dinner we decided that it was a bit extravagant to open the tin of ham and settled instead for some bread and jam, eaten whilst wearing our new caps. During the morning the Rickman's son, Sam, came over to invite us to take part in the church service that was about to begin. Dawn was not in the least religious and I, as a typical Catholic, fully expected to be struck down by a bolt of lightning if I so much as set one foot in a non-Catholic church but it was Christmas Day in the middle of Africa and we didn't want to upset our hosts so we decided to go across. The church was just a simple square building, a far cry from the huge edifices built by the Catholics in Sudan. The pews were packed with excited and beaming locals dressed in their brightly coloured finery, the girls and women sporting the most amazing hair arrangements of tight plaits dividing the scalp into geometric patterns. The service launched into a succession of lengthy bible quotations interspersed with enthusiastically sung hymns. I'm afraid that the novelty soon wore off for us, and after two hours we felt that honour had been satisfied and we quietly took our leave. The service was to continue for another hour or so and besides, Dawn had some washing to do, Christmas Day or no Christmas Day.

At about one o'clock we were called over to the house and met the complete mission complement of Don and Lois, Sam and Bonnie, Betty, Jim, David and Simon. The meal was boiled chicken and various vegetables followed by an excellent mincemeat tart with ice cream. They were a pleasant bunch although they didn't take much prompting before they started preaching, and the conversation never strayed far from religious matters. As a polite precaution, before we went over for lunch Dawn had slipped a simple ring onto her wedding finger. We had been wary of the Arabic attitude towards unmarried couples and had decided that Evangelist missionaries might also frown upon people 'living in sin' and we certainly didn't want to offend them in any way. Just as well because Betty homed in on the ring during the meal and commented pointedly on it being a rather *unusual* wedding ring. As ever, Dawn took this calmly and in her stride and without batting an eyelid she blithely explained it away as being an old family heirloom or some such, although I don't think for one minute that Betty was fooled and she continued to occasionally glance at the ring in a very suspicious manner.

We all mucked in after dinner to clear away and wash up and then Jim showed us round the incredibly clean and neat hospital facility that was part of the mission; such a contrast to the Wau facilities.

All in all it was a very pleasant Christmas day for us. It was sunny and warm, if a little humid, but cooled down nicely in the evening and after we had lit a fire Sam came over with some fresh coffee and stayed chatting for a couple hours.

A visit to the hairdressers before church on Christmas Day

Boxing Day and another shot at an early getaway in order to reach Rafai, some 160 kilometres further down the track. Sam gave us twenty litres of petrol to take to the mission in Rafai and we climbed into the Rover at eight o'clock, started the engine and….no clutch. A quick check revealed no oil in the clutch reservoir so I filled it and then spent an hour struggling to undo the bleed nipple in order to get the air out of the system. We finally left at nine o'clock. It wasn't such a good road and had some very rocky and bumpy sections. Much of it was through thick jungle undergrowth that crowded in on both sides and somewhere it was narrow enough to knock the filler pipe off the water tank, resulting in the loss of half our precious drinking water. We also came across some alarmingly large flies, each equipped with a huge and menacing proboscis. I wasn't sure what a tsetse fly looked like but took no chances and we now discovered the advantage of horizontally sliding door windows that could be flipped shut in an instant.

At Dembia we again crossed the river using a ferry but had no problems with payment. Then there was a second ferry at Rafai, which we had to use to reach the Evangelist mission. After the delayed start we didn't reach Rafai until after five and decided to sneak past the Gendarmerie and onto this ferry to save time. No such luck as there was a policeman at the ferry and he sent us back to register. We felt like a couple of naughty school children. So it was that we eventually arrived at the mission in the dark, met Ray and Eleanor Warburg and handed over the petrol sent from Zemio. A nice place to camp, although we couldn't see much of it in the dark.

The next day I found the clutch reservoir was empty again so I decided to change the seals on the slave cylinder, spares of which were in my box of goodies. We were obviously going to have to spend a second night at Rafai so having fixed the clutch I checked the front axle as I had had some suspicions of its serviceability after a bit of slipping and sliding during the previous day. Sure enough I discovered that the left hand drive shaft was broken. I was prepared for a broken rear half shaft and carried spares for these but not for the front. Whilst I was investigating the situation a local chap puttered up on his moped, introducing himself as Ali. We chatted as best we could with my shamefully limited French. When I found the broken drive shaft he immediately offered to pop into town to see if he could find a spare somewhere. This broken shaft was pretty bad news at this stage of the journey as it meant the loss of our four wheel drive, and although we were given to understand that the worst of the CAR terrain was behind us, we still had the Sahara Desert to cross. Not surprisingly Ali returned empty handed so I had no choice in the matter but to reassemble the front axle sans left-hand drive shaft and cross my fingers. I gave Ali a litre of our precious petrol and he pop-popped happily off home.

We had a nice outing with the Warburgs later in the afternoon when we all piled into their pick-up - Ray, Eleanor and teenage children Cathy, Jeffery and Walter – and drove to the village where there was a dirt airstrip and the boys were able to fly a rubber powered model aircraft received for Christmas. We bought some oranges in the village plus a huge, juicy pineapple.

We had already eaten dumpling stew and banana tart with the family at lunchtime and were now invited back for pancakes and coffee which nicely rounded off a good day, if you ignore the broken half shaft.

The next morning we bade farewell to our latest new friends and headed to Bangassou which was about 150 kilometres away. The road wasn't, in fact, as good as the previous road from Zemio to Rafai but we made good time and fortunately didn't ever need four wheel drive. We met two truckloads of overlanders along the way, both heading east. One was a MAN full of Brits and the other a Mercedes full of Germans. These large parties usually had their own favourite overnight spots and didn't bother the missionaries, which possibly explained why we were always made so welcome, as couples like us were not perhaps so common and we expanded their otherwise very narrow social scene.

The road to Bangassou

We arrived in Bangassou in the late afternoon and dropped off the police mail from Mboki at the Gendarmerie. We then went to the market and were pleasantly surprised to find a bigger selection than we had been used to for some time. There was cooked and charred fish and meat and a greater variety of vegetables. The inevitable tinned mackerel, sardines and tomato paste was available but at remarkably inflated prices. The origins of the cooked meat was brought into some doubt when we were offered a dead monkey by one of the stall holders. There also appeared to be dead rats but perhaps these were just a local variation on the long tailed, furry animal theme. We were not tempted and happily continued with our vegetarian diet.

The other notable thing about Bangassou was the sudden increase in the white-robed Arab population. As in Sudan, these were obviously the local businessmen and traders and demonstrated their wealth by riding around on mopeds and in the occasional diesel vehicle. As ever, the black African remained at the bottom of the pecking order.

During our drive around Bangassou we came across one or two petrol pumps but no petrol and there was no bank there either. By this time we were down to our last eight gallons or so of petrol. According to the map it was 360 kilometres to Alindao and we had averaged just twenty three kilometres to the gallon (or fourteen miles to the gallon) since leaving Wau. Our eight gallons would therefore take us only about 184 kilometres so we would somehow *have* to find fuel before leaving Bangassou.

There was a large Catholic mission but we stayed the night in the grounds of the Baptist mission where, yet again, we were made very welcome.

With our urgent need to find petrol, we headed into town the next morning and came across a helpful postman who hopped in with us and directed us around the maze of streets. After nipping in and out of various small trading establishments, he eventually tracked down four and a half gallons for us, albeit at the horrendous price of £3.50 a gallon, the most we ever paid for petrol during the whole trip. Added to our remaining eight or so gallons this would give us a range of just over 300 kilometres, theoretically still not enough to reach Alindao. It was going to have to be a day of very gentle driving in order to squeeze out the mileage. Hopefully the road would be sympathetic to our situation. Back to the police station for the obligatory registration where we were obliged to wait for over an hour because they were all 'in a meeting', and then at last we were on the road to Kembe at ten thirty.

*A mixed reception whilst passing through Kembe*

The route continued through rain forest along the usual two deep ruts with smooth sections, interspersed with slow, difficult bits, but yet again all negotiable in two wheel drive. The last section into Kembe proved to be the worst, where the road had suffered severe water erosion although it was now quite dry. We were heading for the local Baptist mission again but our requests for directions led us astray a couple of times down some appalling side roads. We had long ago learnt that it was fatal to ask directions in the format "Is this the road to …..?" as this would inevitably lead to vigorous and confident nodding of the head whether it was the correct road or not. It was therefore always necessary to ask "Where is the road to ….?" as this required a knowledgeable answer. So far these interchanges had been in our very limited Arabic but in the French speaking CAR we encountered a slight variation on this theme as we had a smattering of school French between us. It was therefore rather nice to pull up next to a local, peer out the window and with some aplomb rattle off "Excusé moi, parlez-vous Francais?" as a precursor to asking for directions. Unfortunately this would inevitably result in an enthusiastic and lengthy response in fluent French of which we could make neither head nor tail, and at which point we would have to admit that our conversational skills were limited to single words and much hand waving. So much for the sophisticated Englishman abroad.

We eventually found the mission but not before first coming across beer for sale on the way. An opportunity not to be missed and we splashed out on a bottle and it was absolutely delicious. The mission was another immaculate set-up, this time run by a couple in their sixties, Dick and Irene Paulson. Dick and Irene were both qualified dentists and had a thriving clinic as their main occupation in addition to their preaching duties. Generously they invited us to use their guest room. We initially politely refused but they insisted and we were able to have a super shower followed by a meal of Nile Perch and salad, accompanied by an interesting chat and then into a comfy bed. Very nice.

Our visit was rounded off the next day with a breakfast of paw-paw and pancakes followed by an unfortunate hour of what could only be described as bible thumping. This rather took the edge off things. A delightful couple but fanatical scripture preachers. Nevertheless, yet another amazing example of selfless commitment to the welfare of the black African.

We made our escape at nine and yet again struggled through some enormous dry ruts along the road. We crashed and banged and bounced slowly along until suddenly, there in front of us was 'the road gang', progressing towards us from Alindao, still some 170 kilometres away. The road gang consisted of an enormous bulldozer with a pair of three foot tines at the back which ripped up the dirt like a fork through soft butter. This obliterated all the ruts and a grader followed to smooth out the ploughed field effect, in turn followed by a big roller. We waited nearly an hour at a village whilst this process rebuilt the road through it and then as we continued the surface gradually improved and we were able to cruise at fifty kilometres an hour. It was ages since we had been on such a flat, smooth surface and the relief was incredible. No more bracing against bone-shaking jolting and lurching.

Huge relief as we meet the road gang working towards us

We reached Alindao just after lunch and just as we entered a town of the usual thatched mud dwellings we ran out of petrol and the engine died. Actually, not quite out. I still had a couple of pints in the leaky second tank but it had been a very close run thing. The improved road surface must have made all the difference as we had averaged an amazing twenty seven kilometres (seventeen miles) to the gallon since leaving Bangassou. Switching the tanks over we drove a final kilometre and with sighs of relief found shops and petrol. It was still very expensive so we cautiously bought only four and a half gallons at about £2.70 a gallon and then carried on towards Bambari, our next objective.

As we drove along I did some more mental calculations and realised that four and a half gallons of fuel was, in fact, barely enough to cover the 120 kilometres to Bambari even if we were averaging twenty seven kilometres to the gallon. Fortunately the better road surface reduced consumption and I also slipped into 'freewheeling downhill' mode and we arrived in Bambari hardly believing our good fortune. Bambari was a much more advanced town than we had met so far. With more sighs of relief we pulled up outside a store with a hand operated petrol pump only to be told that it was closed and we would have to return the next day. Now we were really sweating on the fuel situation. I drove gingerly off, hardly daring to touch the accelerator. The Baptist mission was three kilometres away and we rolled very gently into the yard and quickly switched off the engine. Yet another generous welcome from Don and Betty Teachout and their sons David, Jonathan and Don Junior. We were given access to a hot shower and were then invited to take supper with them, a very tasty meal of meat and macaroni with salad and home-made bread buns followed by iced chocolate cake. Once again the conversation quickly turned to their religion and we were treated to some intense bible analysis before going home at nine o'clock.

This was to be our last experience of missionaries in Africa. It had been very interesting to experience the differences in approach by the Catholics, the Evangelists and the Baptists. It had been a privilege to meet them and they had all been very welcoming despite the fact that we were not part of their crusade. The Catholic presence had been marked by large, awe-inspiring church buildings and seminary complexes designed to turn out local priests. The welfare side appeared to be handled by overworked nuns who ran orphanages, schools and basic health clinics and who also seemed to have to provide housekeeping duties for the priests. The Evangelists were taking a much more practical approach, not only training preachers and teaching religion but at the same time introducing excellent small industries and craft training in addition to basic education. Finally, the Baptists seemed to be the most ardent bible thumpers and the impression I gained was of them existing in their own sheltered lifestyle, fervently bringing the Word of God to the local population but themselves remaining largely unaffected by their surroundings and the local culture. Classic Americanism. Both the Evangelist and the Baptist missions were staffed by complete American families, including teenage children, and neither of these religions went in for huge ornate churches, managing with very simple buildings. I came away with no conclusions other than that I would have felt much more comfortable if the Africans had been left to their own traditional beliefs. What they needed was education and healthcare with a bit of sympathetic Christianity thrown in, not the other way round. I find it hard to believe that an all-merciful God would have put people on the Earth and then ignored them until they were eventually discovered and converted by white men with their own peculiar brands of worship.

We had breakfast with the Teachouts and Don insisted that we take away a paper on the origins of the world to read at our leisure and then hand in to the mission in Bangui. We were also to deliver a couple of letters there for them. We took our leave and drove into Bambari, expecting to run out of petrol at any minute. In town we at last found a bank so were able to change some money, but it was the last day of December and it looked as if the whole local population was there jostling for their end of month pay. After much good natured pushing and shoving we managed to change ninety dollars and with considerable relief returned to the petrol pump where we took on board eighteen gallons at £1.90 a gallon. Not only was the cost of petrol decreasing rapidly but the availability of food was increasing equally fast. We bought bread, eggs and bananas without difficulty and later in the day some tomatoes from a roadside stall.

We wanted to reach the capital Bangui that day, and celebrate New Year's Eve in what we hoped would be some form of civilisation. We estimated it as being some 400 kilometres away but the huge improvement in the dirt road surface meant that we made good time. The vegetation was starting to become smaller and sparser but the villages still consisted of thatched mud huts. About halfway to Bangui, at the town of Sibut, our road was to meet the north/south road that went from Bangui up to Chad. According to the Michelin maps we had seen, this road was tarmac and we looked forward to a smooth, fast run into Bangui. Our optimism was tempered somewhat as our road deteriorated the nearer we got to Sibut but at last we came to the tee-junction and turned left on the blacktop. We were already running later than planned, after the delay at the bank, and our plans were now further thwarted just down the road when we were waved down by the occupants of a Toyota bus which had a puncture. This wasn't a country where mechanical help could be summoned with a telephone call from a convenient AA box, and the driver had the tools and ability to remove the wheel and the tyre but unfortunately didn't have a patch or a pump to complete the job. I had both but it took forty five precious minutes before the bus was back on its wheels and we were on our way again.

Darkness fell, which was not ideal for driving but we were now committed and determined to reach the capital. Near the city we had to stop at two police check points, but passed through both with no delays. At last we drove into Bangui to be met by some street lighting, proper multi-storey buildings and lots of people obviously milling about preparing to celebrate the New Year. A really nice atmosphere. We had been told by other travellers to head for an area of open ground opposite the Rock Hotel, where all overlanders congregated and camped whilst in Bangui. Surprisingly enough we found this without difficulty and found several vehicles there already and lots of Brits who welcomed us with open arms. It was eight thirty. Dawn did some quick housework to clear the worst of the dust out of the Rover before knocking up a tasty stew. I obtained directions to a local shop where I bought a bottle of wine and a couple of bottles of beer and we settled down to a relaxed meal in friendly surroundings with a feeling of relief and satisfaction at having completed yet another significant stage of our overall journey. We rounded the night off by heading over to an Encounter Overland Bedford truck where we joined in the celebrations with singing, drinking and chatting until three o'clock.

We completed our welcome to the New Year with a lie-in the next morning followed by a leisurely and hearty breakfast of fried potatoes and tomatoes, fried bread and eggs. The rest of the day was spent giving the Rover a good clean out after all the dusty travelling since Sudan, and Dawn, of course, did some washing.

This so-called camp site, just a large open area, was situated over the road from the two storey Rock Hotel which backed onto the Ubangi River. It was surrounded on the other three sides by tall trees and stands of virgin bamboo and was overlooked by the multi-storey Safari hotel just along the road from the Rock. It was a quiet location but within convenient walking distance of the main town centre.

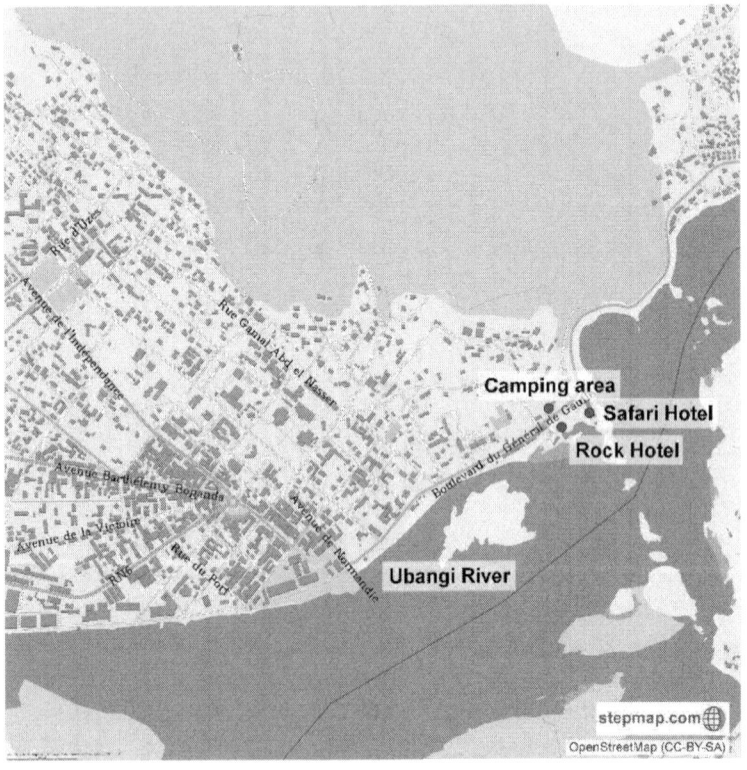

*Our landmarks in Bangui*

In addition to the Encounter Overland truck there was a purpose-built Stonefield vehicle owned by the British Guerba travel company, which catered for the upper end of the overland market. The Stonefield was an impressive vehicle carrying perhaps twenty people in an enclosed body with proper opening windows as opposed to the canvas backed Bedford and its younger passengers. Stonefield was a company based in Scotland that was striving to produce the ultimate four wheel drive vehicle for both commercial and military use. This one was interesting in that it had an automatic gearbox and this led to much discussion with the driver about the pros and cons versus a manual gearbox. They had had some gearbox problems since leaving England and this only increased my scepticism about the choice, being a died-in-the-wool clunky Land Rover gearbox man. The Guerba passengers were generally of an older, certainly more wealthy, breed. We found them to be an amiable bunch but at the same time we were intruiged to hear that they had actually ganged up on and voted off one female passenger who had apparently had a bit of a fling with the driver. Not unnaturally this had left the shadow of a black cloud hanging over the remaining group, not all of whom had voted for the dismissal, and we were somewhat dubious about how their travels and relationships would develop.

The occupants of the Bedford were the usual happy-go-lucky bunch of young people. The leader of this Encounter Overland group was an extremely personable young man called Dave who had all the character and charisma that this sort of position required. I was to run into him again a couple of years later whilst in Kathmandu. I was booking on an Encounter Overland river rafting trip and he was the local representative. He delved into a pile of boxes in his desk and produced a slide showing my Rover in the Bangui car park. Small world. Encounter Overland had an excellent reputation in the adventure travel world and their organisation and professionalism in Bangui demonstrated only too clearly what a shambles the Traks venture had been.

Various other vehicles came and went during our time there, a VW camper, a Dutch guy in a Land Rover and a couple of Unimogs being amongst them. Most were heading in the opposite direction to us and generally crossed into Zaire over the Ubangi River which flowed past Bangui and formed the border between the two countries. Because of this close proximity to its neighbour, Bangui was the focal point for some entrepreneurial types who made some kind of a living out of buying second hand lorries in the UK and driving them down to sell to Zairians who came across the river to conduct their negotiations. The very nature of the business meant that the vehicles up for sale were a real hotch potch of types and marques. One guy had a most unsuitable looking articulated, flatbed Morris truck but after a few days he announced that he had struck a deal and was ready to head back home. How he had driven it from the UK I don't know. He must have been towed across the Sahara.

New Year's Day passed very pleasantly and we enjoyed the company of other travellers. One thing we were quickly told was that Bangui was notorious for thieves, and therefore our vehicles were arranged lager style much like the covered wagons in the Old West. There was an infamous tale of a German Unimog parked there with a small motorbike securely chained to a carrying frame at the back. During a torrential thunderstorm this bike had disappeared without the vehicle occupants hearing a thing. In fact we actually had first-hand experience of some of the nefarious local population later that afternoon. Dawn and I took a stroll into the town, which was all but deserted due to the holiday, and came across a group of lads with whom we struck up a bit of a French conversation in our usual amicable fashion. Part way through I became aware of activity around one of my trouser pockets and looked down to see two brown fingers attempting to gently extract a bank note. Just as gently I reached down and pulled the hand away and returned it to its grinning owner. This attempted burglary had been so amateurish and light hearted that it was hard to take it seriously, although I have no doubt of the fate of my money had I not noticed. I think that Dawn was a bit disgusted that I hadn't been more aggressive, but that isn't my nature and, in a place like Bangui with poverty ridden teenagers of dubious reputation, discretion was the better part of valour. To guard against crime back at the campsite a security system was operated and all the occupants were entered onto a roster so that we all took our turns at patrolling the site throughout the night. A sort of Neighbourhood Watch. That first night I had the two o'clock to three o'clock shift and whilst the weather during the day was warm and very humid I soon found that the temperature dropped to shivering in the middle of the night during the lonely trudge around my beat.

Another feature of the Bangui campsite worthy of mention was the toilet facility. As previously stated, this wasn't a proper campsite, just a large patch of waste ground. There were no toilets and if there had been they would probably have been unusable, but fortunately behind the camp were the huge bamboo stands with pathways and clearings in between. All that was necessary was to keep an eye open to ascertain that nobody else was in there attending to their needs and then boldly stride in with one's bog roll and spade in clear view to signal one's intentions to other people, a bit like moving a cubicle bolt to the 'engaged' position. Once inside, the ground was nice and soft and sandy. The only danger, of course, was that you might dig in the same spot as somebody else had recently, but this never happened to me and the forest was remarkably efficient at absorbing the effluent of countless numbers of people, the bamboo apparently flourishing on it.

On the open road our toilet needs were easily met, we simply went behind a convenient bush with paper and entrenching tool and did the necessary whilst relaxing and admiring the view. Having said this, however, the simple life is great until one runs out of soft toilet paper, which was all too easy to do in Arab areas where it played no part in the daily ablutions. Whilst in the youth hostel in Wau, crumpled pages of the Reader's Digest had borne testament to the desperate straits that at least one sad individual had been reduced to.

Having reached our latest objective we now had to tackle the bureaucracy necessary to enable us to leave the CAR and drive first into Cameroon and second into Nigeria. Our first hurdle to overcome was the fact that Dawn's passport was now completely full and that whilst still valid there were no blank spaces for any more stamps. Each border crossing had obviously necessitated rubber stamping but we hadn't bargained for all the police registrations en route, and many of these, too, resulted in the application of a local stamp, applied with a determined and flamboyant gusto and little regard for the amount of space consumed.

We loaded all the still damp washing into the Rover and set off to the British Consul where we left Dawn's passport whilst they attended to attaching some additional pages. We also changed some money and went off on a bit of a mad spending spree, returning to the Rover with bags containing bread, fresh meat, lots of vegetables, paté (yes, paté), chocolate (luxury), toilet rolls (even more luxury) and a bottle of beer (necessity). During the day we also visited the main post office and managed to telephone our respective mothers back in the UK, which was quite an achievement. In addition I found two Land Rover dealers where I enquired after rubber bushes for the front suspension but met with no success. A rattling and knocking from the front had revealed that the bush in the left-hand leaf spring rear end had worn to the extent that virtually no rubber was left.

Guard duty that night was a more reasonable eleven o'clock to midnight and Dawn stopped up to keep me company. Another damp day with a cool night.

The following day we collected Dawn's expanded passport and headed for the Nigerian and Cameroon embassies. The Nigerian was closed but we obtained the necessary forms from the Cameroon and I had some passport photos taken. It was a pleasanter day with much less humidity. In the afternoon I was chatting to Alan, the driver of the Guerba truck, and he rummaged in his spares box and came up with two of the rubber bushes that I needed for the front suspension. I gratefully accepted one of them and jacked up the Rover and replaced the worn one. Being Saturday we went across to the Safari hotel in the evening where we took the lift up to the bar for a beer and from where we had a bird's eye view of the campsite. They actually ran out of beer at ten o'clock so we went back to bed.

There was going to be no visa business on a Sunday so I continued my maintenance of the Rover by replacing the oil seals on both back wheels, where oil leakage was betraying some wear and tear. Another overland Bedford arrived but these large groups tended to be self-contained and kept themselves to themselves.

Monday morning and time to start the visa chase. With room in Dawn's passport for more stamps we now had to obtain extensions to our CAR visas which, on our present time scale, would run out before we could leave the country. We left both passports and applications at the Immigration Department and then went looking for camping gas. We had been told of a company called Centro Hydro who supplied liquid gas but we had no success in finding it. Abandoning this quest we sought the Baptist mission to return Don Teachout's scripture paper. We couldn't find that, either, but eventually found the Evangelist mission and they promised to pass the paper on for us. Back to the Nigerian embassy which this time was open and where we collected the visa application forms before returning to the Immigration office to be told that our visa extensions were not ready. So the day passed with little progress made.

Leaving Dawn at the Rover I walked to the Immigration office the next morning and learnt that our visa extensions needed stamps costing about US$10.00 each, but of course these could not be bought there. No, I had to walk to a particular office which happened to be behind the old presidential palace where the tyrant Bokassa had once lived and infamously dined on his subjects. Fortunately it wasn't too far but on my return to the Immigration office I was told that our visa extensions could still not be completed until the next day. Unfortunately today was Tuesday, the only day of the week that the Nigerian embassy accepted visa applications so I had to stop the extension process, retrieve our passports and hot foot it to the Nigerian consul, where I submitted all the necessary forms and then sat around waiting for two hours before being told to come back the next day.

Next day there I was, this time for two and a half hours before being told to come back on the Friday. We knew that government offices and officials were always going to be a tedious part of our journey and we strove to remain patiently resigned during this type of delay. There was no point in making a fuss, we didn't hold the whip hand. We were just grateful that it was always possible to obtain the necessary visas along the way, whatever the frustration. Apparently travellers with companies like Encounter Overland going in the opposite direction from the UK to Kenya, for example, could obtain all their visas in the UK before setting off. In fact, *had* to obtain them before setting off. Simple.

The following day the Guerba group were scheduled to leave so in the evening we joined up with some of them in the Safari bar for a last couple of beers. These get-togethers with other travellers were always enormously interesting, entertaining and, not least, informative. We were all thirsty for information about what was to come, and advance knowledge of roads, camp sites, fuel availability etc was eagerly gleaned and mentally filed away. Unfortunately a very pleasant evening was ruined for me as I had the three o'clock to four o'clock morning guard duty. The temperature plummeted and I spent one of the coldest and most miserable hours of my life as I shivered and plodded my way round in the dim moonlight, peering into the shadows for any suspicious movements. Thank goodness for the Rover, a warm bed and a human size hot water bottle at the end of it.

The next day, Thursday, was effectively a free day as all government offices were closed and we could do nothing about our visas. We had chatted with a German chap who was travelling with his girlfriend in a Mercedes Unimog and they, too, needed camping gas. Our search for Centro Hydro having been a waste, we had now been told to go to Hydra Electric so I was going for a ride in the Unimog to investigate. Whilst waiting for the lift I jacked up the Rover and started stripping the front right hand stub axle. I found this to have been damaged in the accident, the stub axle being slightly bent and the whole steering swivel assembly being displaced vertically by about a quarter of an inch. The result of this was that the large oil seal on the big swivel ball didn't align anymore and the axle oil just poured out, which meant, more ominously, that dirt and sand could just as easily get in.

Our German friend came over and I hopped into his vehicle. I knew nothing about the Unimog, only that it was a pretty rugged piece of kit with a large box body on the back, which looked ideal for campervan conversions. It was bigger than the Rover and this one had a diesel engine, but any envious thoughts I may have had were immediately cancelled when I discovered how cramped and uncomfortable the ride was. There was very little leg room and the ride was really hard and bumpy, even around town on halfway decent roads. It was also very noisy. Thanks, but I'd stick to the dear old Rover. Not surprisingly our venture proved fruitless. Hydra Electric did have bottled gas but their fittings were not compatible with our bottles.

Back at the campsite I completed my repairs by fitting a spare stub axle from my goody box and shimming it with washers to lift it and realign the oil seal. I doubt that Land Rover Inspection would have passed it but under the circumstances I was very pleased with my efforts.

Another arrival at the campsite had been a huge, ex-German army MAN diesel truck with a canvas back cover, basic bus seats and a complement of young Australian overlanders, all shepherded along by a young and likeable American lad called Eddie. Eddie came over for a chat and proved to be a mine of useful information. He was a one man band and had bought the truck in Germany, advertised the trip from there to Kenya and filled it with enthusiastic passengers, an assortment of very large cooking pots, some tents and various other basic essentials. He had somehow acquired a copy of the Encounter Overland bible which was supposed to be jealously guarded by each of their tour leaders and which contained all the necessary information needed to plan and run an overland adventure tour group travelling through Africa. It all sounded very exciting and fascinating, although Eddie did put things into perspective a little when he recounted having to have a complete spare engine flown out to Nigeria after a disastrous breakdown. Anyway, one vital piece of information was that we would need proof of insurance at the Moroccan border. Insurance? What was that? Eddie gave a knowing smile and produced an official looking green card from a pile he had in his truck. This proved to be an 'International Motor Insurance Card' issued by 'The Hanover Insurance Company of 14 Fenchurch Avenue, London E.C.3' and 'Issued under the authority of Motor Insurer's Bureau'. All we had to do was fill it in and, hey presto, we were insured. Easy.

The Guerba group had left as planned that morning, leaving a sizeable hole in the campsite, both physically and socially. A large truck like that, surrounded by perhaps eight or ten tents, took up quite a bit of space and we had grown very used to the presence of some very pleasant people.

We went into town the next morning to learn that the Nigerian visas were still not ready and neither were suitable adaptors available anywhere to enable us to have our gas bottles filled. Later in the morning, after my second walk into town, I collected our passports with fourteen-day Nigerian visas in them. This enabled me to take them straight back to the CAR Immigration office where I was told that we would be given a fifteen day extension and…..."Come back tomorrow". Back at the camp, things had been reorganised a bit since the departure of the Guerba group, and Dawn and I were now part of Eddie's group for guard duties and the girls were expected to do their share, too. That night Dawn and I ended up with the two hour shift from eleven o'clock in the evening to one o'clock in the morning. Another very cold night.

*****

The Bangui campsite. The Guerba truck is on the left with us behind it. Eddie's big MAN truck is in the background

Despite it being Saturday the next day, the Immigration office was actually open and we collected our passports with, in fact, a twenty day visa extension in each, which would be ample time for us unless anything unexpected cropped up. From the Immigration office it was straight to the Cameroon Embassy, which was also open, where we duly submitted our applications for passage into that country. They wanted the vehicle details so back at the campsite it was a good opportunity to carefully fill in Eddie's donated insurance card and give it a trial run. We breathed a sigh of relief when all our paperwork passed scrutiny at the embassy and our passports and visas were promised for the Monday. So far, so good.

That evening we went over to the Safari for a beer with Eddie and ended up having a rather intriguing conversation. Encouraged by his experiences so far, Eddie wanted to expand his overland business. He had learnt quite a few lessons and felt confident that he could now create a successful enterprise. However, he wanted to take on a business partner to share the expenses, responsibilities and problems. After our contact over the previous couple of days he suggested that I might be interested. Having given up my job with British Aerospace I had no idea what I was going to do on our return to the UK and, in my current very enjoyable Travel Mode, the prospect of driving truckloads of happy-go-lucky people from the UK to Kenya sounded very appealing, so we quickly moved on to a more detailed discussion of working together. Over the next couple of days Dawn and I discussed this potential venture. She felt rather left out of the plans although I could see no reason why she shouldn't come along on the trips in an official capacity. She remained sceptical but at the same time was prepared to support me if that was what I decided to do. By the time we left Bangui, and after more in-depth discussions, Eddie and I had shaken hands on the future. He was going to complete the current trip and then contact us back in the UK. My commitment to the business at that time was to buy some large aluminium cooking pots in Morocco when we passed through there. To finish the story, a few months later Eddie did turn up in the UK and came to Dawn's cottage to see us. He had suffered a very bad break to his right leg and this was going to leave him unfit for some time and certainly in no state to drive a heavy truck across Africa. I had been fully prepared to go along with the venture but have to admit that it was a bit of a relief when he backed out. The four large aluminium cooking pots remained for many years as a reminder of what might have been.

Talking with other people at the campsite we had learnt that it was possible to visit a Pygmy settlement situated just over 100 kilometres from Bangui. This was a settlement where a small mission with a handful of nuns provided spiritual guidance and basic health care to the local indigenous population. It was situated a few kilometres out of the small town of Mbaiki, near a lumber camp. Apparently visitors were welcome and the Pygmies were grateful for simple gifts such as sugar, salt and matches. With a spare day whilst we waited for our Cameroon visas it was an opportunity for a unique outing, so on the Sunday we packed up and headed out of town. The road was good tarmac and it was a relief to be on the move again. Just outside Bangui we picked up a young gendarme at a police check point and gave him a lift to Mbaiki. He pointed out Bokassa's old residence and other points of interest and we bowled along through tall trees dotted all over the spreading savannah until we reached Mbaiki where we left behind both the gendarme and the tarmac. We drove through the town of mud brick huts, took a left a few kilometres outside and headed off along a reasonable dirt road, eventually turning right towards the lumber camp. The vegetation started to build up until we were in dense, green forest. The road ended for us when we came to a bridge over a small river. The road over the bridge was blocked by tree trunks and a padlocked barrier. This all corresponded with the directions we had been given and we left the Rover and continued on foot. The bridge, in fact, had partially collapsed and didn't look too safe. We walked for about a kilometre and found the nuns' brick but basic quarters. Here we introduced ourselves to one of the nuns and she agreed to arrange a local guide to show us around the following day. We were also able to confirm the correct etiquette for handing over our little packages of gifts. On our return to the Rover we found two local girls squatting in the shallow river fishing for tiny, wriggling creatures.

They had some very battered aluminium pots and simply dipped these into the water and then strained out their prey with their fingers. They took not the slightest notice of us. Once again the prudish imposition of religion was in evidence. They would probably have been innocently naked and comfortable a few years before but now looked rather awkward and ridiculous in tatty old shorts and one of them wore an old dirty bra. The overall impression was of very basic survival and was quite depressing.

We camped where we had stopped next to the bridge and early the next morning were rudely awoken by the unlikely arrival of a large bulldozer and a lorry, both of which squeezed past us, removed the tree trunks, unlocked the barrier and disappeared into the undergrowth, locking the barrier behind them. We walked down to find the nuns again and were assigned a local Pygmy guide to show us around. This fellow was remarkably smartly dressed in a blue business suit.

Meeting our Pygmie guide

The whole area was densely wooded with thick jungle vegetation and narrow paths winding and twisting between small settlements, with just five or six very basic huts in each. These huts resembled igloos and were very simply made with a skeleton of bent branches covered with an assortment of leaves and dried grasses. If our guide could boast a suit, the settlement inhabitants certainly could not. Clothing was barely a nod to decency and it was generally traditionally woven or made from forest materials with only the occasional Oxfam hand-me-down shorts and shirts.

*Getting the Pygmies into perspective*

We were shown basket traps which were used to catch termites smoked out of mounds and also a dug-out canoe under construction, being chipped out of a huge tree trunk.

With the Pygmies we really did seem to have come across a virtually unspoilt group of people who were hardly affected by the twentieth century, and presumably but for the logging camp a short distance away they could have remained totally remote for many more years. Over everything was an almost tangible air of poverty and need, evidenced by the presence of many bellies swollen with the classic sign of malnutrition. At the same time everybody we met was cheerful and friendly and at least they were being left pretty much alone to live as they had done for thousands of years.

Nevertheless the logging industry was continually expanding and eating away at their natural environment and I couldn't see how these people could survive for much longer and even less could I see how they could be integrated into a modern society. Very sad.

We circled through the forest and visited four of the settlements, in each of which we were casually greeted and gently pressed for cigarettes, sweets and salt. Back at the Rover, as agreed beforehand with the nuns, we handed over our little offerings of salt, sugar, matches, an empty jam jar and even more cigarettes. It had been a tremendous experience, made all the better as we never felt that we were intruding and were able to freely take photographs without offending anybody.

We headed back to Bangui, arriving at the campsite mid-afternoon having called in at the Cameroon embassy to learn that our visas were still not ready. Eddie and his tour were still there plus one or two other people that we had come to know, but the usual peaceful and convivial atmosphere was ruined by the arrival of some Dutch guys who played loud music tapes throughout the evening and then again early the next morning. This was most unusual and we didn't experience such inconsiderate behaviour anywhere else on our trip.

What was to be our last day in Bangui was spent in collecting our passports and Cameroon visas and then obtaining exit stamps from the CAR Immigration department. We filled up with petrol which, incidentally, was readily available, carried out final preparations on the Rover and stocked up with some food. It was now obvious that the days of petrol shortages were behind us and we had met a Brit couple, Andy and Sue, who were heading in the opposite direction so we sold them the plastic petrol containers that we had bought in Sudan and re-packed the roof rack without them. As part of the deal Andy gave us a soft collapsible 5 gallon water container which had a slight leak, plus their Michelin road map for North and West Africa. This gave us our entire detailed route from Bangui to Spain and it was a wonderful document to get our hands on after the somewhat unsatisfactory Bartholomews maps.

We were initially to head to the Cameroon border, north and west from Bangui and just over 600 kilometres away. The road was good tarmac and we made good time. At Bouali we made a short diversion to make a tourist visit to the very impressive waterfalls. Back on the main road and 30 kilometres later we came to the roadhead and we were diverted around the road building machinery on a very dusty track before returning to the original road sans tarmac. Nevertheless it was well used and in good condition with the usual thatched hut villages dotted along the way. About 260 kilometres after leaving Bangui we stopped for the night just outside Yaloke. By this time we had completely run out of gas and Dawn was having to do all the cooking over an open fire. That night she produced a very impressive spread of beefburgers, chips and peas, topped with a thick gravy and followed by fried banana and evaporated milk. The lack of gas had no effect on the quality or variety of meals that she could magic up, the only downside being a collection of very black and sooty pots and pans. Early in the evening a local turned up on his moped and once again we were persuaded to hand over a pint of petrol.

We had hoped to reach the border the next day but a combination of a bad road surface and then a one hour holdup due to bridge repairs meant that we still had 120 kilometres to go when we stopped for the night in a small clearing by the roadside. At the bridge holdup there were 3 VW Combis, a Land Rover and a bus full of Italian overlanders all heading from Europe to Bangui. From Bangui the main overland route at the time then headed south into Zaire and it seemed that few people planned to head east to Sudan along the route that we had used. Hence the previous lack of traffic. Also the end of the wet season probably signalled the start of the travelling season.

An unsettling incident occurred that night. We had an early night but were disturbed at nine o'clock by a strange scraping noise from just outside the Rover. The night was pitch black and the sound was a bit like a large stone being pulled over a sheet of metal. Somewhat nervously I took the torch and investigated but couldn't see anything. However, it was unsettling enough for us to grab the two picnic chairs from outside, secure the vehicle and drive off into the night to find a better spot. Of course we had no idea where we were, so continued along the road peering through the blackness until we came across a flat area and the outline of some village huts just beyond. The thought of peaceful villagers not far away gave us a feeling of security and we spent the rest of the night undisturbed.

Not so the next morning when we awoke to find ourselves surrounded by chattering residents and children, no doubt much intrigued by this mysterious midnight arrival. Well, we really couldn't be bothered with it all so quietly dressed, sat in our seats and then drew back the curtains, started the engine and drove off all in a few seconds, much to the amazement of the wide eyed children. We stopped for breakfast on the other side of the village and then continued to the border, arriving at midday. The drive over the past two days had been uninspiring and I had noted in the daily diary that it was 'just a journey'.

Distance across Central African Republic  -  2,464 km

Total distance travelled from start – 13,238 km

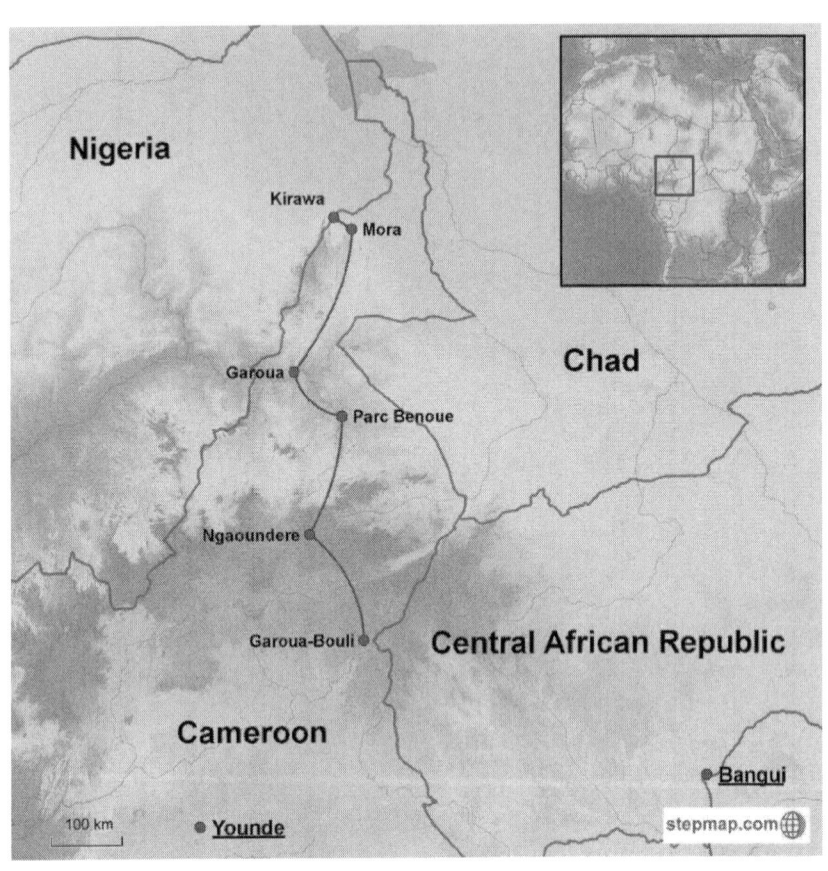

# Chapter 15 – Cameroon

Friday 16th to Wednesday 21st January 1981

Journey days 119 to 124

With formalities taking only a few minutes at each border we were soon in the Cameroon town of Garoua-Boulai. At the CAR border we had met another Brit couple in a Land Rover and now in the town we met a couple of Kiwi lads and a girl and had lunch and a beer with them. We needed local currency but had to wait until two forty five for the bank to open. Once inside we were astounded to be told that they would change neither traveller's cheques nor cash American dollars. This was just the latest example of frustrating banking that we came across. Opening hours varied from country to country as did the closing days, depending upon whether it was a Moslem week or a Christian week, and services such as international exchange could be non-existent, even next to borders. As always, the inability to obtain local currency was very inconvenient. We were able to change our remaining CAR currency but this was insufficient for our needs before we could reach Ngoundere and its banks some 260 kilometres further down the road. A sympathetic bank employee suggested that we try the local American mission, so yet again we set off to seek their assistance and yet again we were welcomed by some very pleasant people who were quite willing to change US$25 dollars cash. This enabled us to buy petrol and engine oil and we then drove about half way to Ngoundere before nightfall.

The red dust of Cameroon

We had had no idea what Cameroon would be like, and the most noticeable thing was that it was red. The soil was the colour of red ochre and as fine as talcum powder so that it permeated every nook and cranny of the Rover. The terrain was becoming hillier and we were slowly but surely climbing as we headed northwest. However, there was a noticeable lack of the late afternoon and early evening haze that had been present all through the CAR. This particular evening the gain in altitude and the clearer air gave us spectacular and far reaching views across the countryside, a refreshing change. Also the villages were different, round thatched huts instead of rectangular and many more with mud walls around them instead of open areas. The inhabitants appeared to be predominantly Moslem, clad in full length white robes rather than the casual and often limited attire worn in the Christian areas of the CAR and Sudan.

Our days now started more slowly. In order to make tea and coffee for breakfast we had first to light a fire to heat the water. This was a beautiful morning, clear and clean and not too hot. Being still in dire need of cash we had to reach Ngoundere before eleven thirty when the banks would close. After a fast ride on an excellent dirt piste we arrived there just after eleven to find the bank firmly closed because, of course, it was Friday in a Moslem country. However there was a Transcontinental Hotel and as Ngoundere had all the looks of a decent civilised town we headed over to it, only to have to wait for one and a half hours for the manager to turn up. This fine fellow very reluctantly agreed to change some travellers cheques for us, and further demonstrated his enthusiasm by quoting a ridiculously low rate of exchange. Unfortunately we had no choice but to accept, but under the circumstances cashed only $100.

This still resulted in us having a relatively large sum burning a hole in our purse and so, somewhat in awe of our modern surroundings and facilities after weeks and weeks of deprivation, we decided to treat ourselves to a posh lunch in the Giraffe Café, a pleasant looking place situated on the edge of an attractive, sun dappled square. Sitting outside under an awning overlooking the tree-filled square, we both selected the Special of the Day - avocado followed by roast chicken, green beans and French fries followed by Banana Surprise. All started well with a beer and an orange juice and we sat back feeling rather contented. The starter duly arrived, just a plain avocado cut in half but there was a whole one each and they were very big and tasty. The main meal followed and looked good until we tried to eat it and found that the chicken, a large and remarkably long leg section for each of us, was as tough as old leather and quite inedible. Our culinary adventure was completed when the Banana Surprise arrived, by which time we were not, in fact, at all surprised to find that it was just a couple of unpeeled bananas lying on a plate.

There was no point in complaining in our poor French so we put it all down to experience, wrapped up the chicken to finish cooking it later and headed back to the Rover. C'est la vie.

We rounded off the afternoon by taking advantage of the amazing range of foodstuffs that this relatively sophisticated and obviously ex-French colonial town had to offer. This was after we had found an Indian trader who changed a $100 travellers' cheque at an agreeable rate. We also found a shop selling camping gas but it was at such an exorbitant price that we left him with it.

Ngoundere was very pleasant. The presence of French ex-pats meant that white faces were common and we attracted no attention and enjoyed our visit – apart from the Giraffe chicken.

At this stage of our journey the next main objective was Sokoto in northern Nigeria, where Dawn had friends who were expecting us. From the Michelin map we plotted a route north through Cameroon to cross the border into Nigeria at Kirawa. The map also showed several national game parks in Cameroon and one of these, Benoue, lay on our route less than 200 kilometres from Ngoundere. Other travellers had told us of decent camping facilities available at the Buffle Noir (Black Buffalo) resort in the park so we wanted to spend the night there. It was a good tarmac road but we still didn't arrive at the main park gate until six fifteen. Here we were told that it was still a further twenty six kilometres to the campsite. In fact we clocked thirty three and it was pitch dark by the time we eventually located the lodge and the adjacent camping area. Here we were amazed to find a very sophisticated establishment with a smart restaurant full of elegantly dressed French ex-pats enjoying a Saturday night out of town. Against this background we felt spectacularly grubby and shabby but managed to buy a cold beer from the bar without being thrown out as undesirables. At the camping ground we lit a fire and when it had burnt down to ashes we wrapped our salvaged chicken legs in tin foil together with some garlic bread and potatoes and put them in the glowing embers for forty minutes. Lo and behold, like magic the previously tough, inedible chicken was transformed into lumps of black, inedible charcoal. The bread and potatoes suffered a similar fate, too, having become just a thick, sooty layer when we unwrapped the foil. We compensated with some fried bananas and went to bed at eleven just as the temperature started to drop.

In the morning and with daylight we were able to take stock of our surroundings and found ourselves in a beautiful setting in the forest. The lodge consisted of very attractive, single storey stone built units with thatched roofs arranged around the smart bar and restaurant. Not quite as sumptuous, perhaps, as its cousins in the Kenyan game parks but decidedly up-market. The situation was stunning, up on the edge of a gorge through which ran the Benoue River. The range of animals in the park was extensive, with hippos, crocodiles, eland and monkeys. It all smacked of prosperity and Lotus Eating French and was obviously provided for, and supported by, the ex-pat population. Not that the animals were necessarily protected. Cameroon was popular as a country where big game hunting still flourished.

To regain the main road we decided to continue north to exit the park near a camp called Bel Elan. At a barrier we were stopped and asked to pay $12 each to continue through the park. We managed to argue our way out of this and trundled slowly along a picturesque track from which we saw monkeys, wild pigs and elands. Bel Elan proved to be just a single cabin with three French hunters in residence. They directed us to the main road and we headed for the next main town which was Garoua. En route and mid-afternoon we saw a sign off to the right for 'Camp Des Elephants'. This was also marked on the map so we turned off for our night stop. At the end of a 20 kilometre track we came out into a small clearing on the edge of an escarpment looking out over dense forest as far as the eye could see. Down below was a wide tributary of the Benoue River and in a flat sand bank in the river were the unmistakeable tracks of a large animal, which we decided must have been an elephant. In the clearing itself was a small, locked cabin plus a covered shelter with an old table and chairs plus a large fire pit with still smouldering ashes. A framework over it made from small branches had recently been used for cooking and there was a pleasant lingering aroma of wood smoke and roasted meat. We must have only just missed the previous occupants who were presumably more French hunters.

The very atmospheric Camp Des Elephants

It was a fabulous place to spend the night. As we were heading further north we were experiencing longer twilights and the atmosphere of the Camp Des Elephants was quite enchanting as the sun sank in a huge red sky, illuminating the broad river below us like burnished copper. It was pleasantly warm, perfectly still and completely peaceful and serene. We rekindled the fire, Dawn cooked yet another excellent meal and all was well with the world. To cap it all the moon rose big and silver and bathed our whole world in its soft, white light. Magic.

This gentle experience continued the next morning. We rose at seven (early for us) and had breakfast whilst still enjoying our surroundings. After retracing our route back to the main road we headed north to Garoua, passing through a small village on the way where bundles of firewood were displayed for sale. We stopped and bought a couple and put them up on the roof rack for future convenience, but a few kilometres further on we came across lots of wood lying around for free. At least we had contributed something to the local economy.

Garoua proved to be disappointing. Back to a poorly stocked market and a small and unimpressive supermarket. Obviously no French ex-pat population in that area. We continued to search for gas and were told that that it was available from the local Mobil petrol station. It was only midday but again, being a Moslem town, everything stopped and closed from then until three thirty, including the petrol station. We decided to wait because a gas refill would make life so much easier. Wasting no time, Dawn promptly settled down for a snooze (there being no laundry facilities handy) and I wrote some post cards until three thirty when we reported to the Mobil station to be told "Non, rien", which pretty much summed up our overall Garoua experience.

Thus it turned out to be yet another short travelling day. Beyond Garoua we managed just a further 80 kilometres, climbing now into the mountains, before pulling off the road for the night. Splendid views again, the moon was bright and full and Dawn knocked up a corned beef curry, a dish which would no doubt raise an eyebrow or two if requested at your local Indian take-away.

We were now within a day's motoring of the Nigerian border, but on the way had to pass through the small town of Rhumsiki which had been developed into something of a tourist trap to exhibit life in a typical Cameroon village. This was an ambitious idea considering what must have been very small tourist numbers but it was nevertheless an enterprising effort so we decided to swop our travellers' hats for our tourist hats for the day. In fact it turned out to be rather enjoyable. As soon as we arrived we were adopted by one of the local guides and abandoned ourselves to his tried and tested (and successful) spiel and manipulation.

Rhumsiki village

The whole area was laid out just as a village would be and first on the list was the 'chief's hut' with his day area and dining area at the front and grain stores at the back. Lounging on an animal skin in the day area was his 'wife'. In the dining area a large black, old fashioned telephone sat ostentatiously on a small, carved table. Presumably this was 'the village telephone' and a firm reminder of who had the status in these parts. Next door in another hut a woman was grinding millet with a hand held stone rubbed on a larger flat stone. We were encouraged to tip her twenty five francs and received a few peanuts in return. A couple of huts down was a woman making little thumb pots from local clay using a wooden mould and a wooden tapper. This lady was turning out dozens of red clay cups and bowls with her standard mould and decorating them with simple patterns engraved with a sharp stick. Once dried in the sun she covered them with a mixture of mutton grease and dung which then produced a dull, black glaze when fired. Firing took place in a kiln which was just a hole in the ground with a fire in the centre. Another 25 francs.

Next was perhaps the highlight of the tour, The Crab Sorcerer. This gentleman sat in solemn meditation and contemplation in the shade outside his hut. Before his crossed legs was a large clay bowl filled with coarse sand. After studying us and asking a couple of pertinent questions he inserted short sticks and shards of broken pottery into the sand in the bowl to represent us, our journey, Africa and England. This whole arrangement was then covered with the top half of a larger water pot which had had the bottom knocked out of it. In turn the top of this pot was covered with a shallow saucer. We were then invited to each ask a question. After some thought I requested when we could expect to be back in England. At this he picked a small crab out of another pot, lifted the saucer, poured some water down onto the sand, kissed the crab, put it down through the hole onto the sand and put the saucer back in place.

The Crab Sourcerer sets the scene

After a few moments he produced a small violin-type instrument with only one string, played a few discordant notes and then lifted the top pot and removed the crab. No doubt in an effort to get away from the music, the crab had quickly buried itself in the sand, disturbing all the sticks and bits of pottery.

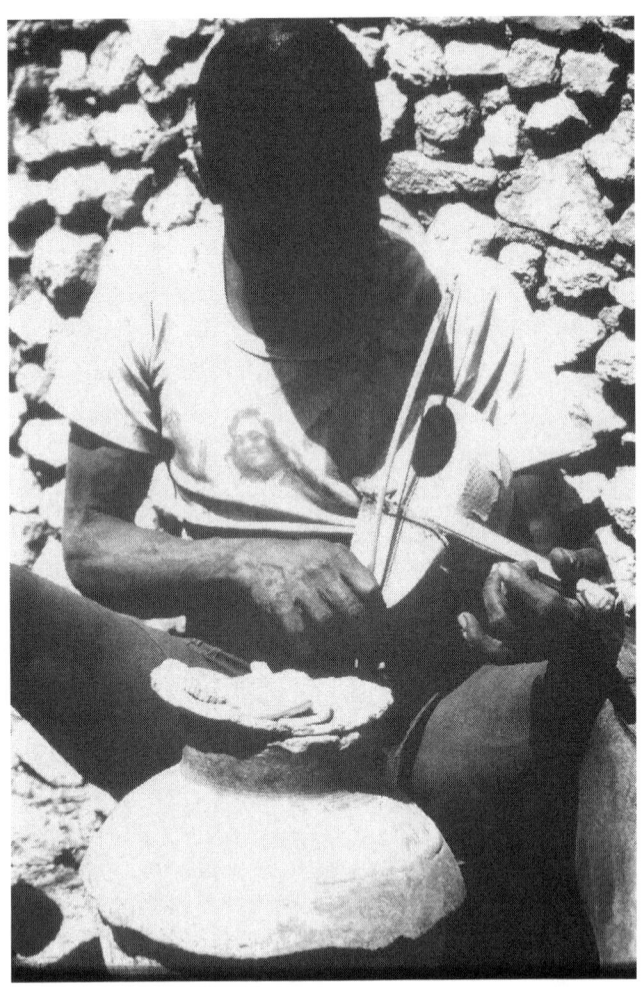

*A little bit of inspirational music......*

The resulting jumble was studied by The Crab Sorcerer who then solemnly advised me through our interpreting guide that I should arrive back in the UK in April or May (a bit beyond our current planned time) and that I would arrive healthy and after having had a good time. I would then have three children, two girls and one boy, and return to Africa within the next two years. Hmm. Dawn then asked where *she* would be that time next year, and after a repeat performance with freshly arranged sticks and shards, but no music this time, he announced that she would be back living and working in Africa but there was no mention of children. Hmm. With these little nuggets of thought provoking information our audience came to an end, The Sorcerer sprinkled water over our feet and we departed after giving him fifty francs.

Next were The Spinners, a group of women transforming fleece into yarn with hand bobbins (twenty five francs). The resulting spun yarn was passed to The Weaver, a gentleman using a small but complicated loom to produce a two inch wide strip of woven material. Multiple strips were then stitched together to make items of clothing. The loom itself was a simple affair lashed together from branches and sticks but which required considerable dexterity and skill using both feet and both hands in order to carry out the necessary sequence of operations.

The very complicated loom

The last visit on the itinerary was The Blacksmith, whose place of work was a 10 kilometre drive away. Unfortunately he wasn't in when we got there so it was just twenty francs to his wife and back to the village. It had actually been an enjoyable experience and quite illuminating. We paid off our guide with 500 francs and some vitamin tablets, removed our tourist hats and continued on our way. To put things into perspective, our apparent carefree scattering of francs cost us about US$3.50.

The road closely followed the Nigerian border, winding through spectacular mountains with huge volcanic plugs rearing up like giant stalagmites. Scattered villages of round mud huts with tall conical thatched roofs completed a scene of rural peace and tranquillity. We drove through Mokolo which was not much of a place but we were able to buy bread, carrots and lettuce. Continuing on to the border town of Mora we came across a cooperative handicraft complex presided over by an enterprising Dutch fellow. We stopped for quite a long chat with him and bought some small pots for souvenirs.

The road between Mokolo and Mora left the mountains and crossed onto the plains which marked the eastern edge of Nigeria. We drove just through Mora and camped by the roadside after darkness had fallen.

Back into Mora the next morning but any hopes of replenishing our food supplies were dashed when we could find no market and very little else, but we did buy three packets of local cigarettes for backsheesh handouts. In typical fashion we drove out of Mora in the wrong direction and had to retrace our steps to find the correct road for the border where once again the formalities were quick and cursory.


\*\*\*\*


Distance across Cameroon - 1,071 km

Total distance travelled from start – 14,309 km

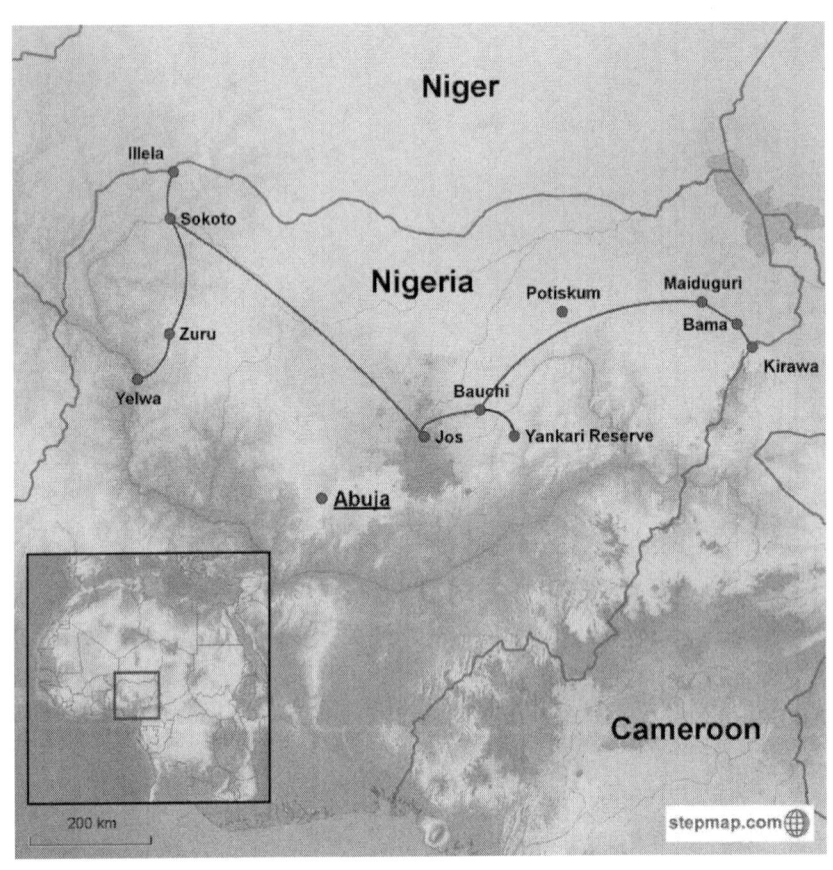

# Chapter 16 – Nigeria

Wednesday 21st January to Sunday 8th February 1981

Journey days 124 to 142

We bade 'au revoir' to Cameroon and after a short drive across no-man's land we were greeted with 'good morning' by the Nigerian official as we at last entered an English speaking country at Kirawa. We took advantage of a filling station to buy ten litres of petrol with the last of our Cameroon francs and then headed for Bama, about 60 kilometres further on into Nigeria and what, according to the map, looked to be a decent sized town. Well, yes, it was a pleasant, bustling little town, but when we found a bank and tried to change cash or travellers cheques we once again were surprised to find that a bank in a town so close to the border did not offer international exchange facilities. In response to our looks of despair we were shown through to the manager's office, a smart and tidy room where a large, beaming gentleman in traditional, brightly coloured Nigerian robes was comfortably ensconced behind an equally large desk. We sat down in the visitors' chairs, slightly scruffy and travel stained as usual, and explained our predicament. We didn't have enough petrol to go much further and had no local currency with which to purchase more but we did have ample American dollars in either Travellers Cheques or cash. To our astonishment this fine fellow dug out his own wallet, selected a five nira note and handed it over to us. This was worth about US$10. He told us that there was a branch of his bank in the next town, Maiduguri, where we would be able to change our travellers' cheques and he simply asked us to leave the five nira with the manager there for eventual return to himself. Try that with your local Barclay's manager.

The five nira bought us twenty five litres of petrol and we set off for Maiduguri, 70 kilometres away. On arrival we discovered this to be a very large town. The size of a place was usually proportional to the odds of us getting lost but in this instance we managed to navigate safely to the bank, change some travellers' cheques and leave the five nira for the Bama manager.

This northern area of Nigeria was just flat, hazy and boring. Fortunately the road was tarmac and we made good time, but it was no place for admiring the scenery, of which there was none. The next major town was Potiskum but this had been bypassed with a new road so we missed it altogether and stopped for the night a little further on.

We were heading for a game reserve at Yankari, which at 300 kilometres on a decent road was reachable the next day. We had learnt of this place from other travellers and it was pretty much on our route. We headed for Bauchi, gradually climbing back up into low mountains, and here at last we stocked up on foodstuffs, petrol, engine oil and brake fluid. We also found some nice looking barbecued mutton kebabs. At the game reserve we paid a nominal fee for entry and drove to the visitors' centre where we found attractive, individual thatched huts. There was a central restaurant and bar but in contrast the camping area was cramped and unattractive. There were 4 other overland vehicles there, a couple of Land Rovers, a VW Combi and a Unimog but the place was deserted, the owners presumably out on safari. We collected together armfuls of washing, donned our swimming gear and walked to the nearby Wikki Spring where a broad stream of crystal clear, warm water gently flowed past a concrete jetty under the dappled shade of overhanging trees. There was nobody else about and with no more ado we leapt in and luxuriated in the sheer cleanliness and freshness of it all, before setting to with soap powder and elbow grease to give everything a thorough wash and rinse. Luxury! All it needed now was a beer, but the bar remained firmly closed until six thirty, although at least when it opened, they did have cold beer.

Dawn in the laundry tub again

From Yankari our next main objective was Sokoto, where we hoped that Dawn's friends David and Helen were expecting us. We had told them of our intentions before leaving Oman but at that stage had had no idea of a date of arrival. Nevertheless they knew that we would eventually find them and, in fact, it was David's birthday in two days' time. We realised that with some serious motoring we could arrive triumphantly in the middle of his party, if he was having one, which Dawn was confident he would. Of course we didn't manage an early start the next day. There was still washing to be done and dried and we spent lunchtime at the bar with a soft drink chatting to a Swiss couple who also had a camper Land Rover. We exchanged travel information and tips and they mentioned the Hill Station Hotel in Jos, waxing lyrical about the wonderful sausage rolls that they had bought there. The mutton kebabs that we had purchased the day before had proved to be delicious so our appetites were already whetted. It was about 230 kilometres to Jos so we wouldn't reach it that day, and managed to get just past Bauchi before nightfall.

We camped by a small lake where we noted in the log that there were lots of birds. I was later to discover that the Jos Plateau Indigobird is unique to the area and of much interest to birdwatchers – not that we would have recognised one if had landed on the table in front of us.

We had thought that we were in a pretty remote area but the next morning we awoke to find a local standing gazing at us. He didn't stay long but soon after we heard the sound of a flute coming ever closer. The tune was quite melodic and the musician came strolling into sight and sat down by the lake, still continuing to play. It transformed the scene and was quite delightful.

In Jos we were determined to find the Hill Station Hotel and stuff ourselves with the fabled sausage rolls. We missed the turn the first time and ended up circling the complete town on its ring road before getting a second attempt but, of course, when we got there they didn't have any. We changed some money and headed for Sokoto, but not before passing for the second time a most unusual traffic policeman who was directing constant streams of vehicles at a busy crossroads. He had the most amazing technique, constantly twirling and dancing whilst sweeping his arms artistically through the air and blowing periodically on a whistle clenched in his teeth. It was tremendously entertaining and very effective, as the traffic remained firmly under his control, no doubt as fascinated as we were by his non-stop balletic performance. Much better than a set of boring old traffic lights.

We ended up covering 750 kilometres that day, much more than we would usually attempt but we now had our hearts set on attending David's birthday party, plus the bonus of sleeping in a proper bed. The road was good tarmac all the way and we pushed on through Zaria and Gusau without stopping. Inevitably we ended up driving several hours in the dark, a dangerous practice as we constantly encountered cars and cyclists without lights plus pedestrians ambling along the pitch black roads. There were ample stark reminders of the dangers in the form of crashed cars, especially taxis, lying at frequent intervals by the roadside. At one point we slowed right down as our headlights picked out some fresh branches of green leaves laid along the road and a local waving another branch in warning. Lying on the road were two inert bodies that looked pretty dead to us.

It was by now impractical to stop and cook a meal. We continually passed through small villages where bustling market stalls lit by bright, hissing pressure lamps displayed tempting displays of cooked meats and kebabs. We stopped at one but it was impossible to tell the origins of the cooked meats, so despite the mouth-watering sights and aromas we took the cautious route and in a larger town bought some kebabs identified as genuine beef.

We arrived in Sokoto at about ten thirty, much relieved to be near journey's end. Not as near as hoped, however. Although Dawn had been there on holiday a couple of years before, things were much different in the dark, despite it being a modern town with good roads and decent lighting. We didn't have a street map and drifted around the deserted town looking for a landmark that would give Dawn an indication of where we were relative to David and Helen's. In total confusion we eventually gave in and sought the help of a Nigerian gentleman in a smart Mercedes who kindly led us to the housing area we wanted. By this time all that was keeping me going was the thought of that cold beer just minutes away. We drove down the street to David and Helen's house, which we could now see was suspiciously dark and quiet. No party? An early night? No such luck. Nobody at home. Exhausted and crestfallen we pulled into the garden behind the house and speculated on all the scenarios. We just hoped that they hadn't gone away for a few days. By this time it was getting quite cold. We lit a fire and made a cup of coffee and sat listening for the sounds of our hosts returning home. By two fifteen we were freezing so gave up and went to bed, wondering what the next day would bring.

The next day, in fact, brought a pair of inebriated and astonished people who arrived home as the sun was rising at five thirty and who started banging on the Rover in excitement and delight. Dawn and I just managed to pull some clothes on before we were dragged out of the vehicle and into the sunrise. David turned out to be a larger than life, exuberant character. He grabbed Dawn and just about hugged the life out of her, then gave me a pretty big hug, too. Helen was a little more restrained but generally it was a huge, boisterous welcome that more than made up for the disappointment of the previous evening.

We adjourned to the warmth of the house and settled down to talk non-stop about everything. David offered me a scotch, which went down nicely but which wasn't too good as a thirst quencher at six o'clock in the morning. But you never knew what the alcohol arrangements were in different countries. Sometimes consumption was limited by liquor licences or local laws. I really wanted a cold, fizzy beer but was too polite (stupid?) to ask. I was only offered scotch so assumed that that was the only tipple available. Consequently, I drank too much, too quickly, too early and on a too empty stomach. Some beers did eventually materialise but by then it was far too late and I was virtually legless. At nine o'clock I crawled out to the Rover and collapsed unconscious on the bed but half an hour later I found myself stark naked and on my hands and knees, relieving myself on the ground by the side of the Rover. I don't think the neighbours saw me and Dawn eventually stumbled across me and guided me back into the Rover where I passed out again for a couple of hours.

This was to be the start of a very enjoyable and fruitful two weeks in Sokoto. Enjoyable because of the great hospitality extended by David and Helen and their many friends, and fruitful because of all the repair and maintenance work I was able to carry out on the Rover. It was, in fact, a return to the carefree, indulgent ex-pat life that we had left behind in Oman, with lots of dinner and lunch invitations and no shortage of alcohol. It was really nice for Dawn to spend so much time with her old friends and for us both to relax.

On the Land Rover front I had the most incredible good luck in that David had a contact at the Ministry of Works, where several partially stripped Land Rovers lay gathering dust in a yard. Maybe you can imagine my excitement when I first laid eyes on them. David obtained an official letter stating that I could take whatever items I wanted from the wrecks and this was like a free pass into an Aladdin's cave. I happily set to and worked my way down the list of repairs that had gradually built up over the weeks of travel.

I was able to fit a whole new stub axle assembly to the front right hand side to replace the one distorted by the accident and which I had shimmed in Bangui. The immediate result of this was much lighter steering. I was also able to replace the broken front half shaft which reinstated our four wheel drive, an essential requirement with the Sahara crossing now looming before us. The universal joints on the front prop shaft had become a bit loose and noisy so I replaced the whole shaft. To my amazement one of the derelict Rovers was a relatively rare version with twin, long range petrol tanks like mine and I was able to replace the leaking one from under the driver's seat. It needed a split welding up but I paid for that and this meant that we were back to the full vehicle capacity of twenty gallons. Another unbelievable stroke of luck was finding a Rover heater unit. This was fairly simple to remove and fit into my vehicle, plumbing it into the engine cooling system and connecting it to the now redundant radio aerial switch to give us a two speed fan control. I don't think that the need for a heater had crossed my mind before this. Our daytime travel had always been in the heat and we had the gas heater in the back of the Rover for cold nights. We were gradually heading further north, though, and would inevitably arrive in Europe in the middle of the winter, so the opportunity to fit a heater was a godsend. These were the major jobs that I completed and, in addition, I fitted a replacement rear door lock assembly and then did a complete oil and filter change.

Typical of our amazing good luck, the engine fan belt broke whilst we were in Sokoto. Digging into my spares box I found two spare belts, both of which turned out to be the wrong size (!). I was able to buy a couple of new (correct size) ones in the town and the problem was therefore easily rectified, but it would have been a very serious business if the belt had broken miles from anywhere.

Our search for cooking gas continued in Sokoto but again without success. We had talked to other overlanders about this and learnt that it was possible to transfer gas between bottles by connecting them with a length of suitable hose and holding the full one upside-down such that the liquid gas simply ran down and into the empty one. This advice was inevitably accompanied by hair-raising tales of explosions, but it sounded quite feasible and we managed to cobble together the necessary connection hose and transferred enough gas from David's large house bottle to ¾ fill one of ours and 1/3 the other before our nerves gave out. We still kept the supply of firewood strapped on the roof rack.

The preparation of the Rover for the continuing journey was completed with the purchase of a new eight gallon plastic jerry can to give us a decent supply of drinking water, again with the Sahara in mind.

On the home front things galloped along at a somewhat frantic pace with lots of socialising. I have mentioned the new-fangled video tape that we had watched in Qatar, and here, too, in Nigeria the video was a source of technological wonder. We watched several movies on a player owned by Paul and Maggie Ricketts and when we finally left Sokoto, Richard and Liz Harding appeared with a video *camera* and actually *filmed* our departure in black and white on their new Sony Portapack system which was a large but fairly lightweight camera connected by a stout cable to a substantial recorder and battery pack carried over the shoulder. Golly, whatever next? Tiny wireless telephones that you could carry about? Ha! Ha! At this point I might add that only one couple that David and Helen knew had a telephone in their house. We tried more than once to contact our respective mothers in the UK but without success – a very typical situation in those days.

With David and Helen in their home made pool

Whilst we had missed David's celebrations on his birthday, we were fortunately able to attend a combined party for him and his friend Moritzio which was held on the following Saturday evening. Attended by about thirty people this was an excellent, if surprisingly quiet, occasion and we were able to help out with the preparations and the catering.

With me busy on the Rover and David and Helen out teaching, Dawn was left to her own devices much of the time. Of course she did lots of washing but also had the opportunity to take a local lad, Umaru, under her wing and start to teach him to read and write English, much to his delight and Dawn's satisfaction. We did have spare time to ourselves to explore Sokoto, however. There was an interesting 'New Market' where I bought a couple of tribal knives and Dawn bought a skin jug. Outside one of the hotels we found a man with a small stall selling tourist souvenirs which included a stylised man on horseback made in metal in a basket-like weave. It was very attractive and very unusual. Dawn immediately fell in love with it and we entered negotiations that lasted for several days but the stall owner refused to budge from his asking price of about five hundred dollars. Dawn tried to beat him down to nearer three hundred but in vain and rather sadly he was left on the stall. She just had to make do with the skin jug which was more in our price range at three dollars.

Our roaming around Sokoto also led us to a pot manufacturing area where huge kilns were filled with clay pots, covered with broken shards and fired with an abundance of black smoke and heat. On another occasion we went to a dusty, open area where wrestling matches were taking place between the local Hausa tribesmen. Much displaying of half-naked, muscle-bound torsos (to Dawn's delight) accompanied by lots of loud drumming.

During the second week of our stay David had to go out on teaching inspections at Zuru and Yelwa and he invited us to accompany him. At Zuru, some 300 kilometres south of Sokoto, we met Keith and Jill, an English couple living in very spartan isolation in order to teach English at the local school. There presumably weren't many opportunities for them to socialise with other Brits and they welcomed us with open arms. Just outside Zuru was the Germache Shrine, a large pool of peaceful water surrounded by thick, green trees amidst flat, brown surroundings. Keith took us over to it, explaining that it was inhabited by crocodiles and was a place for the local people to worship and make sacrifices. We didn't see any crocodiles but as we were leaving some men were indulging in some grass burning which suddenly flared out of control and the whole shrine was engulfed in flames and even the trees caught fire. It all looked like a bit of a disaster and I don't suppose the crocodiles appreciated it either.

We stayed the night with Keith and Jill then continued on to Yelwa the next day. Yelwa was a much bigger town, situated on the eastern bank of the Niger River, which was very wide and slow flowing at this point.

The bustling riverfront at Yelwa

258

David dropped us off for a few hours and we wandered through the town and along the riverfront which was a bustling port area with fish and vegetable markets, boat yards and *men* washing clothes. It was a fascinating visit, but slightly marred when a rather officious man stopped us, showed us some sort of security pass and questioned us about what we were doing there. His attitude was quite aggressive but he eventually let us continue on our way and we met up with David and returned to Sokoto.

And so the two weeks passed by in a most enjoyable fashion, but all good things must come to an end. Dawn was still anxious about her potential job interview in the UK and I was starting to get itchy feet to be on the move again. Nevertheless it was still difficult to make the decision to leave, much as it had been back in Oman, but we finally had no excuses to stay any longer. The Rover was serviced and repaired and champing at the bit, our visas were all in order and we had cashed a UK cheque with Richard and Liz so that we had a big stash of nira to take into Niger. The question of getting money out of the country was a problem for some ex-pats in Nigeria, who were paid in the local currency. There were strict limits on how much could be taken out of the country so cashing a cheque with us was an ideal way around the situation. There were two advantages to us in that they offered us a very favourable rate, and furthermore we were told that we would have no problem changing the nira for West African CFA on the black market in Niger. All we had to do was smuggle the nira out of the country (hopefully avoiding being thrown into an African jail for a few years). This taxed my brains a bit but in the end I rolled the nira notes into a bundle and pushed them up inside one of the hot air pipes connecting our new heater to the windscreen demister slots.

It was only 100 kilometres to the border from Sokoto, and we finally managed to take our leave of David and Helen at midday. Unfortunately Dawn was feeling a little unwell, which didn't help the situation. In the small Nigerian border town of Illela we stopped at its bustling market and bought four locally made blankets, more preparation for the cold weather that we were heading into.

****

Distance across Nigeria - 2,115 km

Total distance travelled from start – 16,334 km

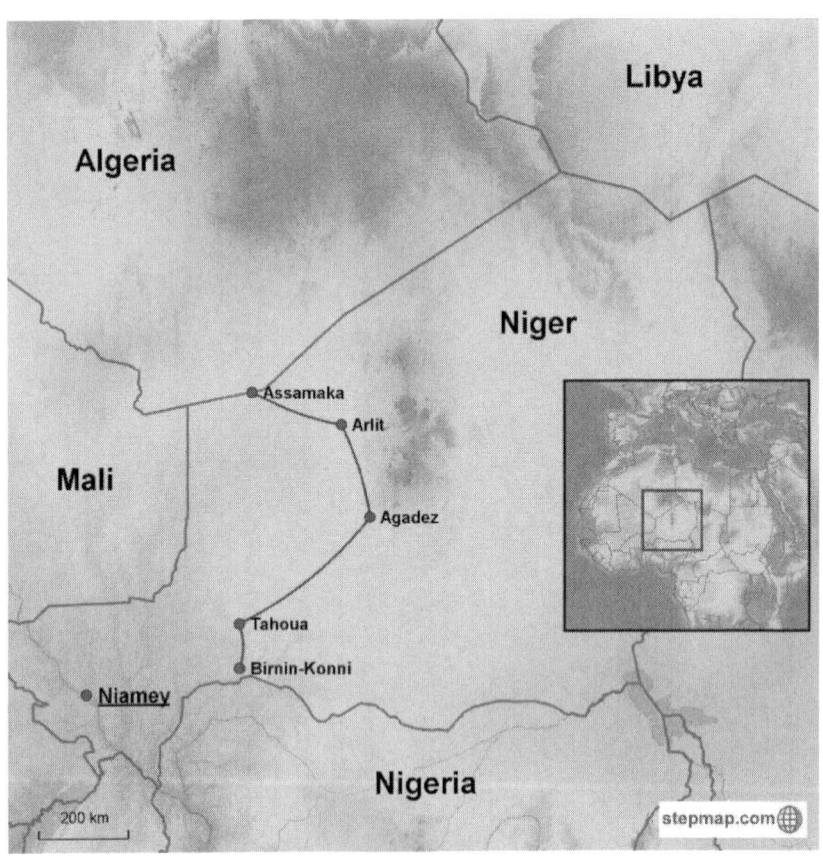

# Chapter 17 – Niger

Sunday 8th to Thursday 12th February 1981

Journey days 142 to 146

The Nigerian border was just a couple of kilometres outside Illela, and although the process was a bit slow we successfully passed through both the Nigerian and the Niger formalities with our stash of contraband loot intact. This despite feeling absurdly guilty which in turn made it ridiculously difficult to act naturally.

Birni-Nkonni was only about 5 kilometres from the border and we wondered how one made contact with the black marketeers once we arrived there. It was a sizeable place with dense single storey housing and huts and there weren't many people about as we drove slowly into the usual dusty town. On the basis that any shady currency business would be taking place close to the border we pulled up fairly quickly to consider our situation and were immediately the focus of attention of half a dozen local lads who appeared like magic from nowhere, crowding at the Rover windows and asking if we wanted to change money. As simple as that! Having agreed that that was our intention they indicated that I should leave the Rover and follow them to conduct business down a side street out of view of prying eyes. This gave us a chance to retrieve the bundle of nira from the heater hose without them seeing it, and I headed off clutching the roll of notes in my pocket.

Once again I blithely stepped into a situation of potential danger without even considering it, just as with my encounter with the wounded man in Jordan, the hijacking ferry operators in the CAR and the pick pocket in Bangui. Just naïve, I suppose. Anyway, I wasn't mugged or assaulted and after a quick haggle over exchange rates I selected one of the boys and we counted out and exchanged our respective piles of notes, I handed over 280 nira and walked away with 64,000 West African CFA equal to about US$190.00, a very satisfactory deal for all concerned.

We drove about another 100 kilometres before stopping for the night, Dawn feeling very unwell and going straight to sleep. As I sat outside at sunset writing up the log a local woman walked up with a crying baby and pointed to its left ear. Despite the absence of a stethoscope I must have looked a bit like a medical man – well, I was white – so I responded to her trust by opening up the surgery, digging out a bottle of ear drops and popping a couple in the offending ear, after which both she and now silent baby went off apparently happy.

Niger turned out to be what can only be described as boring and unremarkable. We had 450 kilometres to go to reach Agadez and it was good tarmac all the way. The countryside changed from sparse bushes to flat, bleak desert by the time we reached Agadez and the only memorable feature of the journey that day was the incessant and incredibly strong wind which swept across the open wastes from the north east and which constantly buffeted the Rover, leaving us driving through a brown dust haze. Not being in the least streamlined the Rover was at the mercy of any wind, and this semi-headwind reduced our petrol consumption to about 4 kilometres to the litre or 11 miles to the gallon. The situation didn't improve on arrival at Agadez. I think I had a romantic idea of this place, I don't know why and I was certainly quite wrong. The name was familiar for some reason. Otherwise it was just another square brown, boxed town amid flat desolation. The only notable feature was the tall mud, timber beam-skewered tower of the Grand Mosque which first rose above the rest of the one storey town in 1515 and which still maintained its solitary dominance of the place in 1981.

Grand Mosue at Agadez

The wind didn't abate at all and we had to camp in an official campsite which was very basic and just brown dust like everywhere else. There were three Unimogs and a couple of Landcruisers with overlanders, all travelling in the opposite direction to us. We chatted with a French chap and changed some of our CFA for Algerian Dinars, again at a beneficial rate. We were also advised to buy a bottle or two of scotch, which could be sold on for a handsome profit once inside Algeria. One has to be wary of this sort of thing, of course, but it seemed churlish not to join in with the customs and practices of experienced travellers that had passed through before us so we hedged our bets and bought one bottle for 3,000 CFA which we were told could be sold over the border for 300 Dinar (7,500 CFA). I still don't understand how these things work. It was a sealed, unopened bottle which bore all the scuff marks on the label of a well-travelled item that had been smuggled backwards and forwards between Niger and Algeria several times, presumably earning money for its current owner every time. Anyway, we hid it away for smuggling purposes and crossed our fingers again.

The town of Agadez proved to be as windy, dusty and uninteresting as the campsite. There was a small market based in rough, tin huts and it was interesting to see that sufficient travellers and tourists evidently passed through the place to support seven individual souvenir shops. The provenance of their wares was a little suspect. Everything was dusty and dimly lit and I had previously found Arabs to be expert at ageing recently manufactured goods to look hundreds of years old in order to become 'instant antiques'. We poked about a bit and Dawn eventually bought a bracelet for the equivalent of about $10. We had no intention of staying in the town beyond one night so after the market and before lunch we headed for the petrol station only to find it closed until three thirty. A familiar situation.

Taking on water at the Agadez campsite

After killing time until we could buy petrol we headed due west out of town, intending to take the clearly marked road on the Michelin map which headed north-west after a short distance and then north to Assamaka on the border with Algeria some 500 kilometres away. Part way along this road was the town of Tegguiddan-Tessoum, a place that made salt in the manner they had done for thousands of years and well worth a visit. The terrain looked a bit dodgy on the map with lots of indications of flooding during the rainy season but it was the only road shown. Just out of Agadez we were stopped at a police barrier and asked to produce some stamps in our passports that we should have obtained back in the town. Back to town to the police station where the stamps were obtained with no delay. We also dropped into the tourist office to confirm the route we intended to take. Back to the barrier to be told this time that we didn't have the necessary permission to travel that road and so the barrier remained firmly closed. Apparently the tourist office issued the necessary paperwork – a pity they didn't mention that fact when we were there – so back into town again to find the tourist office now closed for the day. By this time our patience was wearing a bit thin and Dawn, in her wisdom, said we should make another attempt to talk our way past the barrier, the result of which was another wasted journey and another night in Agadez.

The next morning we presented ourselves at the tourist office bright and early. It was open but we now learnt that we could not take the road through Tegguiddan-Tessoum without having an official guide with us. We also learnt that there was now a good tarmac road north all the way from Agadez to Arlit, Arlit being about half-way to the border. Our Michelin map was dated 1973 so obviously quite a bit had happened since then. We admitted defeat and set off north. This road was to the west of the Azbine range of mountains but avoided the mountains themselves and pressed on along the edge of the vast, desert wastelands to the east of us. We left the scrubland behind and traversed flat desert most of the way to Arlit, arriving at midday. We had a break and a quick look around the souk, where we met an older German couple heading south who were looking in vain for some suntan lotion. We had a bottle to spare and received a can of Lowenbrau in return.

Our 1973 map showed nothing beyond Arlit and, as we had been told, the tarmac ended abruptly there. Beyond the town it was just a wide, flat expanse of sandy gravel with the direction to Assamaka marked by periodic oil drums. All around and as far as the eye could see the featureless plain just disappeared to the horizon. One picked one's own route out of a band of tyre tracks several hundred yards wide in places and generally the going was fast and comfortable although we soon discovered that there were treacherous patches of deep, soft sand lurking along the way and without warning we would be dragged gently to a halt and despite slipping into four wheel drive and low ratio we would remain securely stuck. For the first time on our journey it was necessary to unstrap Graeme's ex-Hunter sand ladders and see if they would do the job. In fact they were splendid, and we found them much easier and lighter to use than Bruno's aluminium tracking, and were certainly at least as effective.

The highly efficient Sand Ladder Recovery Team in action

The only slight problem was that once run over they completely disappeared under the sand and took some finding again. This was resolved by tying a length of rope to each one and Dawn usually had the job of trotting back to retrieve them whilst I started digging again. So started a routine of digging, pushing the ladders as far under the front wheels as possible and lurching forward in short spasms over them until each patch of sand was negotiated and we reached firm ground again

The lonely but glorious beauty of the Sahara

265

We had heard about two enterprising local lads who would appear from nowhere (and I mean *nowhere*) and help stranded motorists. One of them was usually stark naked which meant that he was always given some clothing together with any other small gifts they might be offered. Sure enough they found us on one occasion and were rewarded with a pair of my underpants, some bread, water and matches. They probably managed to run a profitable men's underwear stall somewhere.

*"Everybody gets stuck there, mate"*

It was here that we also started seeing the sad remains of vehicles that had failed to make the grade and which had just been abandoned where they stopped. Most were total wrecks, bent and battered in all manner of contorted positions and relieved of all fixtures and fittings, leaving just the bare metal skeletons which had been stripped of paint and burnished by the blowing sand.

The flat gravel gradually gave way to rolling sand dunes but the piste was firm enough for us to continue without becoming stuck and we eventually stopped in the desert at about six o'clock having covered just 180 kilometres since leaving Arlit four hours earlier. Other vehicles had been few and far between and most people, once on the move, wanted to keep on the move. On one occasion we did go across to a couple of trucks and two buses heading south with three dozen Norwegian kids aboard but we became stuck again for our trouble.

We were now only about 40 kilometres from the border and reached it without incident the following morning. Assamaka turned out to be no more than the remains of an ancient mud walled fort and a handful of old buildings situated hundreds of miles from anywhere significant and being slowly swallowed by the ever creeping sands. More than one building had succumbed to the relentless pressure of the desert, the remains being just low walls with sand piling up and over them. There were a few stunted trees but otherwise this was one of the most remote and desolate places I had ever seen. Pity the poor guys that manned the customs and immigration facilities although they must have been entertained by some almost unbelievable sights as people attempted crossing the Sahara using all manner of weird and wacky forms of transport. No problems at the Niger border and on into Algeria and In Guezzam despite a couple more sand laddering incidents along the way.

Algeria on the horizon

*****

Distance across Niger  -  1,196 km

Total distance travelled from start – 17,530 km

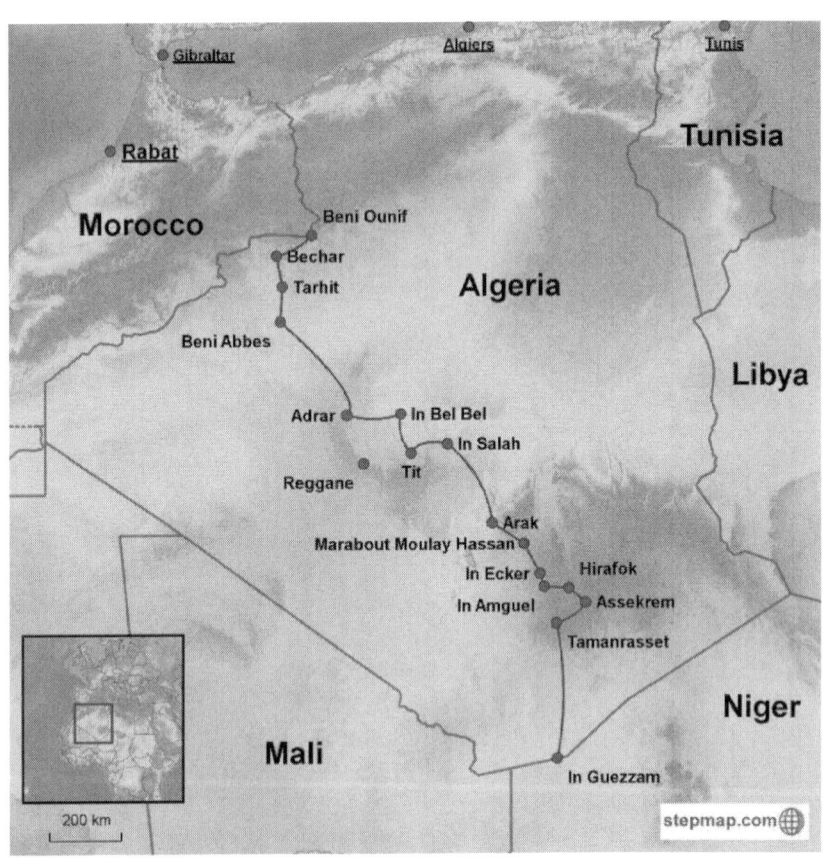

# Chapter 18 – Algeria

Thursday 12<sup>th</sup> to Sunday 22<sup>nd</sup> February 1981

Journey days 146 to 156

Entering Algeria was straightforward but we were subjected to a comprehensive currency check and declaration. In Guezzam was a reasonably sized town of the standard shoe-box design, brown mud houses which were fighting a losing battle with the encroaching sand dunes. Yet again one had to wonder what was the reason for such a remote community and just what did they live on? One can understand the need for a manned border post but considering that the next town was Tammanrasset some 450 kilometres away, what was the function of In Guezzam? Despite the bleakness at least there were actually some petrol pumps that were open and working so we were able to top up with fuel. We also discovered that the official rate of exchange was just 1.56 Algerian Dinars for 100 Nigerian CFA compared to the 4:100 rate that we had agreed with the French chap at Agadez. Another winner.

A good sized banknote

The route left In Guezzam and headed into the open desert to Tammanrasset. The piste varied from fast flat sandy, gravel to agonising corrugations which we avoided where possible by diverting into virgin desert. We managed to get nearly halfway to Tammanrasset before stopping for the night.

The weather was noticeably cooling down now with daytime temperatures in the mid-twenties, and with the nights cooling to the low teens we were using some of our firewood to make fires for warmth. Nevertheless it was the best time of the year for travelling across the Sahara, avoiding the searing forty degree heat of the summer. Yet another lucky fluke of our haphazard planning. It also meant that it was time to get the ammunition box down off the roof rack and dig out our jeans and sweaters that had been carefully wrapped in polythene bags before we left Oman.

The colder nights made it that much more difficult to abandon the warmth of the bed in the mornings and it was nine fifteen before we headed off again the next day. Fortunately the kettle could be put on without getting out of bed and by the time the water was hot the Rover had warmed up from the gas ring. The route was now noticeably climbing and we were leaving the desert behind and heading up into the mountains. The result of this was that the wide piste was being gradually constricted by the surrounding rocks and was becoming narrower and narrower. At lunchtime we stopped under a solitary tree occupied by a solitary bird. There was no other vegetation in sight. Quite remarkable. Eventually the route narrowed to a single track and we were at the mercy of the dreaded corrugations again. Some compensation was gained from the scenery, however, as the mountains rose ever higher and closer and the ground became decorated with bright violet-flowered bushes.

About 100 kilometres from Tammanrasset we came across the first signs of the trans-Sahara highway being constructed down from the north. At first this was just a graded strip but it steadily improved as ballast and fill had been added and it took shape as a firm, rolled roadbed. Eventually we found the tarmac surface but there were no signs of any machinery or workforce and it looked as if the whole project had been abandoned. Our move onto the tarmac was short lived when we found the whole surface to be covered in carefully placed sharp rocks, a simple but extremely effective method of making vehicle progress impossible. We tried to pick our way along but soon gave up and were forced back onto the infuriating corrugations.

Keep off!

The tarmac was clear and useable just 30 kilometres from Tammanrasset. We were well into the mountains by this time and these were very reminiscent of those that we had explored in our beloved Oman, bare and grey and awe inspiring. Once again we had missed a time zone and arrived in the town at six o'clock, believing it to be only five o'clock. Being Friday everything was closed and quiet. We found a couple of overlander MAN trucks full of Brits and parked and settled next to them in the usual grey, bare, sandy camping ground. We had barely come to a halt before a black Toyota tore up next to us in a cloud of dust and the driver wound down his window and said "Whisky?". Once again our dilemma of how to find the black market had been solved for us. A short haggle saw him roaring off with the whisky whilst we sat a little bemused clutching 250 Dinars which gave us a profit of about

US$16 on the original purchase price in Agadez. Mind you, by this time all the shenanigans with currency rates and black markets was leaving us quite confused as to the real price of anything, but we undoubtedly made a profit on each transaction.

It was getting cold and dark. We had climbed nearly three thousand feet travelling from In Guezzam to Tammanrasset and the effect of the altitude change was quite dramatic. Obviously the balmy nights of sitting about in our camp chairs were over. The wind had persisted throughout the day and this had resulted in a hazy atmosphere of brown dust, which together with an overcast sky and the chilly air presented us with a sudden and stark contrast to the weather we had so far encountered. The mountains loomed in the middle distance and it was quite gloomy. We felt that we needed perking up a bit so for once we wrapped up and abandoned the Rover and headed into the nearby town to savour the nightlife. Being Friday this was even more limited than was probably usual and we ended up in a dim little café where we met up with Mark and Pete from the MAN trucks plus a Dutch couple. A bit Spartan with plastic check tablecloths and rickety tables and chairs on a bare concrete floor but better than the cold and dark outside. The menu was in Arabic and none of us could make head nor tale of it. There was a suspicion that camel was one of the choices but we think that we managed to identify and order chicken. We spent the evening as ever, swapping travel tales and experiences. Like everybody else, these people were headed in the opposite direction to us so we pumped them for information on road conditions, routes and petrol supplies to the north and at the same time gave them the benefit of our knowledge of the route to the south. Jan the Dutchman had a Trans-Sahara Handbook which he lent us and we eventually retired to the Rover and copied out bits and pieces from it. With the curtains closed and the little flameless gas heater lit the Rover was very snug and cosy. Thank goodness we had managed to put some gas in the bottles in Nigeria.

In Tammanrasset we had to report to the police station and obtain the obligatory stamp in our passports and we also had to purchase Algerian insurance for the Rover, which cost us the equivalent of about US$10. We pottered about doing the usual travel things, going to the bank, filling up with petrol, shopping for food. In preparation for some rugged driving I topped up the gearboxes and the differentials. During our walkabout in town we came across a young Brit lad called Julian who was cycling down through Africa. He had a custom built trailer behind his push-bike to carry his essential possessions. I just had to admire people like that who set off to the most unlikely places completely alone – on a bicycle! To me, a large part of travelling is the sharing of the experience with a travelling partner, never mind sharing the worries and problems.

We left Tammanrasset after just the one night and headed for La Source, a natural mineral spring of drinking water about 25 kilometres away. We arrived late afternoon and camped there for the night. The idea was to see and photograph the sunset over the mountains but the whole day had been cloudy and we just saw a brief glimpse of the sun before it disappeared. Another cool and very windy night.

In the morning we went to the spring and bought some of the water. It was beautiful and clear and sparkling. We filled our containers with it and the fizz lasted for 2 or 3 days until we had used it all. Probably the best and most interesting water I have ever had.

From La Source we headed into the mountains to visit the Hermitage of Charles de Foucauld at Assekrem. This religious gentleman retired to the Hoggar mountains in the early 1900's and, inspired by the rugged but tranquil beauty of the scenery he built a basic stone refuge where he lived in contemplation and meditation for several years with his library of books before being shot dead by local insurgents in 1914. Not quite as peaceful as he had thought.

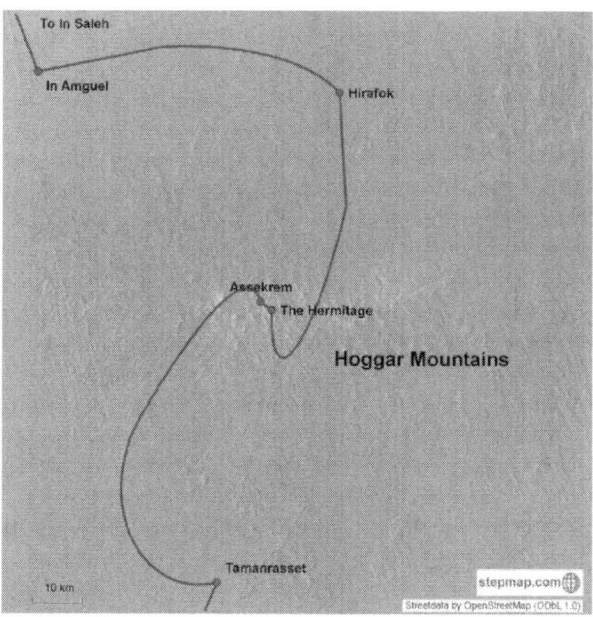

*Our route through the Hoggar Mountains*

The bleak and awesome Hoggar Mountains

It was only about another 50 kilometres to the Hermitage but we were climbing steeply and the Rover flogged uncomplaining up some challenging sections of the gravel road. The Hermitage sat at nearly ten thousand feet, a significant altitude for us after years of living at sea level. All around us the mountains rolled and then reared into massive volcanic plugs like arthritic fingers poking up out of the ground. Despite an hour's holdup due to road works (!) we arrived at the Hermitage compound at lunch time. This was a stone walled area with some stone built accommodation for visitors. The actual Hermitage turned out to be another small, stone building further up the side of the mountain behind the car park, a ten minute scramble up a steep, zig-zag path. Huge views over the mountains, for which the place is renowned, and a quite spiritual experience walking into the refuge with its tiny chapel, shelves of books and a tiny area for sleeping and eating. It was very cold, windy and overcast with lowering grey clouds. Easy to imagine the privations and discomfort of living there all alone despite the comfort and companionship of God.

We signed the visitor's book and returned to the car park, passing through it and out the other side to climb the opposite slope and give ourselves a view of the sunset. Yet again we were thwarted by the non-appearance of the main subject so saved our film and hurried back to the warmth of the Rover.

274

*Time to break out the cold weather clothing*

The next morning was a significant test for a couple of late risers like us. The Hermitage is one of those irritating tourist places around the world where one is expected to get up very early to be in position to observe and photograph the sunrise. We made our preparations before going to bed. The kettle was ready to put on for coffee and we set the alarm clock, the only time that we used it on the trip. In pitch darkness and bitter cold we struggled out of bed at four thirty and into our icy cold clothes. The climb to the refuge was made as the grey and gloomy grey of dawn crept out of the mountains. The sky remained overcast and we just had a brief flare of hazy sunlight as the sun came over the horizon before it climbed higher behind the veil of unrelenting cloud. Nevertheless we managed some satisfactory shots of the distant peaks that looked like the huge ramparts of a giant's castle. It was very cold, very windy, very bleak and it started to rain but there was no doubt in either of our minds that the effort had been well worth it.

*Sunrise over the Hoggars*

275

We scurried back to the Rover where we rewarded ourselves with a fried breakfast and, despite the grey, cold drizzly weather.......Dawn did some washing!

Despite all this activity it was still only eight o'clock when we left the car park. Just a couple of kilometres down the track we came across a Tuareg gentleman and offered him a lift. It took us a little out of our way but the result was that he invited us to his tent for a cup of tea. We left the Rover and walked down a steep, rocky hillside to his tent which sat in the cold drizzle miles from anywhere. Here we met his two women companions but their relationship remained a mystery, mainly due to our lack of a common language. Back to international nodding and smiling. We sat cross legged on a carpet, taking care not to point the soles of our feet anywhere near our hosts, and the tea was brewed in a very elaborate manner using two small teapots, some small glasses, lots of sugar and lots of slurping. Much pouring back and forth before it was judged fit for consumption. We drank the customary three glasses each before the inevitable sales pitch and we bought a couple of bracelets for about US$2 each. Not a bad exchange for the overall experience. Our host then escorted us back to the Rover where we ended up giving him some instant coffee and some jam.

Rather than retrace our steps we noted a decent looking route on the map which wound north through the mountains to Hirafok and then west back to In Amguel on the highway some 100 kilometres north of Tammanrasset. Although this was part of the main route from Djanet in the east to Tammanrasset it turned out to be very basic and neglected. Just a narrow, sandy, gravelly track but which granted some stunning views down into some vast wadis. The wind continued unabated but the drizzly rain gradually eased and it warmed up a bit and as the air cleared we stopped to take some photos of the scenery. I then discovered that the front right hand tyre was flat as a pancake– an indication of the slow speed and rough surface that I hadn't noticed it before. Whilst I changed the wheel Dawn knocked up some hot dogs, chips and fried onions – yes, hot dogs, chips and fried onions.

We eventually rattled into Hirafok where we were flagged down by a Tuareg man and his son and invited in for tea again. This proved to be a pretty blatant commercial interlude when we were offered some cheap and nasty souvenirs (which we declined) and were also told of ancient engravings just outside the village, a 'must see' experience and, by the way, if they showed us the engravings would we mind carrying some firewood for them on the way back? All part of the rich tapestry so after tea two men and a pickaxe climbed in with us and we drove a few kilometres and then walked to a rock face where there were just a few discernible scratches apparently showing cattle and a giraffe. Goodness only knows how genuine they were. Anyway, our companions headed off into the sparse scrub and gathered together a huge pile of dead, stunted bushes which they proceeded to heap up on the roof rack until it nearly doubled the size of the vehicle. Back at Hirofok this wood was unloaded and Dawn was introduced to the man's wife who persuaded her to hand over some Vic ointment and some vitamin pills for their small, ill son. Another somewhat bizarre episode. I have often wondered how long the wood supplies could last but one has to admire the enterprise of these people. Did they just create the 'ancient engravings' themselves to attract travellers and their vehicles to more and more remote places to find and carry firewood? In some ways I hope so.

Collecting firewood

Back on the road again, we dropped steadily back to the desert as we neared In Amguel which lay at three thousand feet. The road continued to be very rough and corrugated and we gave up for the night some 15 kilometres before the town.

We at last found relief from the dreaded corrugations when we reached In Amguel the next day and rejoined the north-south tarmac highway. However, our relief was short lived as the surface was so full of pot holes and we were constantly slowing right down to manoeuvre our way through them. However, it was a nice, clear and sunny day although the breeze was cool enough to justify keeping the windows closed, an unthinkable condition just a few weeks earlier.

Not far up the road we passed by In Ecker. Whilst it was little more than a walled compound with a few apparently abandoned buildings, it had a dubious claim to fame as being the centre for French underground nuclear testing in the 1960's. In 1981 the only evidence of it's murky past were a few rusty coils of barbed wire, but behind the innocuous exterior the French had bored their way into the solid rock and exploded thirteen nuclear bombs, one of which, in 1962, had led to the escape of dangerous levels of radioactive material which in turn resulted in unnaturally high incidences of illness and cancer in the area. Always handy to have a conquered country in which to carry out your risky experiments.

Further along the route we came to the tomb of Marabout Moulay Hassan. This white-painted building was set some way off the main highway but tradition stated that ill luck would befall those passers-by who did not take the time and trouble to circle it three times before continuing on their way. Neither wishing to attract bad luck nor wanting to miss anything, we duly turned off and completed the obligatory three circles. Judging by the huge, sandy bowl that had been created by the passage of thousands of vehicles over the years, we were not the only ones to hedge our bets against displeasing the spirit of Mr Hassan, and even hard bitten local truck drivers routinely paid their rotary homage.

Round and round......and round......the tomb

From the tomb we headed steadily north, twisting and turning with the road as it found its way across sandy stretches and then diagonally across the high, black rocky ridges that streamed down from the north. This wasn't country to be tamed by bridges and cuttings. The only way through was to use the natural topography and we drove along the edges of sand seas and then through deep gorges, one of which was just so long and narrow and deep that it was truly *awesome*. It finally turned through an enormous bend and then the road emerged from the gorge at Arak, which looked to be a totally deserted and abandoned village with roofless houses. Nevertheless there was a new looking petrol station by the side of the road. In fact this was really the only sign of life between Tammanrasset and In Saleh, a distance of some 600 kilometres, and must have been a very welcome sight for many motorists. For once we didn't need petrol and drove straight past. We had covered 450 kilometres that day and spent the night in the open desert, sheltered somewhat by some low dunes. It was a beautiful night, the wind had dropped and while Dawn cooked ham and macaroni I lit a fire and later made some simple desert bread which I baked in the sand under the hot ashes.

In Salah was reached the next morning after a fast run on good tarmac across rather dull bare and brown scenery, flat to the east with low hills in the distance to the west. A nice sunny day but still cool and windy. In Salah was a large oasis town with decent buildings and waving palm trees, loomed over by some enormous sand dunes. We took the opportunity to stock up on local currency, food, petrol and oil and I also had the punctured tyre repaired. After a pleasant cup of coffee in a street-side café we drove just out of town for lunch at La Palmerie, a local beauty spot with, yes, palm trees and golden sand dunes. From here we were heading west to Reggane which lay on the western north-south route through Algeria leading up to Morocco. The road we had been on to In Salah carried on north to Tunisia and was the usual travel route for overlanders, but our discussions with other travellers had led us to decide to take the Moroccan route. This meant that we could also see the petrified forest that lay in the dunes on the way to Reggane, just outside In Saleh. Not being too sure what a petrified forest was, we left the Palmerie and headed west on a piste that looked soft and sandy but was, in fact quite firm. There was no obvious road but vehicle tracks gave us confidence in our direction. The petrified forest appeared over on our left, brown lumps which took on the shapes of leaning and fallen tree trunks with clearly visible wood grain. Up close one could discern roots and branches. Odd.

I should say here that during our discussions with other travellers it had been emphasised that the route between In Saleh and Reggane was ill defined although there was sizeable town, Aoulef, part way along it. Whatever we did, we were warned, we must avoid going to the south as in that direction lay soft, marshy sand and, apparently, certain death! We were left with little doubt that the map down there would be marked with 'Here be Dragons' and with this in mind we sought out any positive tracks that looked to be heading due west.

I should also add that out navigation equipment consisted of just a cheap compass rubber-suckered to the windscreen which I had never managed to calibrate by adjusting the in-built magnets so it gave only a general indication of direction. We eventually came across some locals who waved us down and pointed out that, despite our efforts, we had started veering south. They volunteered one of their number to hop in with us and he directed us to a small village with the unfortunate name of Tit, which still lay slightly to the south of the route we should have been on and which was still some 50 kilometres short of Aoulef. We dropped our guide off in Tit and as we drove out we came across a French teacher in a red Lada, who, after introductions and explanation of our plight, led us to the Aoulef 'road'. By this time it was late afternoon and there was a beautiful sunset followed by a beautiful moon. The temperature dropped sharply and there was a high wind. We stopped for the night.

We were up and away by eight the next morning but lost the road completely after half an hour. Just flat sand and no tracks. Presumably the strong wind had obliterated all signs of previous traffic, which was probably only a handful of vehicles each day, anyway. We were still very wary of drifting south, and now apparently overcorrected and headed too far north, seizing on any signs of a track. After some 80 kilometres we were relieved to meet a Datsun pick-up truck full of locals heading towards us and stopped it to ask for help. To our consternation we discovered that we were indeed well off track and heading virtually due north to somewhere called In Bel Bel. They assured us that we could get from there to Adrar and as one of them wanted to go back to In Bel Bel anyway, we took him on board and he pointed out the route to the town. This was pretty desolate country. We drove across the trackless sand and the barren mountains came closer and closer until we were driving along a valley floor with rock faces rearing up on either side. In the distance, barely discernible against the surrounding mountains, we started to see the specks of a few mud houses together with the greenery of an oasis of palm trees. On the Michelin map this whole area was shown to be dotted with sources of 'eau potable' and 'eau bonne' and presumably In Bel Bel survived by tapping such a source and using it to grow date palms. Nevertheless it must have been at least 200 kilometres from any other civilisation in surroundings that can best be described as a dead moonscape. It certainly looked very poor and impoverished when we finally reached it. Our guide got out and we rewarded him with a cigarette and the remains of an old loaf of bread.

We were now in what appeared to be a dead end until one squinted and realised that at the back of the village an incredibly steep track zig-zagged up what looked like the almost vertical side of the surrounding mountain range. This didn't look right at all, but it was too late to change our minds and we just hoped to come across a visible route to the west once we reached the top. We ground our way up and I couldn't shake off the idea that the whole village was secretly watching us and wondering what on earth we thought we were doing. We emerged over the top and found ourselves on the edge of an escarpment looking down over more moonscape as far as the eye could see. In the flat, stony plain below the escarpment it was just possible to discern a possible track heading west but at the same time we couldn't see how to get down the hundred foot face of the escarpment to reach it. We drove along the edge and at last came across an incline which led us down onto the plain and we headed west following all sorts of tracks that constantly appeared and disappeared. In the end we gave up and put our confidence in the compass, which then constantly led us to escarpment edges that we had to find our way down. We were now hitting huge patches of soft, gravelly ground requiring four wheel drive in low ratio and we only just managed to keep going in the worst sections, although we never had to resort to the sand ladders. Fingers crossed for the engine, gearboxes, axles and differentials. We eventually came across some markers and positive tracks heading in the right direction so feeling a little more optimistic we set off only to be abandoned in terrain like a ploughed, sandy field which stretched on and on and up and up until yet again we found ourselves on the top edge of another escarpment looking out over miles and miles and miles of flat nothing.

The sun was dropping in front of us so we knew that was west, which was some consolation. Otherwise we had to face the fact that, to all intents and purposes we were lost and that lots of better prepared people than us had perished under similar circumstances. On the positive side we had plenty of food, water and petrol and knew that if we could just keeping heading due west we would eventually bump into the main road. A serious mechanical breakdown would be disastrous, of course, as would getting irretrievably stuck, but best not to think about things like that.

The view was both awesome and eerie and totally emphasised our isolation. We were experiencing a total loss of perspective and it was becoming impossible to judge distances without logical reference points to measure them by. I stood on the top of the escarpment and could have sworn that it dropped at least fifty feet to the plain far below. I set off to clamber down and was quite startled when I reached the bottom a couple of seconds later having dropped barely fifteen feet.

In the middle of nowhere

We made the most of the huge sunset but as darkness fell it was a rather subdued couple who snuggled down for the night as the temperature fell and the wind blew across the empty plains. Needless to say, Dawn cooked up an excellent meal, as ever, which cheered us both up and there was always a cigarette to enjoy. We had actually covered 250 kilometres that day, which should have seen us well through Reggane and nearly as far as Adrar, but now we had no idea where we were or how far we had to go. I tried to remember the figures for calculating the distance to the horizon and despite the apparent infinite enormity of the view before us I figured that the horizon was, in fact, only about fifteen kilometres away, so Adrar could be only twenty kilometres away.

The next day was Dawn's birthday but this was not the ideal situation in which to celebrate. However, despite the obvious inaccessibility there was a card waiting on the mat for her. We were up early at seven and heading off at seven thirty, the view looking no less intimidating than the evening before. Not too far along the escarpment we found a way down and set off across the literally trackless wastes trying to keep a heading of just north of west using a combination of the magnetic compass and the projected shadow of the sun behind us. I had never been so lost and it was very worrying. We clung to the fact that the north/south road through Adrar must be somewhere in front of us. The sun was bright and hot and we ground on through the soft sand and gravel in four wheel drive, the Rover never missing a beat and apparently revelling in doing just what it had been designed for. The perspective confusion continued and there were times when I could have sworn that I saw a truck in the distance only to realise that it was a small rock a short distance away. Fortunately the going improved to a firm piste beneath a covering of sharp, volcanic stones. We had been told that Reggane had been the centre for the French atmospheric nuclear tests in the sixties. It was somewhat unnerving to think that we were perhaps driving across a radioactive landscape and that the terrain was the result of nuclear heat rather than ancient volcanic eruptions. In reality, we were a long way from the test sites.

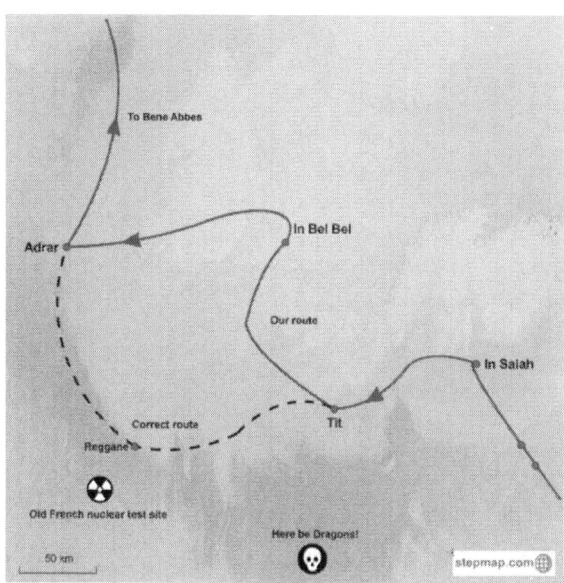

*A not recommended route across the Sahara desert*

After some 35 kilometres we started to see what looked like low buildings in the distance, but the continuing distortion of perspective meant that we couldn't be certain. However, sure enough, there were buildings plus some tents and the ground was covered with lots of small piles of gravel and there were about twenty men scooping the sand and gravel into metal bowls and tossing it into the air to apparently winnow out the sand in the wind. This was very odd. My only conclusion was that they were prisoners on hard labour but there was no evidence of guards and two of them came over when we stopped and in answer to our query told us that Adrar was only about 12 kilometres away to the south west. Relief? Well, under the circumstances it had to be experienced to be appreciated.

As an interesting sideline, just under a year later in January 1982, the Dakar Rally left Tit on a stage to Timeiaouine on the border with Mali some 1400 kilometres to the south. One of the competitors was the UK Prime Minister's son, Mark Thatcher. Somewhere along the way he had a breakdown and despite the fact that he was immediately logged as missing and a massive rescue operation was set underway with the Algerian army and search aircraft and helicopters, it was still 6 days before he and his two companions were located and rescued. With nobody knowing anything about us or our travel plans, it takes little imagination to calculate the chances of our rescue in the event of a similar immobilising breakdown.

Sure enough, Adrar appeared on the horizon and we were soon driving through it, a town of many new buildings and a pleasant atmosphere. We replenished vegetables, petrol and water and reported to the police station where we picked up a local looking for a lift north. We took him a few kilometres to an isolated café. The wind was continuing to blow very strongly from the west, picking up sand and dust and making everywhere very hazy. Our passenger offered us a cup of coffee so we followed him into the café where he also gave us a packet of cigarettes. So far so good but when we came to leave he demanded 'un souvenir' – another common international word associated with bribe, gift, or something for nothing. I think that he had his eye on my Zippo cigarette lighter so we placated him with an old Bic lighter and a felt tip pen.

The wind and blown sand continued through uninspiring scenery until we reached Kerzaz where the Grand Erg Occidental range met the highway in the form of towering, golden sand dunes. We stopped for lunch and scurried up the sandy slopes like kids in the snow. These were really classic ranges of dunes just like the pictures in a National Geographic magazine, constantly moving and changing in the wind and looking like the top of a meringue scalloped with a pallet knife. The edges at the tops were quite sharp and you could see the individual grains being continuously picked off by the wind.

These colossal dunes continued to Beni Abbes, nearly 400 kilometres from Adrar, an indication of our speed along the excellent tarmac road surface. Beni Abbes was a few kilometres off the highway, up a huge wadi and surrounded by tall sand dunes.

This was where our old friend Charles de Foucauld had first settled in Algeria before moving to his retreat in the Hoggar Mountains. In the town were two large and impressive hotels, the Rym and the Grand Erg. These looked relatively new and were certainly smart enough to remind us of our generally travel stained appearance, but the lure of a potential cold beer in the bar was more than sufficient to overcome any reservations, particularly when we wanted to celebrate not only our survival in the desert earlier that day but also the fact that it was Dawn's birthday. We tried the Hotel Rym first. The bar was quiet but when we asked for a beer it was made very clear, by a somewhat unfriendly barman, that none was available. On to the Grand Erg, equally luxurious and, this time the bar had a few local patrons who looked to be quaffing amber, fizzy stuff poured into glasses from typical tall brown beer bottles. Again, our reception was cool and again, we were told that there was no beer. Our protestations and gesticulations at the other customers left us no further forward and as our French wasn't up to complicated arguments, we gave in and just had a coke each, totally bewildered by the whole situation.

We moved the Rover to the base of one of the dunes for the night, where, despite some shelter from the wind, the temperature dropped really low again.

The next day we diverted off the main highway just beyond Beni Abbes in order to go and see some famous rock engravings further to the east. The route followed the edge of the Grand Erg Occidental and the first 30 kilometres were good tarmac. Beyond the village of Igli the tarmac disappeared and we rattled the remaining 60 kilometres to the picturesque town of Tarhit with its red buildings, green palm trees, brown rocks and, of course golden sands. The houses were scattered along the edge of a wide, dry wadi running from north to south, sandwiched between the stunning sand dunes rising steeply and immediately to the east and the bare rock mountains rising immediately to the west. Here we took on board a guide who directed us to the Gravures Rupestres (Rock Engravings), 18 kilometres away. The whole journey was through breathtaking scenery and the engravings themselves were on tumbled rocks on the edge of an escarpment. They looked to be genuinely old and showed all manner of animals – fox, lion, bulls, ostrich, snakes, giraffe, camels and buffalo. I'm not really one for this sort of thing but it was a worthwhile expedition to see them. Back at Tarhit we paid off our guide with about US$1.50 and a Beatles cassette tape.

From here we continued almost north through the arid wadis and valleys until we regained the main road to Bechar, where we were stopped at a police check and discovered that our insurance purchased in Tammenrasset had expired the day before! Fortunately we were able to talk our way out of the problem by promising to buy some extension cover. We quickly found the insurance office in the town and forked out US$12.50 for a further 3 days. Notwithstanding a great position within the mountains and the sand dunes, Bechar was a bit bleak with little in the shops and the overall atmosphere wasn't helped by the unrelenting cold wind from the north.

286

We had now travelled almost exactly 20,000 kilometres since leaving Oman and the tyres were starting to show serious signs of wear and tear. They hadn't been brand new when we left, and were only mediocre Japanese jobs, although I wasn't going to criticise them, not after all they had gone through. But it was time to consider replacing them although despite my good intentions we found nowhere to buy any in Bechar.

Up until this point we had been planning to continue north through Algeria and cross the border into Morocco at Oujda. The Michelin map showed all this route, and that beyond to Ceuta for the ferry crossing to Spain, to be big red main roads and I think that we subconsciously shied away from such trappings of civilisation. Also Casablanca sounded like a romantic place one would like to be able to say one had been to, so we changed our minds and aimed to cross the border about 100 kilometres past Bechar at Ben Ounif and Figuig.

As an indication of how cold the night was, we actually dug out and used the hot water bottles that Dawn's mother had insisted we carry and in the morning the Rover refused to start on the electric starter but thankfully responded to a few hefty cranks on the starting handle. It was bitterly cold but bright and sunny and we reached the Algerian border just after eleven o'clock. A quick and efficient completion of formalities and into Morocco.

*****

Distance across Algeria  -  2,540 km

Total distance travelled from start – 20,070 km

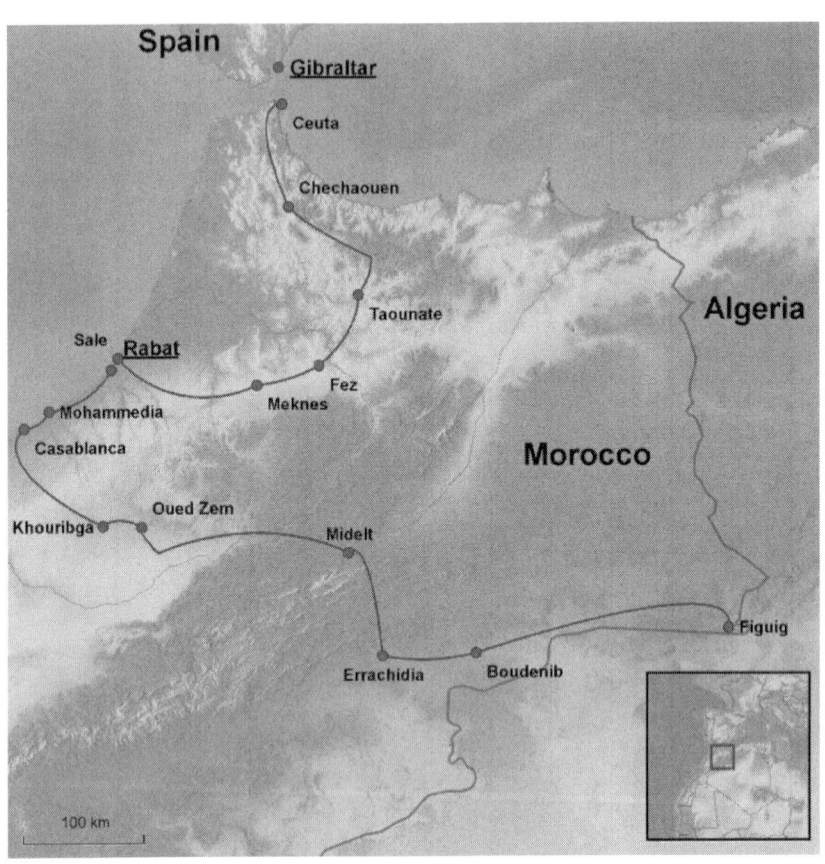

# Chapter 19 – Morocco

Sunday 22<sup>nd</sup> to Saturday 28<sup>th</sup> February 1981

Journey days 156 to 162

It was only a short distance across the border and into Figuig. The road ran through a natural cleft between two rocky hills which reared up out of the flat plain. The resulting valley was filled with green palm trees. At this stage we were a little apprehensive on two counts. Not least was the forged insurance card that Eddie had given us, but in addition to this we had been warned that the Moroccan authorities might take a dim view of excessive quantities of petrol being brought into their country. We had topped up with about thirty one gallons in Bechar so we were bristling with clearly visible jerry cans full of the stuff. With the difference in prices between Algeria and Morocco, however, it was worth the risk. As it happened the Moroccan officials were very pleasant and stamped us in without a query. A quick stop in Figuig to register with the police and then on our way. Figuig was very quiet but perhaps this was just because it was Sunday.

The rest of the day was spent driving along a very wide wadi bed, albeit on a decent tarmac road. It was still barren desert with sandy gravel and brown rocky ridges on either side and it was all rather uninspiring.

At lunch time I decided to fit the thermostat to the engine, having always run without it in the hot weather. We drove off but the temperature gauge soon climbed into the red, clearly indicating that the thermostat was not working so we stopped and I took it out again

The next day we drove through Boudenib, picking up a young gendarme to give him a lift to Errachidia (marked on our map under its former name Ksar-es-Souk). Errachidia was a large modern town with an airport and situated where the country began to climb into the Atlas mountains. The effect of the mountains and the sea not far beyond was becoming evident in the rivers and streams fed by snow melt, resulting in much more irrigated cultivation in this part of Morocco. Some 15 kilometres before Errachidia we came across a sign to the 'Piscine Bleu de Meskine'. Our gendarme indicated that it would be a good place for us to visit and happily hopped out, presumably on the basis that another lift would not be long in forthcoming. The Piscine Bleu was a little tourist trap based on some natural (cold!) springs with a swimming pool, showers and washing facilities. There were also some ethnic shops selling souvenirs and we seized the opportunity to buy a couple of rough woollen coats with integral hoods, which were to prove essential as we continued north in the middle of winter. Dawn got stuck into a pile of washing and I pottered about round the Rover with some sealant mastic in an attempt to find and block the leaks which had made themselves known in the brief amount of rain we had had in the Hoggar mountains. It had become obvious that our cosy little home could quickly become a damp little hovel if we experienced some serious precipitation. We rounded off the visit with icy cold showers in the open air. I suspect that the Piscine Bleu was really a summer attraction, at which time the cool waters would be welcome. Notwithstanding the temperature, it was very refreshing and at last an opportunity for some serious hair washing.

On into Errachidia where we changed some money at the bank and Dawn attempted to telephone the UK about the Shell job, but without success. I did a bit of shopping and although many stores were closed at that time of day, it was obvious that the quality and range of goods was steadily improving as we left Africa behind and approached Europe.

Just through the town was a huge reservoir formed by a barrage built in the early 1970's. We hadn't seen any bodies of water since Lake Nasser and it was fascinating just to be driving alongside it. We were now steadily climbing through ever more awesome mountains. We went over the top at about six and a half thousand feet and were quite excited to see snow-caps in the distance.

Quaint Midelt

290

Dropping down to Midelt for the night we found the official campsite. It looked as if our days of stopping wherever we wanted to were over, as we travelled through increasingly populated and cultivated lands. Midelt was a lovely ancient town with attractive old buildings clustered along narrow streets. It had a really Christmassy atmosphere with the cold, the brightly lit shops and strings of coloured lights across the roads and all surrounded by high, moonlit mountains. We treated ourselves to a meal in a local café and enjoyed an atmosphere of more prosperity than we had experienced for a long time.

The following morning Dawn went to the post office to try and telephone her mother again for any news of the Shell interview. Meanwhile I chatted to three Dutch guys in a Rover and they very kindly gave me a serviceable thermostat, which I immediately fitted. Dawn returned having managed to get through to the UK and learn that there was no news on the job front. Nevertheless this continuing agitation about getting back for what was only a *possible* interview was starting to niggle me a bit, and our happy-go-lucky, no-time-limit journey was starting to be influenced by an urgency to be finished and back in the UK to meet what was just an imaginary deadline.

Whilst in Midelt we took the opportunity to roam around the shops where we purchased a local carpet after an enjoyable haggling session and then bought four large aluminium cooking pots and lids as agreed with Eddie and as a start to kitting out our African expedition company. The only problem was where to carry them and they spent the remainder of the trip getting in the way.

*Last vestiges of snow in the highest passes*

We were heading for Casablanca but intended an overnight stop on the way. We continued driving from Midelt up into the mountains and through some fantastic passes with pastoral valley sides dotted with sheep, finally arriving in some tangible snow although it was mostly thawed. As we started the descent to the coast the scenery went through a dramatic change with more open country, trees and greenery. It was also very noticeable that we were now encountering traffic on the country roads, a novel and not particularly welcome state of affairs. We reached Oed-Zem in the late afternoon and this would have been a good place to stay but we couldn't find a campsite. We carried on to Khouribga, another 30 kilometres, which was a very big place and obviously prosperous from the proceeds of the local potash mines. Our enquiries after a campsite resulted in us being pointed in various directions but without success so we abandoned Plan A and decided to go straight to Casablanca. This meant finishing the journey in the dark, not best for sightseeing and a bit tedious. Casablanca, of course, was enormous and we had no local map. We had been told of the Oasis campsite right in the centre and eventually arrived there at ten o'clock, courtesy of directions from a helpful policeman, still needing to cook and eat.

In the morning we took brief stock of our surroundings which proved to be a very clean and decent campsite. We packed up and headed for the seafront. Unfortunately, wherever the supposed romance of Casablanca was, we totally failed to find it. We expected to come across a corniche or something but all we found were the docks and surrounding poor areas. We continued to the north east and eventually just drifted out of Casablanca, coming first to Mohammedia and then Sale just out of Rabat. Here, at long last, we managed to replenish our two gas bottles but had no success in buying any suitable 35mm film, which we were now getting low on. So we left Rabat and headed for Meknes. Very pretty countryside with lots of grass and trees, including areas forested with trees with cork bark, presumably grown commercially. The flat coastal plain gradually gave way to high rolling hills as we approached Meknes, where we found a nice official campsite and bought a bottle of wine to accompany some rather tasty lamb chops.

In Meknes we found a tyre workshop where I ended up buying a couple of rather cheap and nasty re-cuts to replace my rear tyres which were by now seriously low on tread. The front ones would get us back. It was quite fascinating to observe the skill of the cutter as he zig-zag traced the faint remains of tread with an electrically heated tool which neatly scooped out new grooves, transforming an old, worn out tyre into one that looked remarkably like a brand new one. Life was so simple in those days.

We continued on to Fez, where we wanted to explore the fabled medina or market. We drove into the town and found the Tourist Office. We had been warned that the medina was such a rabbit warren that it was very easy to become lost there, and we knew that if anybody could get lost it was us. The office was closed so we went for lunch in an ethnic café where I had the Moroccan staple of cous-cous for the first time and wasn't particularly impressed. Afterwards we located one of the gates into the walled medina and were immediately adopted by a young 'guide' who set off with us in tow. Indeed, here was a veritable maze of very narrow alleyways which would accept nothing larger than a wheelbarrow and hence the main form of transport was donkeys and horses. The place was huge and was a bewildering assortment of shops selling anything and everything with small industries producing woodwork, metalwork, brass work, leatherwork and woven fabrics. The yarns for weaving were coloured in huge vats of brightly coloured dyes. Dotted throughout were tea shops and snack bars and all too many carpet shops, their owners lounging outside ready to pounce on passing innocents. Our guide, of course, led us only to the carpet shops run by his relations. Not surprisingly, the whole tour turned out to be centred on selling us a carpet, pretty much to the exclusion of the historical interest of the place. We finally settled in a shop where the owner, yet another of our guide's numerous uncles, served us with glasses of tea and chatted amiably in good English about our travels. His sales technique was so soft, in fact, that eventually we almost had to persuade him to show us his wares, which he did with a brilliant show of reluctance. The whole experience was refreshingly laid back and after a bit of obligatory haggling we left with a small carpet and the satisfaction of a deal well done. I bought a small Moroccan tribal knife and then our guide was happy to lead us out, no doubt in a hurry to scurry back for his commission.

The narrow alleyways in Fez

It was a fascinating experience which we enjoyed, accepting our role as gullible tourists, and we were also left in little doubt as to the very real possibility of becoming lost and confused in the network of alleyways. By the time we left it was starting to get very cold and we still had to locate the campsite within the town.

On our way out the next morning we paused on a hill overlooking the medina. It was a beautiful sunny, clear day with a perfect temperature and not a breath of wind. Leaning on a low wall we looked down over the bustling town from which the sounds of the chattering population clearly floated up to us as if through a system of amplifiers and speakers. Quite magical. We decided that we liked Morocco.

Our route was now to Taounate and then Chechaouen via Ketama, initially through rolling hills with clusters of cream coloured, thatched roofed cottages at the tops of the hills. There were lots of people about and it was very agricultural. After Taounate the hills gave way to the green slopes of the mountains as we climbed higher and wound our way up the contours, looking down into fertile valleys with picture postcard scenes of farms and grazing animals against the backdrop of mountains and blue sky. Very, very pretty but marred at intervals by groups of local youths who were determined to sell us hashish in one form or another. It was a case of keep driving with the windows closed. One remote stretch of narrow road was virtually blocked with a parked car and as I started to slow down four or five characters approached us rather menacingly. Things didn't look too promising but the Rover bounced up onto the verge and we just squeezed through.

From Ketama the road followed a high ridge, winding along first on one side and then on the other. The scenery was probably some of the most stunning we had encountered, endless mountains and glorious views and an interesting road to see it all from. Just before Chechaouen we were stopped at a police checkpoint. The aim of it was obviously to catch anybody who had been foolish enough to buy hash further back. They asked if we had been approached and we said yes, but hadn't stopped or bought anything. We must have looked and appeared as innocent as we actually were and they waved us through.

We finished the day's travel in the dark and with very little petrol left. Suddenly, out of the darkness we came upon Chechaouen, a large town ablaze with coloured lights. Once again, with the crisp cold, the quaint buildings and the lights one was instantly reminded of Christmas. We were directed to a camping area in front of a hotel where we partook of a beer and a coffee before retiring to the warmth of the Rover. Here we rounded off our meal in keeping with our surroundings with the Christmas pudding and custard not consumed in the CAR.

The next day started with some general maintenance. Dawn cleaned out the refrigerator and I topped up the oil in the transfer gearbox which had now developed a significant leak from one of the seals. We drove into the town and walked around the quaint, steep old cobbled streets, our new winter coats blending nicely with the locals in their brightly striped winter wear. The sun had come out after a dull, drizzly start and it was really lovely. We even bought some leather wallets as souvenirs for some of the folks back home.

*"That blooming bus is late again!"*

We now had just 100 kilometres to go to Ceuta, where we would take the ferry across to Spain. More stunning scenery through the mountains with the coastline and the blue Mediterranean coming into view to the north-east. Ceuta was the tiny Spanish enclave on the Algerian peninsular so we transferred from one country to another just outside the town. An easy exit from Algeria and an even easier entry into Spain which passed virtually unnoticed. We drove straight to the port and bought our ferry tickets.

We could now see the Rock of Gibraltar across the straits and really did start to feel that our journey was coming to an end. Unfortunately everywhere was just too neat and civilised after our adventures in central Africa. We were now into family holiday country where the Rover started to feel gawky and out of place and it was as if we were on a slippery slope that accelerated our progress towards home with no time or interest for side excursions or delays.

We nipped into the duty free shop and were amazed at the cheap prices, coming out clutching a bottle of Courvoisier and a bottle of Cutty Sark whisky.

Once again we wanted to take advantage of the big difference in petrol prices between the duty free in Ceuta and that on the Spanish mainland. We therefore headed for a filling station and took on board about fifty five gallons to fill to capacity all our tanks and jerry cans. Unfortunately our festoons of jerry cans were not eyed at all sympathetically at the ferry. We had the two sticking out the front, two tucked into the rear wing and the remainder on the roof rack. I'm not sure if the objection was one of fire risk or exploitation of the cheap petrol situation but, whatever, we were turned back with the optimistic suggestion that we return to the filling station and ask them to take some back. Whilst this seemed like a ludicrous idea, we nevertheless went back and tried it – who knows what these people get up to? – but to no avail. We weren't going to pour it away so we frantically rearranged our stocks. One jerry can emptied into the leaking, collapsible water container which we wouldn't be needing for water again, and the empty can went back on the roof rack. The other three cans off the roof went into the back of the Rover along with the collapsible container, all covered with our bedding. This just left an empty water can and the empty jerry can on the roof. This was the best that we could do and we crossed or fingers and headed back to the ferry. By this time it was ready to leave, and our arrival was met with some agitation by the dockers, one of whom tapped the empty can on the roof and, satisfied, directed me to turn and reverse up the ramp onto the boat. At this point the customs official spotted, for the first time, the twin jerry cans strapped onto the front bumper and started to shout and stride towards us but the docker was closer and was urging me to keep going so we bounced up into the hold and the ramp started lifting, effectively curtailing any further intervention by the customs man. Once again a bit of luck had seen us through.

\*\*\*\*\*

Distance across Morocco  -  1,677 km

Total distance travelled from start – 21,747 km

# Spain to England

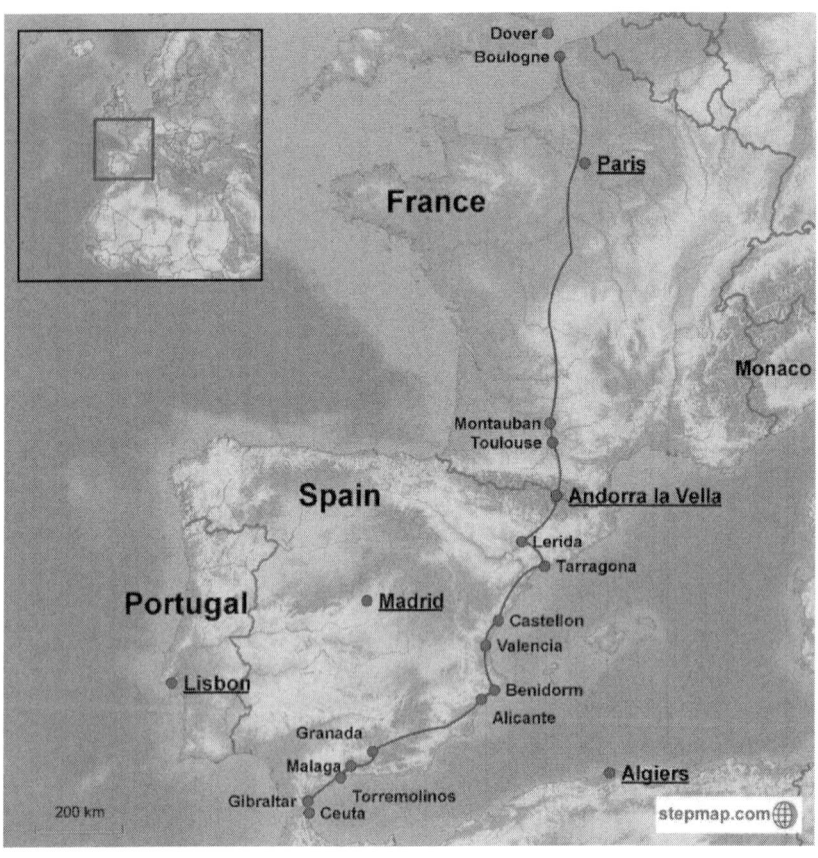

# Chapter 20 – Spain

Saturday 28th February to Tuesday 3rd March 1981

Journey days 162 to 165

What a difference to the shabby boat in the Red Sea! This was obviously much newer and very swish. Unfortunately it was only a brief hour of luxury before we docked in Algeciras, sailing almost beneath the Rock of Gibraltar looming majestically above us.

We disembarked and I pulled up for the usual customs inspection. Nobody appeared so I hopped out and went to enquire what we should do. My English enquiries were met by puzzled Spanish shoulder shrugs and indifference so we eventually just drove off, formalities apparently satisfied by the lack of interest from a little sniffer dog which was having the time of its life skipping from vehicle to vehicle with its tail going like an out of control metronome.

We didn't spend any time in Algeciras, and headed out along the coast road and the Costa del Sol to Malaga, cringing a bit as we drove past countless bars, restaurants and hotels, apparently the promised land of Watney's Red Barrel and Full English Breakfasts. It was all so built up and populated. Admittedly the mountains in the background were scenic but this continuous mass of buildings going on and on was quite claustrophobic after the wide open spaces and freedom that we had been used to over the previous months.

We finally stopped in Torremolinos, a bit later than planned when we discovered that we had gone through yet another time zone without realising it. Too late to do anything, we left our visit to the town until the following day. Torremolinos was inextricably linked to the jokey song of recent years and the dubious reputation of the package holiday business that had blossomed with the advent of cheap air travel in the seventies when stuffed donkeys, paella and cheap brandy had replaced 'Kiss Me Quick' hats, sticks of rock and candy floss. In fact, it wasn't as tacky as we had expected. Admittedly this was the middle of winter and many places were closed but there were still plenty of holidaymakers about, presumably many to escape the English winter weather and to take advantage of cheap off-season rates.

Malaga was full of people and traffic, just what we didn't want, and there appeared to be a local festival underway so we drove through without stopping. Beyond Malaga was Motril. We were now using an AA map of Western Europe and the coast road, whilst very pretty, was very slow. We decided to head north to Granada, where we could pick up what looked like the main east-west road. More very spectacular scenery through the mountains with more than enough hairpin bends before we dropped down into Granada through lots of citrus trees. We went through our usual routine of becoming lost before, eventually, finding the correct road out which promptly led us crawling back up into the mountains. This wasn't the faster route that we had envisaged but it continued to provide an abundance of awe inspiring views. Eventually we dropped down towards the coast again, passing first a row, and then what appeared to be an entire village, of cave houses, for which the area was apparently famous. These looked great, built into the hillside with their chimneys popping up out of the ground.

Just past the village we stopped for the night and I had to top up the transfer box again to compensate for the now significant oil leak.

Definitely travelling much faster. The next day we motored to Alicante, back on the coast, and on to Benidorm, which for me ranked alongside Torremolinos as the epitome of all that was cheap and tacky in the package holiday trade. This was probably grossly unfair on my part. For the diary we stopped there and had a picnic lunch on the beach, which was totally deserted for as far as the eye could see, which was a considerable distance. A bit different to Benidorm in the summer. The day we were there it was overcast and gloomy.

After Benidorm we drove across to the motorway which lasted for just 35 kilometres before coming to an end, at which point we were charged a toll of US$1.50 about which we were quite indignant about at the time. On to

Valencia where we did some food shopping in a supermarket, almost overwhelmed by the selection of goods on the shelves. A stark contrast to the bread and onions and tins of sardines and tomato paste that had sustained us for thousands of miles through Africa.

My, what an intrepid traveller!

The beach at Benidorm  "Wish you were here"

Out of Valencia and back on the coast road, although it was pretty much inland now. We camped in a deserted campsite at Castellon.

The temperature was noticeably dropping day by day. Dawn took advantage of the campsite facilities to do some washing and I attended to my now daily chore of topping up the transfer box. I also washed my hair in some very cold water. We had decided that Andorra looked an interesting place, so further along the coast we headed north from Tarragona to curve around west and meet the Andorra road at Lerida. It wasn't much of a road, tarmac but well overdue for maintenance and a slow, bumpy ride. Things didn't improve after Lerida as we bumped our way higher into the mountains with snow-caps on the mountains in front of us. Fabulous scenery again

\*\*\*\*\*

# Chapter 21 – Andorra

Tuesday 3<sup>rd</sup> to Wednesday 4<sup>th</sup> March 1981

Journey days 165 to 166

A brief glance at our passports at the border and we were soon driving into Andorra de Vella where we found a campsite not far from the town centre. It was a bit shabby and appeared to cater to itinerant gypsy travellers, but was very conveniently situated. The town itself was built in the bottom of a narrow valley with mountains rearing up on either side, densely wooded to the south and more barren to the north. A bit Alpen in atmosphere and building design but not looking at its best during the spring snow melt. Sadly it all looked rather drab and grey and wet. I walked into the town before dinner and once again had to marvel at the mind-boggling range of goods in the elegant, brightly lit shops, and I think that alcohol was as cheap as I have ever found it anywhere. It was very cold up there in the mountains with the remnants of snow all around. Thank goodness for the gas heater and a hot curry that Dawn cooked for dinner.

The next morning we awoke to a really cold day. We had nothing for breakfast having run out of money and having had no opportunity to obtain any. We quickly headed for the town and a bank and then walked in amazement around a huge supermarket full of just *everything* - and all so *cheap*. The booze section looked like the duty free area of a large airport.

Fortified with a gourmet lunch of bread and pate, it was time to fill up with petrol again and head for France. Petrol came in at only 25p per litre (US$0.45) so we once again filled all tanks and containers with the aim of a cheap run across France.

The road climbed and climbed out of Andorra La Vella and we flogged on for kilometre after kilometre in second gear, eventually arriving at the still active snow resorts where the slopes were busy with mid-week skiers. We stopped to stare for a bit. The sun was out in a bright blue sky and it was very crisp and clear, and such a contrast to Oman and the deserts of North Africa that had been our environment for so long. On through the mountains then down and down to the French border, the final section being through the Envalira Pass where the road twisted and turned in a frantic manner in order to negotiate the drop through the steep valley out of Andorra and into France.

The Rover, just as at home in the snow
as in the heat of the desert

*****

# Chapter 22 – France

Wednesday 4<sup>th</sup> to Friday 6<sup>th</sup> March 1981

Journey days 166 to 168

With minimal border formalities and after just cursory glances at our passports, we drove into France, the road continuing through the mountains until just before Pamiers where the countryside became flat and cultivated and of little interest to drive through. By this time we were well on our way down the slope to the UK and just wanted to cover as many kilometres as we could each day. Toulouse came and went, memorable only for a traffic holdup, and we eventually stopped for the night in a small, deserted campsite at Montauban.

The next day dawned with shrouding, damp fog and a thick layer of white frost over everything. The surroundings that we could see were bare, harvested vegetable fields with their unwanted residue of sodden brown stalks draped with dead yellow leaves and surrounded by leafless hedges and trees dripping with water. All a bit depressing. Soon warm in the Rover, though, and a hot bowl of porridge charged up our central heating. It was too damp and cold to do anything but pack up and move out. Dawn didn't even want to do any washing, which was an indication of how cold and bleak it was.

We bought some French francs in the town and then headed north again. The fog cleared and the sun shone but it remained pretty cold outside. I couldn't imagine what travelling would have been like without the heater acquired and fitted in Nigeria. It was continuous rolling countryside, not very inspiring and all looking very damp and wet as if after continuous weeks of steady, soaking rain. Lunch was wine and pate and I took the trouble to check the Rover oil levels, which remained satisfactory. It was probably too cold for the gearbox to leak. The afternoon passed in the same monotonous fashion with just a short entertaining break when we stopped for delicious hot French fries at a roadside caravan. The owner was a Spanish lady who spoke just a bit more French than we did but nevertheless we managed to have an enjoyable and jolly conversation. She was a cheerful soul and probably glad of some company on a cold winter's afternoon.

With nearly 500 kilometres on the clock that day, we pulled off into a picnic spot for the night, reckoning that Calais was about a day away. Another very cold night.

Not good in the morning when we awoke to steady rain, although this did mean that it was a bit warmer. The additional bad news was that my attempts at waterproofing the Rover had obviously not been completely successful and it was decidedly damp inside and the roof lining was starting droop rather despondently. This also meant that our clothes were feeling damp when we put them on. Definitely time to get home as soon as possible. A quick breakfast and then a transfer of petrol from jerry cans to the vehicle tanks. Too wet to crawl about checking gearbox oil.

The day passed totally uneventfully. The roads were good but the weather was not conducive to sightseeing. Except for a brief few minutes in the Hoggar Mountains, this was the first time that the windscreen wipers had been called upon to do anything, and we rumbled morosely along, peering through the streaky arcs on the windscreen at the black tarmac stretching endlessly before us, every now and again flinching as the billowing spray from approaching trucks engulfed us and rocked the Rover. Lunch was paté and wine again, with some French cheese this time, but sitting huddled inside was in such marked contrast to sitting out in the shade in our camp chairs in the middle of nowhere that it served only to remind us of what had been and that this was nearly the end. Difficult to be cheerful.

We were planning to reach Calais and spend the night there before catching a ferry to Dover the next day, the seventh of March. However, by late afternoon we were within reach of Boulogne and although we didn't really discuss it, we were now both itching to get back to the UK. We had friends in Lewes on the south coast who we planned to descend upon and where we could unwind and get drunk for a day or two before heading for Fovant and Dawn's mother and her warm, dry house and a soft bed.

Fate continued to smile upon us, and at the ferry terminal we bought a cut price ticket on a boat leaving just half an hour later, at six fifteen. No delays with too much petrol this time, and we were soon relaxing in the warmth of the saloon having a drink after spending all our remaining francs on cigarettes and wine.

Close to journey's end – Boulogne ferry terminal

# Chapter 23 – England

Friday 6th March 1981

Journey day 168

Unfortunately what should have been a joyous arrival in the UK was considerably marred by the treatment we received at Customs. We still had a pile of African firewood on the roof rack and we had planned to ceremoniously burn this in the huge fireplace at Dawn's cottage. Not according to Customs, however, who zoomed in on it to the exclusion of everything else. Potential source of nasty bugs, apparently, so it was confiscated and we were issued with a formal receipt, the process taking about half an hour. The interior of the Rover and its contents was totally ignored. By this time all the other vehicles on our ferry had disappeared into the night and we were left alone in the empty customs area. With the firewood removed it was time to get the Rover into the country. Over the past few months we had entered sixteen foreign countries with our British passports, relevant visas and the vehicle carnet. With the exception of Egypt this documentation, with sometimes an insurance certificate, had allowed us to cross each border within a few minutes and with no problems. We had now arrived in our own mother country and a self-important Customs official held up a big hand to clearly signal 'Thou shalt not pass'. Initially he insisted that I must there and then import the vehicle and at the same time pay the necessary duty on it. I knew that this was incorrect and that I was entitled to bring the Rover into the country as a visitor, without charge, on the basis that I export it again within one year or, failing that, pay the necessary duty at that time. As with all the other countries the Carnet should also have sufficed in the UK, I supposed, but he didn't seem to be familiar with that option. It was now getting later and later and even the customs offices were deserted of staff, so there were no other officials to appeal to. I continued to argue with our man, who gradually, and very reluctantly, backed off and finally processed the Rover in as a temporary guest, and we drove out of the port an annoying and wasted two hours after docking.

****

We were back. It was all over.

Total distance travelled from Oman 24,247 kilometres (15,154 miles)

# Chapter 24 – Epilogue

The next 5 months or so passed very pleasantly, lazing about at Dawn's cottage in Hindon in Wiltshire throughout a glorious hot summer.

We caught up with friends and JVC came down to inspect the vehicle that he had inspired with his 'tiny piece of toughened glass'.

*JVC poses on the slightly the worse for wear Rover*

I spent some time on the Rover in order to bring it up to a saleable condition, but generally very little needed doing. I resprayed sections of the galvanised metal bodywork where the paint applied in Oman had peeled off, knocked out a few dents, fitted a new back carpet and gave the whole thing a decent clean out. I placed an advertisement in Exchange and Mart and received just three responses. One was from a young couple from the Cambridge area who had just signed a contract to go and work in.......Oman. They wanted to fill the Rover with their personal goods and ship it out at their company's expense. I am happy to say that they both appeared to inherit my love for the vehicle and I duly delivered it to them in Cambridge, and the proceeds of the sale pretty much covered my cost of the journey.

Dawn didn't get the Shell job but ended up going to Papua New Guinea to start up a primary school for the children of English ex-pats building a new cane sugar factory and refinery out there.

I answered a newspaper advertisement which offered 'A challenging career with worldwide travel' and headed off on a new tack as a down-hole surveyor in the oil industry, with an initial two year contract in Saudi Arabia.

*The priceless cup presented to me by JVC to commemorate the journey. So priceless, in fact, that it didn't even contain the original pencil sharpener.*

Thus the forecasts of the Crab Sorcerer in Cameroon proved to be rather wide of the mark. Neither of us returned to Africa and Dawn and I subsequently went our separate ways.

I wrote the first draft of this account in September 1981 whilst spending a few weeks working in Dubai prior to the Saudi contract. The final version was not written until 2014 and 2015. With the technology of the Internet it has been fascinating to retrace the whole route using Google Earth. Also Google has been invaluable in researching the history of many of the places that we visited. The big shock, however, has been the realisation that such a journey would not now be possible. Egypt is still very unsettled, South Sudan and the Central African Republic have enormous political and religious problems, Cameroon has suffered much internal strife and north east Nigeria is suffering lawless rampages by Islamic Fundamentalists. Finally, it is not possible to cross the Sahara through Algeria.

We were therefore not only lucky but extremely privileged to experience these countries during what turned out to be just a brief period of peace for many of them. Followers of Michael Palin's 'Pole to Pole' travels will know that even by 1991 Sudan had been through another civil war in the eighties as the Christian south continued to strive for independence from the Moslem north, and much of his journey across the Sahara in 2002 had to be accomplished by air.

Finally, I look back and am so glad that we travelled before modern technology shrank the world with mobile telephones, satellite navigation and the Internet. We weren't 'Great Explorers' by any means, but back in 1980 it was still possible and feasible to set out into the relative unknown like we did and I think that we can justifiably and proudly claim to be described at least as 'Intrepid Travellers'.

Dawn's cottage 1981. The author sorting 35mm slides.

On the basis that you have now read my book, I say thank you and hope that you enjoyed it.

www.peteredwardfleming.com

If you have enjoyed this book you may be interested in reading the author's second book which tells the story of the ten years that he and his wife spent farming macadamias in Australia. This is another example of jumping in with both feet, based on the simple principle that you only live once and that everything will work out right in the end.

Here is an excerpt from Chapter 1.

The completed book is scheduled for publication during 2017 both as an ebook and as a paperback.

For information on publishing see:-

www.peteredwardfleming.com

# In the Middle of Macadamias

## Growing Money on Trees

Peter Fleming

'As usual, there is a great woman behind every idiot'

*John Lennon*

# In the Middle of Macadamias

# Chapter 1 – Finding and buying

Back in 2003 I don't think that I had even heard the word 'macadamia', never mind knowingly seen or eaten one. On holiday from the UK with wife Claire, we were driving up the east coast of Australia from her parent's home in Toronto to visit her sister in Gympie in north east Queensland. A long journey, this had to be broken half way and we stopped for the night in a place called Ballina. Ballina sits on a flat coastal plain a few miles from an inland escarpment which leads up into some beautiful rolling countryside quite reminiscent of England in places. The area is renowned for being a major macadamia producer. Strolling up the high street in the dark looking for a suitable place to eat, we were innocently browsing in the windows of some real estate agents when a couple of advertisements for macadamia farms caught our eye. The prices looked remarkably low, by which I mean that they could just be within our potential budget at the existing currency exchange rate and based on selling up in the UK. Despite Claire's Australian nationality neither of us had actually fancied going to live there, but the scenery in Queensland was quite a revelation and much more attractive after the drab greens of New South Wales. Drab greens! I hear some of you cry. Well, yes, I had found the countryside around Toronto to be totally un-inspiring with dull green gum trees looking tired and listless with a sort of "can't be bothered" attitude when it came to colour. Yes, I know that Dorothea Mackellar loved her 'sunburnt country' but to me her 'brown land' and 'filmy veil of greenness' was slightly depressing – and I am someone who has revelled in the dead, brown empty spaces of the Middle East and the Sahara.

The following morning we had a chat with one of the real estate agents and this further added to our intrigue about the possibility of becoming macadamia farmers.

Deep down I admit that I probably just had a secret yen to own a tractor, and the thought of owning a farm to go with it was a very tempting prospect. We would not have considered a place with animals, and soft fruits sounded terribly risky. Arable farms were right out of our sights and price range but a 'hobby farm', as this sort of venture is known, sounded quite feasible. On top of this, the thought of saying "bugger it", giving up our jobs and heading into the proverbial unknown was very exciting. You only live once.

As it happens this sort of decision was not new to either of us. Before we had met we had both thrown caution to the winds at different times in our lives and walked away from steady jobs to indulge in some world travelling. It had done neither of us any harm, and I have an unshakeable belief in the notion that if you close one door another one will always open.

As far as macadamia farming was concerned, it sounded as if a mechanical engineering background would be ideal, and Claire liked gardening, so what else did we need? We'd grown vegetables and had also owned a couple of sheep at our Norfolk cottage. Should be easy.

We returned to the UK. Me to my job as Engineering Manager in a small firm associated with the defence industry and Claire to her position as PA to the owner/CEO of an equally small company wholesaling imported garden furniture. I actually thoroughly enjoyed my job, in which I had remarkable freedom, and I repaid this responsibility with hard work, enthusiasm and innovation. Nevertheless, it rather peeved me that my bright ideas were to someone else's benefit and not my own. In addition the owner of the business was notoriously tight-fisted when it came to salaries and as the years went by I found the increasing cost of living was easily outstripping my income and realised that I would soon have to do something about it. Claire was not so happy, was pretty fed up and ready for a change. I suppose most of us feel that we are overworked and underpaid – well, who would admit to being underworked and overpaid? - and this discovery of what appeared to be an exciting and viable alternative to the frustrations of employment caught us at just the right moment.

As it happened our immediate future was ordained by the age and health of our dog. Tessa was an eleven year old Golden Retriever, the centre of Claire's universe. Too old to be subjected to the stress of emigration to Australia, we agreed that our plans must wait until she was safely tucked up in that Great Kennel in the Sky. Perhaps you have to be an animal lover and owner to understand the emotions involved but suffice it to say that it was to be two years later before we found ourselves in a position to put our plans into action, and the very night that we lost Tessa Claire said "Right, time to sell the house and go to Aussi", as much to take her mind off things as anything, I think.

And so it came to pass that a few months later our worldly goods were in a twenty foot container on the high seas and we were in an aeroplane with our 'essentials' crammed into a few suitcases. It had all been a bit of a whirl but with meticulous planning all had gone smoothly. The professional packers had been magnificent. No material was spared in wrapping everything up. I was also taking my beloved Fireblade superbike and this was firmly supported inside its own custom made wooden frame inside the container. Of course it had been an opportunity to throw away lots of stuff that had been stored for years, but nevertheless the pile of packages that gradually filled a couple of the bedrooms increasingly looked like too much for a single container. Come the last day and a container was dropped off in the road and the transfer commenced. Claire slaved away cleaning and dusting and washing as cupboards and rooms were cleared. I'm not sure what I did, but I know I was jolly busy. Many years later Bill Bailey was to say of men "We carry things, we try to keep out of the way and then we die".

I do remember nipping backwards and forwards continually comparing the rapidly reducing space left in the container against the apparently not *increasing* space in the house. Not my problem, of course, but difficult to ignore. Back amongst the dusters and the soapsuds and in typical female fashion Claire had no interest in this complex logistical exercise and my frequent reports along the lines of 'It won't all go in" and "It might just go in" and "It's looking a bit tight" were all met with calm indifference – which didn't help one little bit.

The final result was an empty space about the size of a cardboard carton of tins of baked beans. I can also say that whatever we threw away we neither missed nor regretted apart from a four metre length of hefty tow chain that I had to immediately replace once we were on our farm.

It is rather sobering when you see a lifetime's collecting of furniture, clothing, ornaments, tools and everything else fitting into a single twenty foot container plus sixty kilograms of suitcases.

\*\*\*\*\*

We landed in Brisbane on the ninth of September 2005 and were met at the airport by Claire's older sister Anne and her friend Richard. It was a two hour drive to Anne's house in Gympie. Relaxing in the car and very relieved to have put everything behind us, I casually remarked that all I had dreamed of for weeks was arriving at Anne's and having a cold beer on the verandah. There was a short silence of the 'Uh, oh, here comes bad news' variety and I was horrified to be informed that not only was it too cold to sit outside but also *there was no beer in the house*! Australia? Too cold? No beer? Must be in the wrong place. Fortunately the Aussis, being a resourceful and thirsty lot, had provided late opening drive-through bottle shops for just such a contingency.

Anne's house was a very attractive place just outside Gympie. It had two spare bedrooms in the dormer roof and sat on five acres of land, not an unusual small plot size in Australia. Anne's daughter Sam kept her horse in the paddock and it was a very nice setting with great views over grazing land in all directions. We were scheduled to stay there for a few days to get our breath back and then head for Ballina – eight hours drive away - to look for a farm. Before our arrival, however, Anne had looked into the possibility of a farm in the Gympie area and it subsequently transpired that it, too, was a major centre for the macadamia industry.

Thus, having arrived on the Friday evening, and ignoring any jet lag, we found ourselves being taken to see a farm on the Saturday morning. Although this proved to be unsuitable we then ended up doing the rounds of Gympie estate agents in the afternoon.

Gympie is a small town which in 2005 had a population of only around 10,000 with a regional population of just over 40,000. Nowadays largely a country community with dairy cattle and milk production the biggest industry, Gympie became famous in 1867 when a certain fellow by the name of James Nash discovered gold in the area. This led to a gold rush and the proceeds of this are credited with saving a near bankrupt Queensland at the time. In recognition of his efforts and the foundation of a settlement in the traditional gold rush style of tents, rough wooden huts, mud and chaos, the resulting town was named Nashville. The honour was short lived, however, and in 1868 the place was renamed Gympie, after the Aboriginal Gimpi tree or Stinging Tree, which was in turn named after the anti-social behaviour of its leaves. Personally I think they should have left it as Nashville.

Gympie is a rural town with one main high street still tracing the route of the original shanty town road between some impressive and original two storey buildings, best viewed by ignoring the ground floors which were populated with the usual ugly plate glass and aluminium shop frontages so beloved by cut price developers under the heading of 'modern premises' (find yourself out the back of these places and the word that sprang to mind tended to be Dickensian rather than Modern). Many of these shops were sadly empty and fly posted by the time we left in 2015. Mary Street, as it is known, is a pleasant avenue with some beautiful old trees down both sides which provide very welcome shade in the hot weather. As a side line they produce large, slippery, black seed pods which they distribute willy-nilly over the pavements. The council, in the infinite wisdom of councils the world over, decided that these potential WMDs should be ripped up and consigned to the compost heap before any upstanding, law abiding citizen decided to fall over and jump on the compensation band wagon. Fortunately local opinion, not to mention common sense, prevailed and the trees were allowed to remain.

I have to say that at the time Mary Street was distinguished by its never ending population of pierced, tattooed and somewhat overweight young mothers perambulating countless offspring in a variety of wheeled appliances. It also had what appeared to be a disproportionate number of coffee shops. As the main high street it descends quite steeply, gradually running out of shops and eventually leading to the main highway and then the Mary River. The Mary River is a seemingly innocuous large stream barely glimpsed far below in a narrow ravine when viewed from either of the two road bridges spanning it. In fact most of the year you can drive over the bridges and not notice the river without craning your head out of the car window. Come the summer rains, however, and any delusions as to the might of the Mary are pushed inexorably aside as the masses of water from upstream meet the Gympie bottleneck and the level of the river rises many metres to eventually creep into the shops at the bottom of Mary Street. This is such an inevitable and unavoidable phenomenon that, lured to some extent by cheap rents and rates, several businesses have been there for years and the process of evacuation and repossession is well oiled and slick. Each business has its pet electrician, plumber, carpenter, plasterer and decorator. The flood water rises quite slowly and is quite predictable so shops and businesses are emptied, electrical fittings and plumbing removed and the water allowed to take over, to the roof tops in some cases. As it retreats the workers move in and hose the filthy water from the walls and floors, repair and re-plaster as necessary, refit the electrics and plumbing and all is ready to go again, all in a matter of a few days in some cases. There is at least one very large warehouse with a high shutter door through which they float a small boat when the water level is down to about 4 metres. From the convenience of this boat the walls and ceilings can be hosed down as the flood level recedes and the boat slowly sinks to the ground.

When we first arrived in 2005 Gympie had a magnificent heritage steam rail system based on a train called the Valley Rattler. The old station and marshalling yards are near the centre although the modern rail route completely bypasses the whole town. The Heritage line owned an impressive 40 kms of track which wound its way through beautiful countryside and over some magnificent wooden trestle bridges. Popular with tourists, the Rattler was very successful but the track was slowly deteriorating in places and in 2012 the line was closed for safety reasons. Nevertheless there continued to be strong support to re-open it, despite the eye watering costs involved, and one keeps ones fingers crossed for success in the future.

As for the gold town image, this had virtually disappeared along with the major working gold mine, leaving behind a honeycomb of miles of tunnels beneath the town which were once access routes for trucks and heavy machinery. There was the Gold Museum but like all volunteer run exhibitions there wasn't enough money available at the time to bring it up to the standard that modern tourists demand and it was just a conglomeration of rather sad, dusty old buildings and exhibits. This was despite the praiseworthy efforts of a small band of dedicated and hard working enthusiasts.

With the existing potential benefits of a superb heritage railway line and rolling stock, plus an old gold mine, it seemed a shame that Gympie could not capitalise on both to become a first rate tourist centre.

In conclusion, Gympie cannot be described without mentioning the annual Muster, which takes place in the National Forest a few kilometres away. The Muster is a country music festival lasting perhaps 4 or 5 days. It attracts the big names in Australian country music plus the most amazing crowds of all shapes and sizes shoe-horned into be-tassled cowboy outfits and pointy toed boots, topped off with baseball caps or huge Stetsons (is a ten gallon hat now known as a forty five point four six litre hat?). The venue itself is buried deep in the forest and consists of some permanent but very rough stages with are augmented by large marquees during the event itself. The surrounding forest becomes a temporary town for thousands of happy campers and revellers who set up friendly bars amongst the trees with strings of lights and who then settle down to the serious business of consuming copious amounts of beer and Bundaberg rum in between roaming between the different acts performing on the stages. It is, of course, the Gympie version of the Glastonbury Festival (or perhaps Glastonbury is the English version of the Gympie Muster?) with a different style of music but exactly the same type of mud when it decides to rain. Despite the incredible informality and apparent lack of policing, there never seems to be any serious trouble and it is a fine example of the cheerful Aussie free spirit in action.

\*\*\*\*\*

Printed in Great Britain
by Amazon